Under the auspices of the ADL

A ... School
With best wishes from the author
Who hopes your generation will be
kinder and more tolerant than his

(The U.S. edition is available from
THE PERMANENT PRESS,
Noyac Road, Sag Harbor, NY 11963)

WHEN TIME RAN OUT

WHEN TIME RAN OUT

Coming of Age in the Third Reich

Frederic Zeller

W H ALLEN · LONDON
1989

Copyright © Frederic Zeller 1989

First published in Great Britain by
W. H. Allen & Co. Plc

Set by Input Typesetting Ltd, London
Printed and bound in Great Britain by
Mackays of Chatham Plc, Chatham, Kent
for the Publishers W. H. Allen & Co Plc
Sekforde House, 175–9 St John Street,
London EC1V 4LL

ISBN 0 491 03614 0

Dedicated to the people of Holland.

All author's profits on the first editions of this book in all translations will be donated to *Pro Juventute*, a Dutch children's charity.

WHEN TIME
RAN OUT

MOABIT

It is early spring and I'm looking up at the windows of the tired, grey apartment building at Wilsnackerstrasse 40. So it had survived the bombs. It still stood, stony as ever, exhaling the same boiled cabbage, carbolic soap odour I remember from many years ago. The house where I was born. In a city I never wanted to see again.

Behind which window? Was it the third or the fourth floor? My first memory, my first love affair. She was tall, blonde and about seventeen years old. I was short, dark-haired and about two. I was quite sure that our love was mutual, and forever. How could there be doubt, looking into those true blue eyes, feeling the warmth of her tender, just-the-two-of-us smile?

At lunchtime Marie, Mariechen, who worked in my parents' store, would take me by the hand, lead me upstairs, feed me and entertain me. It had become hard for my pregnant mother to walk up and down the steep flights to our apartment. Besides, lunch time could be a busy time at our yardage goods store just a little further along the Wilsnackerstrasse.

I must have worshipped Marie. Whereas my mother had to plead with me, bribe me, to eat food that was Good For Me, Marie was her own reward. Invited to her house, I demurely ate what my mother would have called "a pauper's meal" of watery, unpeeled, boiled potatoes and Matjes herring, the saltiest of salt herrings. True, I

1

would have liked a little more butter on the potatoes and a little less salt on the herring, but love . . . love changes all.

Mariechen's special treat for me, was playing 'Snow White'. Her job was to mime-munch an apple, cough delicately, lie down and play dead. She did it beautifully. And now I was the prince who had to come along and wake her with a kiss. I never really got it right, the kissing bit. We were hugging and kissing all the time when she was fully awake. So there had to be something different to make her come alive again. I tried pinching her affectionately, nudging and pushing her gently. I crawled all over her, loving the warm feel of her body, her softness, and her enchanting smells. Instead of a princely kiss I found something else that worked. Very carefully, with gentle fingers, I would open one of her closed eyelids and look, utterly taken, at the blue, blue, beautiful blue eye now revealed. After a pause she would suddenly come alive with a great cry, "Mein Prinz", embracing and nuzzling me while I shrieked with delight.

But, our love was not forever after all. A few months after my sister's arrival, Mariechen disappeared and I grieved.

Now, standing there fifty-five years later, seeing her in my mind still as a young girl, I faced for the very first time that, like anybody else, she must have grown up too. That she would have been twenty-three years old when Hitler seized power. And for the first time I wonder.

After she left my parents' store I did see her again, just once, briefly, when I was about six. On the day of the shooting.

I was doing the forbidden thing; hanging out in front of bars, newspaper stands, cigarette kiosks, cadging cigarette cards from total strangers. I was crazy about cigarette cards, with their pictures of football stars, aeroplanes, racing cars, animals. I couldn't get my father to smoke

2

more than two packets a day, so any smoker, anywhere, was my mark.

"Do I have what?" asked the seedy-looking, fair-haired, short man who had just left a bar, and I repeated my question.

"Do I have cigarette cards?" He shook his head and shrugged his shoulders. "No kid, all I've got is trouble."

Suddenly a loud crack-bang, shouts . . . running men, more bangs . . . my potential benefactor disappeared, simply disappeared. He obviously knew more about crack-bangs than I did. A youngish man, his face all bloody, was running along the street on the opposite pavement, pursued by two jack-booted storm troopers. I could hear the sounds of his gasping for breath, and as he was running he twisted his body back awkwardly, pointed his arm and hand holding something black, and then there was that sharp explosion. But that was the last one. Just beyond me on the opposite side of the street the storm troopers jumped the exhausted gunman.

They beat him to the ground, kicked his head, kicked his body over and over again, then pulled him up. Holding him by his wrenched-back arms, they half carried, half trailed the limp body back the way they had come, back to their headquarters down the street.

It was unreal. I didn't believe what I had just seen and just stood there with my mouth open.

The face of the seedy man appeared in the glass pane of the bar. He opened the door, stuck his head out, looked both ways and came out. With a brief nod in my direction he walked away.

I was still standing there gaping when someone came up from behind, covered my eyes with cool fingers and asked, "Guess who?"

I jumped with fright, but the hands were gentle and then my heart, not my ears, seemed to recognise the voice. I was speechless even when I was finally permitted to turn round and see Mariechen, my beautiful Snow White, smiling at me with sparkling eyes. Two other young women were by her side, also smiling.

"Don't you remember me, Fred? . . . I'm Marie!" she said, stroking my hair. Total red-faced confusion. I just looked at her with a strange pain-joy glow inside me. Still smiling she hesitated for a moment, then laughing, leaned over, gave me a brushing kiss and then seemed to be walking on, and on, and on, dreamlike, down the street with her companions.

My mother found out about the shooting, and I heard my parents discussing it. Something about Communists and Nazis. And for endless days I was not permitted to play outside. Eventually, our maid, driven to despair by my nagging restlessness under "house arrest", allowed me to play in the street—but only just where she could watch me from the window. And I must obey, immediately, if she were to call me.

I can conjure up the visual image of that bloody incident most vividly, but time has glazed over the horror. After all, here I was only a witness. Perhaps that is why the even earlier, other dreadful memory, the arrival of my sister, overshadowed the shooting. As Suffering Sibling I had a major part in this drama.

After waiting impatiently all day, I insisted, at bedtime, that the maid must wake me to see the new arrival the moment the stork arrived. I remember waking to a voice in the dark, being lifted out of bed and carried through a long dim corridor. Then suddenly, I was in my parents' bedroom. There was one light only, a lamp on the bedside table that threw deep shadows, highlighting a small area of the room around the bed. They sat illuminated dramatically, like a painting, and like a painting, nobody moved, nobody said anything. They just sat there.

My mother was in a white, lacy nightgown. Her eyes looked black and huge, and she was propped up . . . half

4

sinking into one of those big, square, bulging, German feather pillows. She was looking at me, but with a strange look. As if she didn't know who I was. And my father, sitting at the edge of the bed, next to her, was looking at me also, and there was a question in his eyes too. Next to them, lying on my mother's hand there was this white bundle with a funny, shrivelled, red little face looking out of it. They sat like people in an old, dark, Dutch painting, a complete family group. Without me. Nobody moved. I don't remember whether the maid still held me in her arms or had put me down, or what happened next. All I remember is that I was in the dark, all alone, a million light years away, and they were over there in the light, together.

Why didn't my mother smile and hold out her arms? Why didn't my father get up to kiss me and carry me over to the bed? I never asked myself that question until many, many years later, and then suddenly I knew it all. The clues to blow away those infinities of pain had been there all the time.

I remembered what Cousin Nina replied, when I was about eight, during an argument. Mother's sister, Aunt Cilly, had thrown up her arms and cried exactly like my mother:

"Dear God, what have I done to deserve such children?"

Nina had answered, "Well, Mother, you never wanted us in the first place."

Perfect, I thought, and couldn't wait for my next "Dear God". Once, I had answered, "and what have I done to deserve such a mother?" but that didn't sit too well.

When I used Nina's line about not wanting children in the first place, Mother went pale and I thought, boy, I'm really going to get it this time. But she wasn't even screaming. She made me sit facing her and questioned until she knew where I had got that idea. Then she took

5

my hand and explained at great length just how much she had wanted children. How difficult it had been for her to conceive. And how much the doctors had been against a second child. I was a breech baby, and she knew that the next one would have to be a Caesarean.

So that was it. My sister was a Caesarean. Mother must have been terribly weak and unwell. And Father was afraid to shake the bed if he got up to greet me.

Apart from the nightmare of Lilian's arrival, the earliest clear memory I have of my sister is of her sitting in a spotless crib playing with a steaming product of her own making. I could not believe my eyes, when with a cherubic smile, she offered me a generous lump of it. Running in horror to my mother I was told that I had been chosen for a great honour, a gift of love. Well.

Disillusionment with the world came to me at the age of four in the year 1928, the year of the Great Daylight Robbery—an event that led to my discovery of the Wild West. On my birthday, Uncle Max, my mother's brother, had given me a marvel of a movie projector, complete with some 35 mm films. Had I ever been afraid of the dark, this was the end of it. Standing all alone in total darkness I was in seventh heaven, cranking the handle of this hot-smelling, hot-to-touch machine, watching on a crinkled bedsheet the flickering black and white magic of Charlie Chaplin and other strange beings.

One day, playing in the street, I was raving about it to my friends. A couple of the older boys overheard my boasting and came over to tease me.

"Oh go on," they said. "You've got movie film? You're lying."

Indignantly, I ran upstairs, got one of my films and showed it to them proudly. Nonchalantly, hardly looking at me, one took the roll out of my hand, put a straight finger through its centre. The other, taking the leader of the film, started walking. The roll unwound and unwound.

A third boy walked along the stretched out band of film, stopped at about a third of the way along and asked "Here?". My heart started pounding. At a nod from his accomplices, he tore the film. I burst into tears:

"NO! NO, that's mine! Give it back, it's mine."

But the nightmare continued, for the next and last division of my film. The boys rolled it up, calmly put it into their pockets and started to walk away. I was beside myself with helpless outrage. It was my first experience of betrayal. I ran after them crying so bitterly that one of the thieves experienced an unlikely pang of conscience.

"Oh shit, stop blubbering," he complained, prodding me with his finger. "It's only a bit of film. Come on. I bet you've never been to a real film. Come on. Oh stop blubbering, come with me, I've got a friend who's working for a real cinema. Cm'on . . ." He grabbed my hand and pulled me through the street, my face wet with tears.

"That's my film," I kept on sobbing as he pulled me around the corner, into the Turmstrasse. He dragged me into a dingy, smelly lobby full of coloured photographs and big posters. He whispered something to a fat man and they both pushed me into a dark room.

For a moment I could see nothing but a bright light shining towards me. The light came out of a hole in the wall and it was like when I looked into the lens of my movie projector, only much bigger. I begun to see rows of wooden seats with some people sitting in various places and stumbled on, too scared to cry any longer. Holding on to the side of a seat I turned around. I saw this huge white, flickering wall with hundreds of white and black spots appearing and instantly disappearing. Then I saw rocks and mountains, and a man on a horse wearing a black hat riding like crazy, kicking up dust, turning back and shooting a pistol . . . and then another man, with a white hat, also on a horse, coming at me. The horse got bigger and bigger and I held my breath and ducked,

7

expecting to be trampled down. He just missed me, and then, when I dared look over the seat in front of me again I had to hold my breath once more seeing the rider and horse jump madly from one huge rock to another over a dizzying chasm. Tom Mix, the greatest of cowboys— Hollywood had entered my life.

So did art, and music, at this time. I owe Mother's brother, Uncle Max, my first exposure to culture . . . and with it the earliest appreciation of my musical talent. He took me to a live concert. Seated on a red plush seat in the first row of the balcony, I was overawed by the long rows of low-lit, glittering chandeliers, the giant plaster figures flanking the stage, the blue velvet curtains and gilded balconies. Everybody was talking to everybody and then suddenly the noise of the audience changed into a strange sound. I looked around. Everybody was clapping their hands together, making that noise.

I looked at my uncle and, at the question in my eyes, he said something, pointing down. I jumped off my seat to look over the parapet. In front of the curtain there were a lot of people in black suits, with ties like black butterflies, sitting on chairs, close together, with white paper in front of them. A man with a beard was climbing on to a box and it was getting dark quickly. But the lights down there stayed on and the man on the box started waving a thin stick around. And right away those people down there started moving, and music came up very loudly, and everybody stopped talking. I felt my uncle's hand on my shoulder. He pulled me back gently and whispered something I couldn't understand but I felt his folded overcoat on my seat and he helped me get up on it. Now that I could look down better, I saw the curtains opening and gasped, dazzled. A huge wheel, lit up in the most beautiful colours. It started to turn round slowly, with lots of glittering and flashing. And then I noticed people fastened to the wheel and something moving. It

8

looked like snow falling up and down, but it wasn't. Big feathers like the ones on Mother's old hats, . . . big white feathers, moving and moving again. Then I recognised what it was.

"Ladies," I said to my uncle, utterly charmed. "Ladies with nothing on except feathers."

My uncle smiled.

"And throughout the performance," he added, in reporting to my father later, "he tapped his foot to the music . . . right on the beat too".

Needless to say, such appreciation of my musical sensitivities and his taking me out all on my own, without my sister, or his two sons, made me see in my uncle Max a Very Important Uncle. Unfortunately however this promising relationship was nipped in the bud. It's not easy to be the rich man of the family. Shortly after our cultural outing my parents were no longer on speaking terms with him. Apparently he was not always eager to bail out or finance impoverished family members.

Perhaps my Uncle Mulu, who had a rival yardage goods store in the Turmstrasse, played a major part in this drama. Unlike my father Heinrich, his brother, Mulu lived for business alone. Though somewhat of a gambler he was eventually successful, yet his family had to live quite modestly behind the store in Moabit, so that every pfennig saved could go straight back into the business. Uncle Max, his brother-in-law, on the other hand, was both successful and lived very well, on the Hansa Ufer, in a splendid apartment with balcony and river view.

Mulu was definitely not on speaking terms with anybody who was on speaking terms with Max. Nor was his family. And what applied to Mulu's family was certainly expected from ours.

Though very unlike each other in looks and temperament, my father Heinrich (Henjou) and his brother Emmanuel (Mulu) were very close. What made the

9

relationship even closer was that they had married two sisters, Leona and Fanny. So Mulu and Leona's children Susi and Norbert were, so to speak, "double cousins". More like brothers and sisters, we used to say.

Norbert and I were the same age, but there all similarity ended. He was Nordic, blond and blue-eyed which turned out to be quite useful later. I was Mediterranean, dark and brown-eyed, not a wise choice for what was to come. Our differences in intellect and temperament were equally extreme. Nevertheless, we got on amazingly well and in all those box camera snapshots, wherever you see little Norbert, you see little Fred.

Quite a few family photographs, some dating back to the Austro-Hungarian Empire, have survived. I insisted on taking a few with me on my flight into Holland. Others came later in the small crates of pots, pans, brooms and Rosenthal china my parents managed to ship to Antwerp, with the help of German Christian friends. They got to me in England, just weeks before the German invasion of Belgium.

Now, looking at the photographs of my mother before I was born, in her 1910 graduation gown and cap, or elegantly dressed, late Victorian style, with wide-brimmed hats and softly flowing, ankle-long skirts, I can see how strikingly beautiful she was. And I see in every one of those photographs the same soft-eyed sad and lost look. In every sepia image there's that quarter-smile, not quite of this world. Elegantly poised, she looks remote, vulnerable, lonely. I can't remember ever having had the gift of a happy, carefree laugh from her.

The earliest pictures of my sister or myself show the same concern for appearances that can be seen in all my mother's photos. We look like expensive dolls. Perfectly charming. Soigné. Dressed fashionably with impeccable taste.

There are quite a few studio photos, from the 1880s,

10

of imposing grandfathers and meek grandmothers I never knew. None of them lived until I was born.

There's Uncle Max (cavalry officer in the 1914 Austrian army) with horse, a cigarette dangling rakishly from the corner of his mouth. And other uncles in Austrian uniforms of the 1914 war.

Uncles, aunts, Mother, but hardly any photographs of my father. Just a small, blurred, street photographer's snapshot of a tall, slim man walking, wearing a half-open, dark coat over a grey suit, white shirt and tie, the face half hidden under a 1920s wide-brimmed, grey hat. The one close-up I have of him is on a snatch of photo, clipped from a double parental portrait, dumped by my mother as unflattering, rescued by me secretly from the waste-paper basket. Shiny nose, hair flattened down, it is indeed unflattering. But it does catch a little of him. There are also a few eleventh-hour group snapshots, taken in some Berlin back yard in 1939, in which he looks gaunt, haggard, sick. Not one of these photos resembles my tall smiling, gentle father, always ready to listen, whose hand I held with so much love and to whom I looked up so proudly as I tried to match my childish steps to his longer strides walking through the park.

In a photo taken on one of those walks one can see my five-year-old self grinning from the lower steps of the Tiergarten bandstand. I submit this as evidence that my excursion to the burlesque show with Uncle Max was not my only early exposure to culture. There was that bandstand. There was Rossini. Or more precisely there was Rossini's *Thieving Magpie* overture. It was the first piece of "real" music I knew by name. It was the one piece that was bound to be played at the Tiergarten on almost any Sunday afternoon by the resident group of moustachioed, close-cropped, round-headed, military gentlemen wearing peaked hats. They looked like caricatures of the proverbial Prussian. Quite appropriately, military melodies dominated their programmes; the second piece of music I knew by name was the inevitable "Radetsky March".

They played, stockily resplendent, in uniforms laden with gold braids, shiny buttons, glittering epaulettes. They all looked like generals. But not as impressively so as the silent general of the Siegesallee. The one called Bismarck, who stood way up on a pedestal, wearing a funny hat with a spike on it. He was bigger and more powerful than all the pale marble puppets of the Siegesallee, the wide "Avenue of Victories" that traversed the park not far from the bandstand. Berliners used to call it the "Puppenallee," Avenue of the Dolls, because on both sides of this avenue one could admire statues of kings, of knights, princes, and other rulers of the German lands. They were displayed in various moral or imperious stances, sternly staring, hand on chest or sword, or holding up the Cross. They dominated, tall on pedestals, whilst at their feet, in a semi-circle, granted a bust only, resided artists, composers—lesser mortals, like Immanuel Kant, or Klaus Sleutter.

My favourite was Count Otto the Lazy. This sloth in white marble, wearing the latest in Crusader's fashion, pointed Persian helmet, chain mail and cloak, is shown languidly leaning on his sword, head nodding, eyes glazed, knees bent and just about to give way beneath him.

These tableaux were dedicated to the edification of the general public and for the enlightenment of youth. In the autumn haze they acquired a spectral eeriness. Walking with my eyes to the ground, looking for glowing, reddish-brown chestnuts, I would often not be aware of the Siegesallee until I was standing in it. And there they were, the frozen marble pictures. Silent, greying, ghostly groups, one after the other, smaller and smaller, dimmer and dimmer until they converged and disappeared into the autumn mist.

Parks in summer, cafés in winter, had an important social function in the Berlin Jewish life. They took care of the lesser relationships, the acquaintances you did not invite to your home but enjoyed greeting noncommittally. A great opportunity for the marriageable to look over the field too. Cafés were soon to become dangerous, not so the parks.

The Sunday afternoon pantomime in the Tiergarten, the walk-and-nod, was a most serious affair. Families walked in their Sunday best on the gravel-crunchy paths, men in front, women and children a good few feet behind. Another family group could soon be seen approaching. As they drew level, their men nodded to our men, lifted their hats politely, and then nodded again. As they got to our women, hats off again and another round of nods and smiles on all sides. Now, of course, their women have reached our men. More raised hats and nods, and nods again when they pass our women. As the children passed each other they winked and grinned conspiratorially, waiting for the next group encounter.

Occasionally, in the more open areas, there would be an even more interesting scene in the park. Men running with banners and flags, being chased by policemen on horses. I liked that. Many of them wore brown uniforms, but father told me they were not policemen.

One afternoon we ran into a lot of them. We had moved to the Essenerstrasse in 1929 and were in the Turmstrasse on our way home from the store, my sister and I, holding Mother's hand. Suddenly, in front of us, there was a tremendous commotion. Hundreds of people, many of them in brown uniforms, were pouring out of the Little Tiergarten, running to and fro in the half-dark of this dank autumn afternoon. Quickly they filled the Turmstrasse, side to side, from the park to the Ufa-Palast

13

cinema. There were shouts, screams, waving flags and placards on sticks. People were pushing and punching each other, cracking each other on the head with fists and placard-sticks. A roaring, seething mass of people, spreading rapidly. Suddenly two brilliant light beams seemed to carve right through the crowd, coming slowly towards us. An armoured car, belching tremendous white clouds that spread and billowed in all directions from its turning turret. Like Moses, it parted the seething sea in front of us, the crowd scattering in panic to either side. "Gas," shouted people in front of us. "Gas," screamed Mother, and clutching our hands harder, turned and started running with us, fleeing before the spewing monster. The monster moved faster than we could. Mother screamed, and clutching us to her body, faced death. But it wasn't death and it wasn't gas—just water, a fine water mist. She was crying with relief and kissing our wet faces. Soon everybody knew the bluff, and it was no longer successful at dispelling political street clashes.

There were steadily more of such confrontations now, but my parents still permitted me to play in the street. Up to now most of the clashes seemed to take place in parks, squares or in front of public buildings. But with that shooting incident around the corner from our house and others confrontations all over Berlin you never knew where or when violence would explode next.

Unfortunately, this did not prevent my parents from sending me to school. So in 1930, life started in earnest, with the traditional first-day-of-school gift from my parents, the "cornucopia", a colourful, tinsel-papered, funnel-shaped container full of sweets, biscuits, marzipan, chocolate, dried fruit, coloured pencils in a yellow, wooden pencil box with sliding lid, pencil sharpener. Joy after joy to fool you into thinking that school was a good thing.

I used the pencils for drawing only. The sensibly frugal

school system decreed that you were to waste no pencil or paper on illiterate children. Instead parents provided a little wood-framed slate writing board and a hard chalk writing stylus that scraped and screeched as you laboured in cross-eyed concentration over those first, painful, spiky Gothic letters. With a bobble of natural sponge, attached by string to the writing board, those first literary efforts could be amended or erased using a little water, or, if no one was looking, a little spit. Licking out a mistake worked too, but it didn't taste good.

For a little while Mother took me to school and waited for me after school. Then, reassured that her little boy was not afraid, she permitted Gretchen, our maid, to do the honours. Finally, having reminded my mother repeatedly that I was almost already six and a half and practically grown up, I was allowed to navigate the short, safe walk on my own.

Occasionally, after classes, Gretchen would be waiting outside school with my little sister. She did it, she said, because she missed me. Even though it deprived me of driving home a locomotive, a ship or truck, I was pleased. Gretchen was a different kind of love from my blue-eyed Mariechen. But a love it was. Gretchen, homely, dwarfed, hunchbacked, walking with a limp, looking so much like the witch in my fairy-tale books, was at once the subject of frightening dreams and the giver of love and confidence. I experienced great tenderness, caring and kindness from her, and she had a way of making me feel competent. Every child should have a Gretchen.

The only memorable event in connection with my first school was the boy with the Indian joss sticks. A moon-faced, embarrassed little boy in short pants, holding two thin, smoking incense sticks which soon filled the classroom with a strange and pungent odour. He was led into the class by the normally distant, starchy principal who proudly explained that this child's father had returned

15

from that strange, mysterious country, India, with these smoking marvels. "They use them for prayer," he said, adding, "Once you light them, they keep on smoking, they don't go out." This made a great impression on me. For the longest time I saw, in my mind, the boy's father, laden with baggage, carrying the two ever-smouldering sticks on to the boat, the train, the street car, trailing that strange smell all the way from India to the Bochumerstrasse, Alt-Moabit.

Perhaps I have so few early school memories because life outside, in the streets, was so much more interesting and exciting.

Graffiti blossomed on practically every empty wall space—red, black, blue, green . . . swastikas, hammer and sickles, triple arrows and other party insignia, words, sentences, complete political slogans, calls to action, insults. Quite helpful to a boy learning to write, read and spell. Mind you, the spelling on the walls wasn't always correct. Soon I could distinguish between real words and abbreviations of political party names like KPD, SPD, NSDAP . . . Communist, Socialist and Nazi party. This was not all that easy because there were at least three dozen political parties in the fray at the time. Soon I could spell tough words such as *verrecke* (perish) double-r, of course, and *Generalversammlung* (mass meeting), double-m.

Apart from being educational, the streets were also a lot of fun. I was playing in the Essenerstrasse when round the corner from the Krefelderstrasse rumbled a big, open, flatbed truck. A man in a brown SA uniform, yelling something into a megaphone, was sitting precariously on the roof of the driver's cab, his feet dangling over the windshield. Clouds flew up behind him. The open truck was full of storm troopers wobbling, shaking and bobbing up and down in uneven unison as the truck rumbled over rough cobblestones. They were making the clouds, they

16

were making snow in summer. Yelling and laughing, they threw lumps into the air that burst apart and snow came down. And in the snowstorm the street turned white, next to and behind the truck. A dozen kids followed, squealing in the white blizzard. I ran and looked at the snow on the ground. It was made up of thousands of white swastikas, stamped out of very thin paper, each half a finger long.

I couldn't contain my enthusiasm any longer and joined the other kids following the truck, picking up handfuls and throwing them up into the air. Finally, tired, I went home with fists and pockets full of neat white swastikas. Gretchen did not share my enthusiasm, seemed ill at ease, but said nothing. In the evening when Mother came home, she told me to throw away my lovely little swastikas. The people who made them are not nice, she explained, they are very mean to other people. Ready to defend my treasures, I saw something in her eyes that stopped me from protesting. Like Gretchen before, she looked ill at ease, as if she did not really want to *have* to tell me to throw them away. Meekly I dropped them into the dustbin.

My more usual street toys were marbles or balls of clear, milky or coloured glass. With an incantation to the gods and a beating heart, the player half threw, half rolled his marble towards the hole in the pavement. Proletarian pavement golf. Oh, the thrill of winning. Oh, the agony of going home a ruined man, head hanging, pockets empty.

We had some brand new games. A complete change from Cowboys and Indians, or hide-and-seek. We played Communists, Nazis, and Social Democrats. We addressed "mass meetings" through funnel-shaped, rolled-up newspapers, resembling the mechanical megaphones used by agitators in those pre-electronic days. We strutted up and down and gave fist or raised-arm Nazi salutes. The Social Democrats were out of luck, nobody volunteered to play those, they had no salute. We yelled party slogans at each other, staged street battles complete with "police" who rushed in with water hoses. We had the perfect water hose. Bought for pennies at any self-respecting newspaper kiosk, it was called "Mannekin Piss". You plugged this small, moulded metal, pants-down urchin into a water-inflated rubber sack looking like a clear glass ball. To avoid a watery disaster it was advisable not to let the ball grow above fist size as you filled it under water pressure at the tap. Once attached to the Mannekin, you held the "pressurised" water ball with the left hand, the Mannekin with the right, index finger blocking the business end. When you lifted the finger the Mannekin could piss a good five feet. It dispelled "mobs" faster than the armoured water mist sprayer.

At this time I heard about some new political parties from the boys. They were called Prostetants, Cartolics and Jews. And together they were also called Christians. What puzzled me a lot was that these new parties were also at the same time Communists and Nazis and Social-ists. And some of them wouldn't go to a church, ever, it was said. Well I never went to a church either, I thought. All very confusing.

One thing was sure though. There were more parties and more uniforms every day in 1932. Brown uniforms especially. And the men who wore them exuded a brutal arrogance and confidence that even a child could feel. The uniform did something to bind these men together. It gave them purpose. And lent each one of them a bigger than individual presence.

"There's nothing to stop them," said my father. "They smash anybody who tries, anybody who doesn't agree with them. They're killers." He read aloud from the newspaper a long list of attacks on people, offices and institutions. "They're smashing windows, wrecking print-ing presses. They're beating up, even killing important people, Deputies in the Reichstag." Mother asked, "Why

doesn't someone stop them? We're living in a civilised country, aren't we? What are the police doing?"
"The paper says it's a reign of terror."
"Oh the papers always exaggerate. There are plenty of decent people in Germany who are going to stop it," insisted Mother. "This is a civilised country."
Uncle Mulu, who was visiting, shook his head and said: "Civilised? Fourteen million people voted for Hitler just now."
A few weeks after this conversation, the SA suddenly disappeared off the streets. Not a single uniformed Nazi could be seen and my mother told my father, "You see, they've been banned by the Government. They didn't get away with it. This is a civilised country."
But in June they were back in the streets, cockier and more violent than ever. Only the Communists seemed to stand up to them. There were street clashes and large-scale battles between them all over Berlin. There was broken glass and blood on the pavement all over Moabit. I was no longer permitted to walk to school alone or play in the street.
It was a great relief for me, now under semi-permanent "house arrest", to hear that we were leaving Moabit. My father's business was doing badly, and my parents wanted to try their luck in Spandau, an outer district of Berlin.

SPANDAU

Compared with our Moabit apartment this was the country. There were trees along the broad Askanierring and plots of undeveloped land, where an eight-year-old could play. We were close to my new school where I soon made a friend, my classmate Lothar, who lived just a few hundred feet further along the Askanierring. His apartment building was similar to ours but had one feature I envied him: a spy mirror, mounted diagonally outside the living room window, through which one could check who was ringing the doorbell below.

Our house was modern too, but there was no spy mirror. Rain or snow, when the doorbell rang we had to hang out of the window surreptitiously to discover whether we were at home or out. Comparatively few people had their own telephone those days and, welcome or not, visitors just dropped in. This led to the invention of the family whistle. Not the single note, taxi whistle, of course; nobody would know who was being called, or calling.

No, the family whistle was discreet, melodious, correct . . . and if you had a composer in the family . . . unique. Your very own code of musical notes and only family and special friends knew it.

On Sundays, with many visitors, the musical offerings could be quite entertaining. But for Jews, before long, there would be quite another note to the family whistle.

It could make the difference between opening the door to an uncle or an SS man.

But no amount of whistling consoled me for the loss of the court musicians of Moabit who came to sing, hat in hand, with or without a hurdy-gurdy, fiddler or accordian player going from gloomy courtyard to gloomy courtyard of the older, unguarded apartment buildings. Most of them came in patched rags. Many were invalids of one kind or another, crippled by sickness, hunger or war. A motley crew, on crutches, with a wooden stump for a leg, one-eyed or blind, hunchbacked, careworn. A real-life Beggars' Opera. Some would just start performing. Others, to be sure of some audience, addressed the blank windows in a politely stentorian voice, graced by many a *Meine Damen und Herren*, announcing their programme until a few curious housewives, children and maids looked down.

They usually played popular street music or sang sad, romantic street ballads. Most of them just performed a tired routine and then waited for their meagre shower of pennies wrapped in paper to come falling from their window audience. But a few, by the quality of their voices and artistry, by an indefinable something, created a special tension, a haunting magic that hung in the courtyard like smoke long after they had gone. I missed them all. There were no inner courtyards in the Askanierring.

But that was just about the only thing about Moabit I really missed. Here there was more sunshine, and everything seemed so much quieter. Less political agitation, too. Or perhaps I had just become so used to it that only special events had the power to stand out.

On the outside, my school and Lothar. Inside, parents, sister and the maid who looked after us while our parents were at the new store in the Breitestrasse, Spandau's main street. Also inside and very important, was 'The Family'.

Feuds or no feuds, we were close-knit. Although my

parents now lived in the outskirts of Berlin, family would descend upon us frequently. Or vice versa. I was especially close to my double-cousin Norbert. A little less close to Susi, his sister, who was two years older.

We did terrible things, Norbert and I. Like driving that truck. Not one of those dinky little vans Americans call a truck, but a nice, big, flatbed truck, dilapidated and down at the wheels, standing lost and lonely in a nearby back yard. We would climb into its cab and spend happy hours behind the steering wheel. You could move the wheel just a little and there was also a sort of metal stick topped by a round knob that could be pushed around. Nothing else worked. Nothing that is, until we discovered THE knob. When I pulled this knob one day, there was a terrific clang and the whole truck shuddered forward. It whined, it squealed and it moved. The first time this happened we nearly died of fright. But I quickly pushed the starter knob back and the truck stopped. Then a little scientific experimentation and Eureka, we discovered that if you pushed that long stick down and to the left, the truck drove backwards too, grinding and groaning hideously.

That's how we learned to drive. Nothing to it. We had a lovely time until one day a nasty man came screaming and we had to run for it. A minute later our doorbell rang and he was confronting my mother, still screaming. About his batteries and those dreadful brats wrecking his truck.

We were hiding in my bedroom, ears to the door, hearts pounding, scared he would push past Mother and come right after us.

Poor man. He didn't have a chance. My mother was livid.

"What? You leave your truck unlocked so little children can climb right in and kill themselves? Unbelievable! Outrageous! What kind of a man are you? I should report

22

this to the police!" I had never heard my mother shout like that before. Not even at me.

Of course, the moment he had gone it was our turn.

"What? You climb into a truck that doesn't belong to you and nearly get killed? Unbelievable. *Jaj istenem*, what have I done to deserve such children? The two of you, just wait until Father comes home!"

Norbert tried, quite politely, to point out to her that my father wasn't really HIS father . . . and I certainly agreed with that. I was my father's only son, absolutely, and I said so too . . . but it only made her madder.

Well that was the end of driving trucks, but we soon found another useful occupation. Making and perfecting bottle bombs. Some kid showed us the basic technique and with some research and development we considerably improved the explosive effects.

Before bulb and battery, carbide was used to light lamps for carts, bicycles and street signs. When you combine carbide with a little water, it produces acetylene gas. This could make a mantle wick glow brightly, but in a beer bottle, closed with a snap-lock porcelain top, the gas pressure would build up, and up, and up, until, bang— the bottle bomb. Procedure: put a little water in the bottle, add carbide, snap-close . . . and run like hell. Not only is there a gratifying explosion, but glass, sand and stones will fly through the air.

The large field in front of the Spandau town hall was just perfect for this game. Our innovation was to dig a hole first, arm the bomb, push it into the hole and run. Better bang, bigger sand explosion and a super dust cloud. Just like in the war movies.

Can you make water burn? Sure you can. Another ingenious application of carbide. Throw a handful, wide, like a sower of wheat, into a puddle of water. Let it bubble, bubble . . . throw a lit match after it and jump

23

back. Pow! But of course, timing and speed is all, unless you don't mind singed eyebrows and frontal baldness.

Luckily, we had little money to buy carbide and liked chocolate and cheap cigars at least as much as bombs and arson.

European children had relatively few toys and often fabricated their own out of a mixture of junk and imagination. We made "racing cars" out of wooden crates, broomsticks, discarded roller bearings or stroller wheels. They were powered by gravity.

For indoor locomotion nothing beat the German feather bed, a giant red, down-stuffed pillow that covered the whole bed. It was inserted into an equally giant white pillowcase with buttons at one end. Well, you can unbutton those buttons and crawl in between pillowcase and pillow. Invite a sister or cousin, or both. Then giggling, and wriggling, this monstrosity of bagged arms, legs, heads, bodies and billowing feather bedding, edged expectantly towards the side of the bed until the inevitable crash, in one heap, to the floor. Shrieks of delight half-muffled in the feather womb.

But the indoor-outdoor toy I pleaded for most and always in vain, was man's best friend. Mother was adamant. Dogs were dirty and bad for children. Hardly a month passed when I did not come home with one all the same. I was always finding starving, lost dogs, or they found me. When neighbours saw me coming they grabbed their dogs and looked at me defiantly.

I think I owe this passion for dogs to our butcher in Moabit. He had this ferocious, snarling, brown, Doberman bitch tied up behind the counter. She terrified everybody, but I always exchanged a few polite greetings with her when I was in the shop. She growled but I took no notice, that was just her way. Then one day she got loose, ran into the street and found me. One moment I was standing there, four years old and all alone, the next there was that Doberman madly licking my face. A bit sloppy and wet—but what warmth, what affection. She was formally adopting me as her puppy. Mother stopped talking to our neighbour, swooned, came to—and with an incredible shriek, defying snarling teeth, she grabbed my nice Dobie by the collar and in one fell swoop yanked her back into the butcher's shop. I think the shriek did it; Dobie was completely cowed. Neither dog nor butcher ever got over it, and Mother became a temporary local heroine. I was crying in the street because she had taken away my nice doggie, and cried again in the bathroom, where she was ferociously scrubbing my face.

From that moment on, I desperately wanted a dog. But all I ever got was a carp. And he didn't last too long either. My father brought him (or was it her?) in a bucket, ran cold water into the bath and there was Carpy swimming around, wagging his tail, opening and closing his mouth. Sitting on the edge of the bath, I talked back in fish language and was suffered to pat the head and scratch the rather slimy, scaly back of my pet. And he kept wagging his tail.

That evening I could not bear to eat my poor friend who was staring at me reproachfully from among the onions on the oval dish. I asked to be excused from the table, causing my mother to fear that I would starve to death. This, because I was healthily skinny, was one of her major preoccupations.

Another preoccupation was disease. Hence a wholly unnatural need to constantly wash children's hands and faces. Hence also, her no pets rule. Dogs were unclean animals who gave children diseases and worms. Quite reasonably, I pointed out to her that she had owned two Boxers before she had children and had never caught worms or anything else from them. But it got me nowhere. Nor did my argument that I was allowed to make do with Norbert and Lilian as pets. And they certainly weren't clean—and they were certainly always giving me colds and other diseases.

It was about this time and with Lilian that I had the first conscious intimation of my sexuality and "manhood". It came one sunny morning during my school holidays. The maid was drawing a bath for us. In the meantime Lilian and I, waiting naked, were one moment wrestling on the bed, the next jumping up and down, using the bed as a trampoline. During a brief pause for breath I noticed my sister looking at a portion of my anatomy with particular interest. Then she looked up at me questioningly, her black eyes wide with surprise. I looked down and saw something standing up that had never stood before, at least not that I remembered. Now what? I shrugged my shoulders, unable to explain the phenomenon, puzzled as to what to do about it. Then I thought of something. Soon a clear little stream was rising upwards then descending in a graceful curve on to the rug. That seemed to satisfy the needs of the occasion and my sister looked impressed.

In spite of what Lothar and other boys our age said about girls, Lilian and I got on pretty well at this point. I played big brother to the hilt and was most protective of her. I got up in the middle of the night if I heard her crying, and braved darkness and lurking ghosts to prove, by turning on the light, that the monster in the gloom was only a dressing gown. Frankly, I was relieved it was nothing more than that myself.

She loved me to read her books, and I enjoyed some of her favourites too. Especially *De Puppe Wunderholdt*. This was the saddest tale of a beautiful, porcelain-faced, big-eyed doll and her fall from love, grace, and happiness to hairless, eyeless, scuffed oblivion. I had to read parts of that story over and over again, but didn't really mind. Lilian and I would burst into tears at the same places and sob sadly in happy unison. I loved the book for its vividly colourful cover and beautiful colour plates. Colour had a strong effect on me. Even single primary colours could have an emotional impact and affect my mood for a little moment. There were times when I even thought I could just about taste and hear colour.

My parents took due notice of this and, to keep me quiet and out of trouble, supplied me with crayons and watercolour sets. One temporary embargo came as the result of an early attempt at fresco painting, to improve our delicate but boring floral wallpaper.

Generally however, being practical was the one area in which I could always earn my mother's approval. When I had done anything well, mended her electric iron, built a shelf, ran an errand competently, she wouldn't say much, but there was something in the way she looked at me that made all my efforts seem worthwhile. Soon she would need my help more than anyone could have foreseen.

By the end of 1932, in Spandau as much as elsewhere in Berlin, the writing was on the wall; figuratively as well as literally. Gone was the German respect for private and public property. Painted, postered, and written everywhere were swastikas, hammer and sickles, calls to action, slogans like *Deutschland erwache, Juda verrecke*, (Germany awake, Jews perish) or "The Jews are our misfortune." Swastikas were painted over hammer and sickles, hammer and sickles smeared over swastikas. But the swastikas predominated.

More and more Nazi flags appeared at windows. I thought all those flags, brightening up street after street, looked rather pretty. But violence in the streets increased, and I was getting old enough to understand that violence could really hurt somebody.

During the 1933 January sales, my mother took me on a shopping trip into town. It was a dismal, grey, chilly day; everything seemed to be one dull colour. The street was noisy, and we neither saw nor heard the two trucks

27

that suddenly pulled up right next to us. Instantly SA storm troopers poured out of them, spilled over the pavements, and pushed past us, rushing into the shop on our right. There were explosive sounds of breaking wood and shattering glass, somebody was screaming inside, large chunks of thick, jagged glass fell forward out of the big store window into the street. A man who had not been there before was now lying on the pavement in front of the broken window. He groaned and started crawling away on all fours through the legs of some onlookers. A woman inside the store kept on screaming and another man came flying through the window, carrying still more glass with him. He was lying quite still, just a few feet in front of us, sharp-edged glass pieces all over his body, blood all over his face and hands. Two storm troopers came running out of the store and started kicking the prone man in the head with their jack boots as my mother moaned loudly and started to pull me away from the scene. We had stood as if paralysed.

I don't remember what happened next or how we got home. I was frightened and sick at the sight of so much blood and glass.

Uncle Mulu and Aunt Leona came to visit that evening and the grown-ups talked. It was happening all over the city. We had been caught in the midst of an SA raid on a Socialist election campaign office, just one of many Nazi attacks on political opponents that day, that week, that month.

Where were the police? the grown-ups kept on asking. How can this be happening? They're killing people. Where were the police? My mother made signs and moved her mouth speaking wordlessly:

"The children, the children," I read on her lips . . . and they changed the subject.

Later, when the children were safely in bed, they listened to the radio. But I couldn't get to sleep. I still heard

28

the glass shatter and saw the glass-covered, bloody man. I opened the door a crack and listened to the news with the adults, they in the light, I in the dark. There was a lot of news. The radio man kept on talking and talking about street battles, about Nazis and Communists, about hundreds dead and wounded.

"It's war," I heard Uncle Mulu say for the third time. "The only ones standing up to those gangsters are the KPD, and who the devil wants the Communists?"

"Where are the police?" Mother again.

"Where are the police," mocked Mulu. "Fifteen million Germans voted for those Nazi swine and she asks about the police."

At the end of January, 1933, Hitler became Chancellor. In February the Reichstag, the Chamber of Deputies, was on fire, set by the Communists the Nazis said. The fire was followed by the Nazi usurpation of power, the immediate suspension of civil liberties, the introduction of new laws for "high treason", very loosely defined—and the death penalty, quite clearly defined. Thugs turned cops; the SA and SS were given police power.

As an eight-and-a-half-year-old, much of this was beyond me. But the glass-covered, bloody man and the newspaper pictures of the burning Reichstag, the strutting, arrogant storm troopers—those were easy enough to understand. Their smug self-assurance and brutality marked for me the beginning of a new awareness, a quiet fear that went beyond the shock of any single, terrifying event. It was reinforced by the anxious eyes of the grown-ups close to me. Feelings ran so deep, you could read them on the faces of strangers. Exuberant, gloating faces; anxious, uneasy faces. People started looking back over their shoulders as they walked.

I learned a number of new words and names. Often there was a whole set of meanings that went along with a single word. For instance, "Oranienburg". That wasn't just a place. It had something to do with playing cards in a café on the Kurfuerstendam and getting arrested. It had something to do with disappearing. It was something very terrible. It was like "Dachau". And that was also called "ein KZ", pronounced *kaah-tset*.

"What is a kaah-tset?" I asked.

Mother looked oddly at me, hesitated, looked at father who replied hesitatingly, "Well. Well, that's not easy to explain. KZ means Concentration Camp. You see, they don't have enough prisons for all . . . Look, a KZ is a bad place . . . a sort of prison camp where people are taken who have done nothing wrong."

"Why?" I asked.

"Well, that's hard to explain. You see, something very bad is happening in Germany. Times are crazy. But it will pass."

"Do they take children, too, who've done nothing wrong?"

"Oh no, don't be afraid. They don't take children. Not at all." I was about to ask him whether they would take him or Mother when he continued. "Fred, look . . . don't talk about this to anyone else . . . outside the family, I mean. Don't talk about anything we say about these things to anybody outside. Not even to your best friends. It's dangerous for all of us. You understand?"

I didn't but nodded.

New words kept cropping up all the time and you got to know the meaning eventually. Some of them had something to do with KZ too, like "Schutzhaft" (protective custody). Aunt Leona said Schutzhaft is what happens when the SA arrests people in their homes or in the cafés. There was also the word "denounce". And "ransom", which meant—paying the SA or the SS a lot of money to get out of the KZ. But often they didn't let you out even after you paid them, I heard Mulu say to my father.

April started with another new word, "boycott". It was

a sunny Saturday afternoon and two SA toughs in brown were flanking the entrance of our store as my mother approached, holding Lilian and me by the hand. The pudgy one stepped into our way as we showed signs of wanting to enter. He had one thumb pushed in his belt and the other pointing back over his shoulder.

"Don't shop there, lady," he grinned amiably. "They're Jews. Shop in a German store, *Gnaedige Frau!*"

"I am German," answered Mother quietly, "and this is my store."

For a moment the fat-faced, jowly storm trooper looked uncomfortable.

Then shrugging his shoulders he stepped aside to let us pass. As we did, my mother halted for a moment, still holding us by the hand, looked up at the man and pleaded with a bewildered face:

"*Aber was haben wir Ihnen denn angetan?*" (But what have we done to you?)

He crossed his arms over his beer-belly and looked over her head into the distance. I saw his fat fingers partly covering the red armband with the black swastika on a white field.

The other storm trooper, standing motionless, also with crossed arms, also looking into the distance, had apparently not seen or heard any of this.

A woman slipped past the unseeing storm troopers, and quickly entered the store just before us. Inside she turned and I saw pain in her face. She was an old customer. After hesitating for a moment she awkwardly snatched my mother's hand and burst into tears.

"Frau Zeller," she sobbed, "we have nothing to do with this. I'm so ashamed. I don't know what to say! I don't know what to say."

My mother embraced her and tried to console her. They stood in the middle of the store holding each other, crying together.

I thought it all rather odd, those two women crying together, but soon there were other things on my mind. Like lining up toy soldiers in battle formation, Lothar's on one side, mine on the other, and taking turns pelting them with wine corks until the winner had knocked down all his opponent's army. Even better, as soon as it got warmer at the end of May, we were splashing naked in the Havel river at the shipyard owned by Lothar's father.

When I got back home after one of those splashings I asked Mother why was I different from Lothar down there.

"Christians are not circumcised," she replied.

"Oh!" I said, but hadn't the vaguest idea what she was talking about.

I still did not quite understand this Christian business. Or why, after the Easter break, when school had started again, the three Jewish boys in my class were made to sit together, separated from the others. It was strange. "An order from the top" we were told, and the teacher pointed at the ceiling. The other kids were puzzled too.

Yes, somewhere I had learned that Christians believed in Christ and Jews didn't. But I was also told that Christ was a Jew. And I wasn't at all sure what that meant either. But now, unwittingly, just by having to sit apart from the class with some others they called Jews, I was starting to think for the very first time in terms of "Us" and "Them". They did too, before long, but, of course, we were really "quite all right". They knew us. We were "their" Jews versus "those" Jews. Besides, two of us were football aces and that made quite a difference.

Cousin Maecky came to see us. He told my parents that a cousin of his father's whose husband had disappeared a month ago had received a package in the mail containing a pot. A pot in a cardboard box, wrapped in buff paper. It had official seals all over it. A note inside explained that her husband Aaron had been shot while trying to escape from the Dachau KZ. Here were his ashes. My mother was crying again.

"A frail little old man of seventy trying to escape . . . the murderers! How can God permit such a thing!"

Mother was still wondering where the police were.

One dark morning the maid woke me to get up for school. As I rose I felt a terribly sharp jab of pain in the abdomen and cried out in surprised protest. She thought I was faking as I did from time to time, especially when important matters had kept me from doing my homework.

This morning, however, I was not faking, but the maid of little faith yanked at my arm to get me up. I screamed as if she were jabbing me with a knife, which was exactly what it felt like. The quality of that scream summoned my mother instantly. She rushed in, questioned me and threatened "doctor". I said, "Yes, please", and now she was really alarmed. That wasn't like me, not even when I was really sick.

Dr Kallner materialised. White-bearded, majestic, tall and gentle he leaned over me, prodded me delicately here and there. Acute appendicitis. He beckoned my mother away from my bedside, talked quietly to her, but I heard the words "hospital" and "operation" and all my resolves to be brave turned into liquid terror. I howled in agony and protest.

Dr Kallner agreed to wait until lunchtime for a decision. By the time he returned the pain was so acute I couldn't even protest any longer and they dressed me slowly, carefully. Whimpering, I protested after all. Please, no operation. And Mother assured me there might not have to be an operation. We're going to the hospital for an examination. Dr Kallner picked me up, carried me gently in his strong reassuring arms and held me on his lap in the taxi.

In the big building Dr Kallner laid me on a tall, skinny bed that rolled. A nurse in white pushed it into a big lift, up and out again. I saw the ceilings of corridors moving over me and raised my head just as we entered a door that said in red writing, "Operating Theatre". Turning anxiously to the nurse I asked:

"Am I going to have an operation?"

She nodded calmly and I tried to jump off the bed, howling with pain. I'd been betrayed. The nurse, Dr Kallner, my mother, and another attendant were now all holding me down on the bed as I was being rolled under the big lamp and lifted on a hard table. I was still screaming murder when another person in white came rushing at me carrying something that looked like a fencing mask. He put it over my face. I could just make out the big lamp through the gauze, which smelled terrible. Hundreds of arms were holding me down, and that smell of chloroform was choking me. A distant voice told me to breathe deeply and start counting. I had difficulty in thinking straight and counted a little. The hands that held me loosened and I was up like the furies, bashing the mask off my face and jumping off the table in spite of the pain. They grabbed me, lifted, and I was back on the table. I heard laughter and someone saying "some kid" and hands appeared trying to fit the mask on my face. But I had warped it beyond repair. Another mask. The sickening smell and counting against my will. Everything went black, the blackest black I had ever seen. Loud humming. My whole head was humming and vibrating. Against the deep black appeared a brilliant silver sliver of moon, and stars and stars.

A month later I went back to school a hero. I had to tell all and bare my belly to show the scar. But no football, tag or any other physical game. What a bore. And only too soon I was yesterday's hero, a has-been at nine.

One thing was different on my first day back at school. Before, when a teacher entered the class we had to jump up, click our heels and stand at attention. The teacher would say *"Guten Tag"* and we would give him back our "Good day" in a snappy chorus. He would tell us to sit down, there would be a grrrrrummmmph sound as thirty bottoms hit the wooden benches. Then class would start.

But now he entered, clicked his heels, raised his arm sharply and shouted:

"Heil Hitler."

"Heil Hitler," responded the class in chorus.

"Setzt Euch!"

And grrrrummmmph, the bottoms hit the benches.

I was still standing there with my mouth wide open. The teacher smiled and said quite kindly:

"The Jewish boys are excused from giving the Hitler salute. They will stand respectfully as before, hands to the trouser seam, chest out, shoulders straight."

I had often seen that *Heil* Hitler stuff, of course. Usually by brown shirts, the SS and Hitler Youth. But now it was becoming a veritable passion, taken up by everybody, young and old. Somehow I had always looked upon it as some form of military salute. It seemed a bit peculiar now, coming from people out of uniform, like little old ladies or the snot-nosed street urchins who were running up and down my street going *"Heil* Hitler", *"Heil* Hitler", at each other.

I couldn't resist and practised it in front of our full length mirror, though I knew I could not do it in public. A left view, a front view, side view . . . then I burst out laughing because I remembered a joke our postman had made, raising his arm high but instead of saying *"Heil* Hitler", exclaiming, "That's how deep we're in the shit."

Apart from not being permitted to give the Hitler salute and other such minor hardships, my life flowed along quite nicely during that first part of 1934. I had developed a passion for reading which made the stay-at-home part of winter quite acceptable. There was one book, however, that disturbed me a lot. It seemed to have some connection with the violence I had experienced in the streets. Someone gave me a coloured picture book with verse text called *Struwelpeter*. Along with the Bible, this opus was put into the crib of just about every German child to teach those minors morals by way of example.

Little Pauline plays with matches, she catches fire and the last picture shows her two cats crying over a heap of ashes. To make sure you know whose ashes they are, her miraculously preserved slippers lie in front of the remains.

But the Nobel prize goes to the story of little Konrad, warned by his departing mother not to suck his thumbs. Disobedient Konrad does, though. A round-faced gargoyle in the arch above his head looks grave and for good reason. The door opens and in flies a tailor with his huge pair of scissors who cuts off both of Konrad's thumbs "as if they were paper" . . . big drops of blood dripping into crimson pools on the floor. In the last picture naughty Konrad stands sadly thumbless, the gargoyle above his head smiling with obvious satisfaction. "See what happens if you don't listen to your mama."

The only socially redeeming feature of this hideous book was a surprising appeal for racial tolerance. A black boy is ridiculed by three white boys. Big Nikolas dunks the tormentors into a huge inkwell so they look even blacker than their victim. Still more amazing is the last picture of this story. The three inky tormentors are shown still pursuing and ridiculing the black boy, totally unaware of their own blackness.

If only Big Nikolas would dunk Hitler into an inkwell. All the grown-ups seemed to be able to talk about now was persecution. How this or that Jewish friend lost his job and was not permitted to start another in the same or a similar profession.

Many of Cousin Lotte's friends were in the cinema and theatre. Or rather, had been.

"But how can he earn a living?" she said about one of

them. "They have two children. They told him, the German Stage is for Germans. Jew, go and shovel coal."

Mulu talked about a friend, a government lawyer, injured fighting for Germany in the 1914 war. He's still got his job. At least that much was decent about General Hindenburg who sold out to Hitler, said Mulu, he took care of the Jewish veterans. Not for long. A few weeks after Hindenburg's death in August, 1934, veteran or not, the lawyer got kicked out, along with all remaining Jewish veterans in government offices.

I didn't pay heed to these stories, they didn't seem to have much to do with me. I had a nice little party for my 10th birthday . . . with cousins, sister, Lothar and two other boys from my class. Mother didn't like my two new friends too much. They smell like poor people, she said. Lothar gave me a toy sailboat he and his father had made for me. I worshipped his father, who owned a boatyard on the Havel. The first time I met him he had asked me to call him Kurt. I thought that was quite marvellous— no adult had ever done that before. He made me feel that some grown-ups were almost human. Usually they wanted you to stand up straight, hands to the trouser seam and call them Herr, or Herr Doktor, or Herr Professor. There was one who insisted on being called Herr Professor Doktor Justizrat Langenberger. And his wife was Frau Professor Doktor Justizrat Langenberger.

Kurt took Lothar and me to his wharf quite often, even when it was too cold to swim. I loved the boats, the water, the smell of tar and paint, the heavy ropes, the mud.

Lothar's mother was good-looking and very polite. I spent quite a lot of time at their house, but she never asked me questions or talked to me the way my mother talked with Lothar. There was something about her that made me wipe my feet on the doormat most carefully before I entered their apartment.

One day in June, Lothar turned up in Hitler Youth

37

uniform. I looked at the belt, the buckle with the Nazi emblem, the leather shoulder strap. I was both uneasy and secretly envious. The uniform made him appear somehow changed. We had been friends for two years, but now he looked like a stranger. I was puzzled and then I suddenly understood. The others, that's what it was, I could sense the others in their uniform when I saw him. They were a group, I was not one of them. And I felt a distance, a great pain, a new kind of loneliness. Lothar intended to wear the uniform only for his meetings. He wouldn't want to get it dirty at play, he said.

That evening I asked my mother hesitatingly, sort of sideways, avoiding her eyes, "I can't join the Hitler Youth, can I?"

From her tone I could see the surprise in her eyes without even looking at her. "But why on earth would you want to do that?"

I told her about Lothar and she asked: "Did Lothar want to join?"

"I don't know. He told me his mother thought it would be a good thing."

She started to say something, then stopped. Then she started again, hesitatingly: "Maybe you should not be such close friends with Lothar."

I couldn't believe my ears. "But he's my best friend, my very best friend!"

"Yes, but you know, he is going to be kept busy with his Hitler Youth. He might not have a lot of time for you now. Anyway, I thought Norbert was your best friend?"

I looked at her, shocked. Lothar not have time for me? Out of the question. Mother saw my look, shook her head and walked away.

She was quite wrong. Now that the big school vacation had started, Lothar had plenty of time for me. The weather was warm and we went almost every day to splash around his father's boatyard. Lothar's father took us out for a wonderful run with a sailing-boat.

During those first days of July there were rumours, more rumours, and excited, hopeful, hushed conversations among the grown-ups. The Nazi Party was falling apart. They were killing each other. They murdered somebody called Roehm and were smashing their own SA. Everybody was talking about the end of the nightmare. And then everybody stopped talking about it; Hitler came out of it stronger than ever.

I developed a passion for fairy tales and Miss Dietrich, the children's librarian. She was a strikingly handsome, buxom lady in her thirties with long blonde hair who sat enthroned in a large wooden armchair behind the heavy library table. Like my mother, she wore a silver mantle of stillness and very rarely smiled. If it had not been for all those incredibly interesting fairy-tale books I would not have been able to take my eyes off her. She noticed my worshipful glances, looked back with a faint trace of amusement, but it wasn't only amusement. I felt there was an odd tension between us.

She became the embodiment of the almost unattainable princesses in the stories I was reading. Won only by courage, kindness to animals, the solving of riddles at the risk of your life, or heaven knows what other ordeals.

One particularly nice August morning I went, as arranged, to Lothar's house thinking, "If his father is home perhaps he'll take us to the wharf today." I pushed the bell button and waited for Lothar. Nothing happened. I waited for a while and rang again. And waited. No call from the window, no Lothar. That was strange. I tried again, and still no answer. I wondered—did I make a mistake? Was I too early? Or too late? No, we had said ten o'clock. I rang again, stepped back, and looked up to the third floor. In the diagonal spy mirror outside their window I saw two faces, Lothar and his mother. They pulled back quickly when they saw me looking up and I watched the curtains fall across the window. I stood paralysed. It felt as if a huge hand were squeezing my chest. Almost involuntarily I raised my finger to ring again and stopped in midair. I stood for a few seconds, finger an inch from the button. The pain descended into my gut and, crying, I slowly put my arm down without pushing the button. At home, creeping into my room, I fell on the bed, still in tears. Mother, who had not left for the store yet, followed me into the room. She sat down next to me, held my hand and told me:

"No, you didn't do anything bad. They're doing something bad. Very bad. They all are."

That was the first time I really understood that I had been made into something different. That the word Jew was more than just a word. That it was a feeling in the chest and in the gut. A pain that someone else could put there for you.

Oddly enough, my own most overwhelming experience of grief came at a moment when things seemed to have calmed down a little. The firing from jobs continued, but there were fewer street arrests and disappearances. Hardly any beatings, or slogans and swastikas on Jewish shop windows. Uncle Mulu stopped talking about war. My parents seemed more relaxed. Perhaps they'll leave us in peace now. Fewer people talked about emigration, only the people who had lost their jobs and couldn't find other work.

My mother told me not to blame Lothar, it was his mother. And sooner or later it would have been the Hitler Youth anyway. I didn't even want to talk about it. I was sure I would never have done such a thing. Norbert was around, but he did not replace Lothar. I didn't know any Jewish children in Spandau and now was afraid to trust the others. At the end of August, Mother sent me off with Norbert and Susi and a whole bunch of other children

40

on a camping trip arranged by some Jewish organisation. I briefly fell in love with a girl—my age for a change—and visibly cheered up.

A cold October wind blew through the streets. The brown shirts were singing a new marching song that was very frightening.

"Wenns Judenblut vom Messer spritzt, gehts uns noch mal so gut."
When Jew-blood squirts from the knife—things are going well for us.

I looked at their tough, proud faces. Some of them smiling, obviously most content with themselves as their boots hit the ground vigorously, terrramp, terrramp, in perfect rhythm, resounding and echoing along the whole length of the marching column. Their arms swung forward and backward, left, right, left, right; the street, wet and grey, smelled of smoke.

At school someone put a copy of *Der Stuermer*, Streicher's prurient, viciously anti-Semitic newspaper into the desks of the three Jewish boys in my class. Each of us had a different copy, months old; mine was dirtied by food and coffee stains. There was something repulsive, disgusting in the leering caricatured faces of vile, hook-nosed Jews with side curls, bending over scantily dressed, helpless, fair-haired, Nordic girls. I wanted to tear the paper to shreds, but I didn't. I looked at it briefly, put it back into the desk and left it there. The next day it was gone.

Lothar did not know me at school after the holidays. I was dreading and at the same time anxiously awaiting the encounter. He was not unfriendly, he just didn't see me. Not even when we found ourselves face to face. I remembered the two unseeing SA men who were boycotting our store and began to loathe him.

Obviously our position had worsened considerably: Now it was quite clearly Us, the Jews—and Them. Not so much in my own class—a few of the boys were even protective of us—but the older boys at school baited us during recess and waited outside school to harangue or beat us. The first time they hit me I went home bloody-nosed and crying. Mother turned white at the sight of my face and started crying too.

When my father came home he told me, "I wish I could help you" and helped me already by putting his arm around me, "but we're defenceless. The police will not protect us either. There's only one thing you can do . . . fight back. It might not stop them, but you'll feel better."

Mother looked away. I didn't think she agreed with him but she said nothing. They rarely contradicted each other in front of the children.

School turned into hell. Quite a few of the teachers were now baiting us too. Ridiculing us in front of the class.

"Zeller?" questioned Herr Schroeder snidely, "that can't be your real name, can it? I bet it was something more like Schmu-le-witz, or I-saaak-sohn . . . right?" Then he snapped furiously: "Stand to attention when I'm talking to you. What do you think this is—a Jew school?"

The class roared with laughter and little dried-up Herr Schroeder grew inches taller. His face crinkled into a self-satisfied, tiny, thin-lipped smile. Almost benignly, he waved his hand in dismissal, bidding me sit down.

One by one, the Jewish children in my school disappeared. At the end of 1934, in mid-term, my parents transferred me to a private, Jewish school.

The Theodor Herzl School was located, of all places, at the Adolf Hitler Platz. The word Platz has two meanings in German. "Square", as in village square, as well as "explode", as in bomb. One bus conductor, announcing the stops, regularly paused for a fraction of a second too long between Adolf Hitler . . . and . . . Platz. This made the interpretation of Platz lean towards "explode" rather than "square". But only just. One couldn't swear to it. There were a few secretly amused faces, a few hesitating-whether-to-be-angry faces, but it went past most people.

I loved the location of my new school. It was close to the Funkturm, Berlin's answer to the Eiffel Tower, as well as to the huge, modern exhibition halls with their fascinating trade shows. The best one was the motor show. Cars were one of my great passions, second only to fairy tales. I not only managed to smuggle myself into the show here and there but watched the cars arrive and depart. I could actually go and touch the silver racing cars as they were being unloaded and once helped to push one into the hall with my own hands. Hanging out in front of the halls, I collected brochures from show visitors and out of waste-paper baskets.

But above all, there were the badges: little metal insignia pins given away by the different car makers. Four interlinked circles from Auto Union, now Audi; the round, blue, white and black chessboard enamel of BMW; the Mercedes Benz silver star in a silver circle. I wheedled them out of exhibitors entering and leaving the building, wore three makes at a time, and got stabbed sleeping with them pinned to my pyjamas until higher authority intervened.

The Theodor Herzl School was an utterly new experience. It took me a good few months to get used to it. It was co-educational, progressive and, as the name implied, Zionist in orientation. This meant that the Hebrew we learned in place of Greek or Latin was Sephardic, as spoken in Israel, rather than Ashkenazi, the Hebrew of the Western Diaspora.

The biggest surprise was that teachers talked "to", rather than "at", you. They asked, rather than com-

43

manded. There was no standing to attention or military heel clicking. You could raise your hand and on a nod from the teacher ask a question while remaining seated. Nobody screamed at you. There were no more unprovoked beatings in the schoolyard.

Another staggering discovery: You could be openly critical of authority, bureaucracy, government, your country, without being struck down by lightning. Mr Gaertner, our History teacher, talking about the spread of the Black Death, told us that we still did not do enough about hygiene. Germany is supposed to be a civilised, clean country. In reality we're pigs. How often do people change their underwear? How often have you gone to a public toilet that has no paper, no water to wash your hands, never mind soap and towel. I'm anxiously looking over my shoulders for the Gestapo to come in and arrest us all. And, my God, this is our teacher, not some kid, talking with us about dirty underwear, toilet paper and other unmentionables.

Well, if this is what Schroeder meant by "a Jew school", I was all for it. Not only that, the stuff we did here was a lot more interesting than what we did at Schroeder's rotten school.

I discovered the joys of Geography, History and Science. Even Maths was not that terrible here. But a diary tells that my favourite three subjects were Sports, Art and Music . . . and that I hated English and Hebrew.

Around the corner from school, the Café Haman. Expensive, but they gave you an ice cream that was almost as dense and heavy as halva, quite unlike the watery stuff you got at the Ice Bar in the Havelstrasse. Haman made their own chocolate and candy, too, and every so often for ten pfennig you could buy the best little bag of "Abfall"— leftovers, broken pieces, crumbs.

Life was looking up, I decided. I had a new best friend, Fred Weil, a classmate. And more.

I was in love with black-haired, blue-eyed Susanne Aaron. She had been around in my class for months. But I suddenly became aware of her in a different way. I couldn't imagine how it happened. I looked at her for the fiftieth time and suddenly my stomach took a plunge. Aching all over, I kept following her after school—walking a little distance behind her all the way to her house, pretending to be utterly unaware of her existence. She became utterly aware of mine, her stricken knight in knee-pants. One day, suddenly, she stopped short, turned round and stood there smiling, in the middle of the pavement, challenging, waiting. I seemed to be walking at the bottom of a lake of jelly, lead in my socks.

Somehow I managed to reach her and squeak in hollow surprise, "Oh, it's you!"

"Yes, it's me." Smiling she told me that she'd been secretly watching me stand and stare up at her apartment window, walk up and down, down and up, finally back the way I had come.

I was watching the vapour her voice made in the cold and thought, how beautiful, she is making little smoky whiffs of air. Since I had totally run out of words she admitted she felt flattered, flirted with me a little and allowed me to walk her home. I did the kazatske with high jumps all the way back to my bus.

I was often permitted to be her escort and soon found words again. Speechlessness was never my greatest failing. We enjoyed each other's company and conversation. I was happy. I loved just looking at her. Once, just once, she held my hand briefly. One afternoon in March.

As we reached her home she hesitated, reached out and took my hand. After a searching look that frightened me she spoke quietly and sadly:

"We're going to Palestine."

Pause. Finally I asked, equally quietly, "For good?"

She nodded. "I've been trying to tell you for two weeks

already." After a look at my face she took my hand to her lips and kissed it.

I burst into tears, tore my hand away and ran back to my bus stop. The next day she failed to show up in class. She had promised to write, but I never heard from her again.

Cousin Maecky, blond and blue-eyed, turned up at our house like a movie hero returning from the battlefield, his face and head all bandaged up, his arm in a sling. Not a frequent visitor, but a welcome one, he was decidedly my mother's favourite nephew. This surprised me. He said "Scheisse", shit, every five minutes, even in front of her, and all she would say from time to time, with a mock-shock smile, was "Shhh . . . die Kinder", pointing in my direction with her eyes. Whenever she started her "Shhh. . . ." I always entertained the faint hope that she was going to say "Shit" too, but she never did. If I ever said that word, even once, even quietly, I would be in the doghouse right away. Not Maecky. He was always smiling, cracking jokes and getting away with murder. I worshipped him.

But he wasn't smiling much this time. We had not seen him for several weeks, because he had been dragged into the hallway of an apartment building and beaten up, Ironically, it was his strictly Aryan looks that got him into trouble. Three SS men had felt personally insulted because he had not saluted the Nazi flag as it was being carried past him on the street by a company of marching storm troopers. When he tried to explain that he wasn't supposed to salute the flag because he was Jewish, they hit him some more as a bonus.

Now he had been beaten up even more viciously for saluting the flag. Two neighbourhood Nazis saw him. They knew he was a Jew, and that Jews were not allowed to salute the flag. Right. So they pulled the frail eighteen-year-old into a courtyard and beat him. Then they

46

"arrested" him and half carried, half dragged Maecky, bloody and totally dazed, along the ground on their way to the SA Headquarters. Passing a bar they decided they were tired, thirsty and deserved a drink. They pulled Maecky into the bar and left him lying at their feet among the rubbish and cigarette butts.

Someone must have slipped out quietly to call a Schupo, a regular policeman. Maecky had no idea how long he had been lying there, but his mind was starting to clear a little when he heard the policeman asking the storm troopers what that man was doing on the floor. They explained the situation, about his offence and that they were taking him to SA headquarters. The big policeman looked grave. Yes, Maecky had indeed committed a serious offence. It was his duty to arrest him immediately and take him to police headquarters.

"And you, *Meine Herren*, would be free to have a little drink."

"Up," he commanded, pulling Maecky roughly to his feet. "March," he yelled to the groggy, swaying boy, pushing him brutally out of the bar, along the street, and around the corner. There he stopped, looked quickly behind him, relaxed his grip and asked Maecky quietly where he lived.

"Can you make it there on your own, *Junge*? . . . *Na gut*. Go home quickly. And don't show your face on the street for at least a week, or we'll both be in trouble. Wait . . . do you have a handkerchief? *Na ja*, take mine. Cover this side of your face, it's a mess . . . No. Go. No time for thanks . . . go . . . quickly."

My mother was crying and repeating over and over, "Thank God he was a decent man, or we would never have seen you again. We would never have seen you again."

"It's scary," said Uncle Mulu. "They're starting again. At the end of last year they seemed to be calming down.

Well, not completely, but they didn't make all these arrests, and they didn't boycott stores. But it's starting all over again. They're raiding the cafés."

But that did not stop my Uncle Mulu, the card player, my father's devil-may-care brother, who insisted on going to the cafés to play "Skat" in spite of the danger. One afternoon he even dragged my father along because he needed a third man for this three-player card game. My father came home much later than expected which caused the only loud, heated quarrel between my parents I had ever witnessed. And it was also the only time I ever got angry at my father. When a Jew was late you feared the worst. We had waited in mounting terror for over two hours, and the fact that he had been playing cards at the Café Dobrin, a dangerous place, did not improve matters.

"If Mulu wants to risk his life that's his affair . . . he doesn't seem to care much about his family, but you do, and . . ." At this point Mother stormed out of the room in tears.

Mulu had always been a daredevil. Like almost all the males in my family, he had been a front line soldier in the Austro-German army during the First World War. A somewhat coarse, but strikingly handsome man with thick, black hair brushed straight back, oval face and classic Russian features, he was taken prisoner by the Russians in 1916. Escaping from the prison camp half-starved, he walked and freight-trucked all the way from the Urals straight though the Russian Revolution, to China. He arrived back in Austria just in time to serve another few months in the army. He talked as non-chalantly about this odyssey as if he were describing a little Sunday afternoon outing in the park. So was he going to let the Nazis spoil his Skat game?

Mulu talked nonchalantly about the past, but at least he talked about it. My parents never did. When I was young

48

I wasn't all that interested. I had no grandparents to make it come alive. Then the present became so overwhelming, there was no time to be concerned with the past. Finally, when there was time for the past, there was hardly anyone left to ask about it, especially on my father's side. Except for Sam Neustein. This was a delightful older cousin of my father's I had never even heard of until 1957 when I got to the United States.

Sam had known my great-grandfather, a tall, stern, God-fearing man who had amassed a most unlikely collection of worldly possessions in Sanok, a rural town in the Carpathian mountains. He owned a dairy farm, a brewery and a bank. For fun he bred Arab racehorses. He had three sons: one inherited the brewery, one the bank and one the farm with the racehorses thrown in for good measure. This last one was my grandfather Hersh, another tall, stern and God-fearing man. He worked the farm and got rid of the frivolous racehorses. My father was born in 1894 while the family was wintering in Vienna, his brother Mulu was born in Sanok. Thus my father was Austrian and his brother Polish, which was to make a significant difference later.

I remember Father telling me that he worked for his father in the office of the farm expediting cheese and butter, and handling the distribution of milk until he was called up to serve in the army. The farm was wiped out by war and taxes.

Sam had no idea of when or why my father and his three brothers and one sister went to Berlin.

The Zellers and the Gottesmanns, my mother's family, met there and tied the knot in two places. First came the passionate match between Mulu and Leona. Somewhat later, in 1922, the more sensible, affectionate match between Fanny and Heinrich was made.

But in May, 1935 there were weightier matters on my

mind than my origins. My eleventh birthday for instance. A terrible disappointment, as it turned out. A nice present or two, yes. Candles and the usual sweet-scented little bouquet of lilies of the valley, yes. But no party. Instead, we were packing. Everything. We were packing store and apartment and moving everything to Havelstrasse 20 in the Altstadt, the old Spandau. We were going to move in right over the Odeum Cinema . . . and that was good, maybe I would get free cinema tickets.

We had to move. Earlier that spring, another bunch of thugs had started to boycott our store. And this time not just for days at a time. They kept coming back for weeks, blocking our door and molesting people who tried to enter. Very few dared. Our business, already feeble, collapsed.

Moving meant I had to pack all my books and toys. A lot of books. I had become an avid, indiscriminate reader and book collector for several reasons. Besides the obvious pleasure of reading, there was the joy of discovery. I was insatiably curious about almost everything. And, since my mother was a maniac about putting children to bed early, tired or not, I would be wide awake at the crack of dawn, long before anyone else. Well, what can you do at that hour noiselessly besides read . . . or draw. Fairy tales were still my favourites; but next came *Tom Sawyer*. I read and reread "Tom" at least a dozen times. In German, of course. The fact that it was set in deepest America did not make the slightest difference. I completely identified with Tom. And I saw my mother in Aunt Polly. I quoted the book on innumerable occasions in my efforts to educate Mother. I read her the cat story in which Tom forces a spoonful of hated tonic down the throat of the poor beast which then runs screaming up and down every wall of the house. When his aunt remonstrates, Tom says angelically, "But Aunt Polly, I'm only doing what you're doing for me. Giving her the tonic for her own good, to make her healthy and strong." This little story so echoed my experience with Mother that I jumped up and down in glee after reading it to her. Mother was not amused.

I was, of course, referring to her repulsive habit of forcing cod liver oil down her poor children's throats . . . for their own good. The first time, on request, I opened my mouth wide, unsuspecting good little boy that I was. When I felt and smelt that vile ooze in my mouth I practically choked with nausea and spat it out all over her. She was upset. I, less so. I felt there was poetic justice in it somewhere. I never again opened my mouth that easily for anyone. Yet nothing deterred crusading Fanny from forcing another spoonful through my clenched teeth a minute later. And another, and another, day after day. How I envied my cousin Heini, Max's son. He could throw up at will and did so loudly, emphatically, right under the second floor balcony on the Hansa Ufer where his parents were still having the breakfast he had been forced to share.

I quoted "Tom" so often, it was a wonder Mother didn't burn the book. But since the Nazis, book burning was not popular among us.

I was beginning to inherit books from emigrating family and friends. Grown-up books. Just having them around made me start to nibble tentatively at Goethe, Kant, Schiller . . . but I preferred roaming through the science fiction world of Hans Dominik, the Wild West of Karl May, and the wastelands of utter trash.

Ultimately everything was packed. Finally, in order to rid herself of two considerable burdens during the move, Mother parked Lilian and me *chez* Aunt Cilly in Charlottenburg.

CHARLOTTENBURG

I have only to hear or think the word Charlottenburg to experience a wave of feelings and sensations. At first there are no individual memories, just a surge of awareness of childhood enchantment and quiet happiness. Then faces, events, and places emerge, singly or in sequence, complete with villains, angels, magic moments, and the fear of death.

On the side of the angels; the Bobaths, Aunt Cilly, my mother's sister, and Uncle Ignatz. Their house was the second home of my childhood. I could not go there often enough partly, no doubt, because there at least I enjoyed centre stage without a little sister to steal my thunder. It's not that my aunt didn't have plenty of children of her own, but she had been considerate enough to have them early, so that by the time I came on the scene they were all grown up and represented little competition.

It is here that I found out a little about my roots on Mother's side. I could never get my mother to talk. My grandfather Hersh Gottesmann and his wife lived the nomadic life of a railway construction supervisor. Aunt Cilly was the oldest of the seven children of different nationalities, born in the various towns and countries that marked the progress of the trans-Carpathian railway from Hungary to the Ukraine. So my mother was Hungarian, her sister Leona Polish and Aunt Cilly Czech. There was a Ukranian brother.

Cilly grew up to be a spirited, promising young woman and then spoiled it all by falling madly in love with the owner of a coffeehouse in the little Galician town in which they happened to be living at the time. It was not a match made in Hersh and Esther Gottesmann's heaven. They accused the poor man of being a gambler, wastrel and womaniser—and came running with various matchmakers to get her settled into something "more appropriate to her standing". Cilly escaped to Vienna to stay with her maternal aunt. She enrolled in a millinery course and was concocting spectacular hats until her mother finally appeared in Vienna and led her back into the bosom of the family. Apparently they had moved to another town, well away from the dangerous coffeehouse owner.

Soon the matchmakers came running again, and Cilly was married off safely to Ignatz Bobath, overseer at a large local vineyard. He was apparently dashing enough for undaunted Cilly to go along with the whole business.

After the First World War, the whole tribe wound up in Berlin where Uncle Ignatz, after trying his luck at being a wine merchant, turned to the more elevated calling of antique dealer. Though not a great businessman, he became quite knowledgeable in the field, prospered and raised a family of doctors and the like, almost, it would seem, in spite of himself. He was fiercely anti-academic and anti-intellectual.

Year after year I was always the only young child staying with Aunt Cilly over the Jewish holidays. That was just fine, because for days and days I could enjoy my very own exclusive, magic kingdom. In fact, there were two kingdoms, the upper and the lower.

The lower one, Uncle Ignatz's antique store in the Krummestrasse, was full of sweet-scented, exotic furniture, wood carvings, fine carpets, old paintings, candelabra, chess sets, silver, ivory carvings, spinning wheels, and all kind of other outlandish paraphernalia. That's what I always imagined Ali Baba's cave would look like and often called out "Open, Sesame" on opening the door, amusing Uncle Ignatz no end.

"Here comes Ali Ba Ba Ba," he called back.

Pity. The treasures of Ali Baba's cave would soon be confiscated, looted and strewn all over the street.

My upper kingdom, the huge Bobath apartment above the store, also overflowed with incredible treasures. Once I earned a reputation for being dexterous and careful, I was permitted to explore, touch, and play with anything.

There were glass vitrines and drawers full of surprises: Japanese masks; silver spoons with miniature enamelled pictures of towns; Indian chess figures of maharajahs on plump elephants; darkly glowing garnet jewellery; turquoise scarabs.

At home I had toy cars; here I played with a miniature Chinese silver rickshaw complete with straw-hatted coolie and reclining passenger. Or with a medieval aquamanile in the shape of a brass horse that poured water from its mouth.

In one of those rooms, not exactly a toy or treasure, but an amazing discovery all the same, my first naked lady. I opened a door and there she was, stark naked, waves of overflowing flesh, plump thighs and pendulous breasts, one arm in the air, exposing a big, black bush of hair. With her head thrown back she was admiring herself, or perhaps the black bush, in the mirror. For a few moments neither of us moved. Then I slammed the door shut and ran for my life. I ran out of the house and didn't stop until I had run at least four times up and down the Krummestrasse. When I finally returned, out of breath, I dared only make it as far as the store. Uncle Ignatz prodded me until I talked and then laughed until tears rolled down his face.

"Someone should have told you. We've rented out a

room since you were here last. Well? Nice and plump and juicy?"

I looked at him in crimson confusion, and he laughed even harder.

"You'll have to knock on doors from now on," he grinned, patting me on the head.

And so I did. Nobody could have knocked on doors more diligently. For a while I even knocked before entering my room at home.

I found out that with the Nazi boycotts, and Jews dumping rather than buying furniture as they fled, business was bad and the Bobaths were forced to rent rooms.

Besides the naked lady I also discovered "Books" in Charlottenburg. Real books, I mean, not the children's stuff I had at home. There were Lotte's art books, volumes of literature and poetry. There were some that I simply could not understand. In them people were doing the oddest things to each other, or on each other. Like the con-cu-bincs in Chin P'ing Mei's *Lotus* and Tsao Hsaeh Ch'in's *The Dream of the Red Chamber*. When I asked, "What's a concubine?" Lotte told me it meant "woman friend" in Chinese.

The *Arabian Nights*, in four volumes, un-ex-pur-ga-ted, translated from the French, proved equally dull. Some porter or another was always going on and on, page after page, calling something the hall of bliss, the pathway to paradise, the soft pink plum of the gods . . . and other such nonsense. I had a shorter, much more interesting and adventurous Arabian Nights at home. With coloured pictures, too.

No, in Charlottenburg, I never complained of being lonely or bored. Fidgety Fred even sat quietly fascinated through the entire length of the Passover seder, which was amazing, considering that Uncle Ignatz did not believe in shortcuts. He performed, silver-haired, round-faced and Russian-looking, dressed in a flowing white smock and silver-embroidered white cap, droning and droning, mumbling Hebrew in an endless, endless chant. That part I liked least, but what made up for all the mumbling was the festive table, the candle-lit faces, the theatrical quality of the ritual, the singing, the food and especially staying up late into the night.

Lotte was the one cousin always attending the seder. This was surprising considering that Lotte, minuscule, a little mannish, not quite pretty, was deep in her Red Revolutionary and Bohemian phase, "living" with Korle Kirstein, a "goy", and a Communist to boot. It'll end badly they said. And it did. The family scenes, the uproar! Frequently raiding the larder, Lotte would go off in the morning, take the booty to her Korle, "live with him", and dutifully reappear at home in the evening of the same day. Behind that wild Bohemian exterior lurked a confirmed bourgeois. And right to the end, her devotion to Aunt Cilly went far beyond the call of daughterly duty. The harsher life treated them, as they fled from country to country, the more they would become the centre of each others' lives.

The other Bobath "children" would be at the seder table reluctantly, trapped by guilt or having no excuse to be elsewhere. Pretty Nina, earnest Karl and smiling Arthur, all atheist to the marrow, would sit and suffer. They had heard it all before, but I, propped up on three cushions next to Uncle Ignatz, was all eyes and ears. I had learned the "*Mane stanu halaila hazseh . . .*" and was eagerly awaiting my turn to pipe up with the Passover question, "Why is this night different from any other night?" Then, basking in the afterglow of the inevitable praise, I would watch the candles burn, look at the pictures and illuminated Hebrew text of the Haggadah, sniff the odours of herbs, eggs, wine and chicken soup with matzo balls.

I had carefully carried a brim-full glass of wine through

the apartment, setting it down outside the front door, so the Prophet Elijah could take it as a refreshment, should he by chance pass through the Krummestrasse. Now I too was offered a sip of this heavy, over-sweet, ruby wine from Mount Carmel. Wincing, I swallowed one sip, bravely.

Finally, when it was all over and I had helped to clear the table, it was time to go to bed, to Lotte's bed. This was another Charlottenburg treat. It was so special to have company in bed, her head at one end of the bed, mine at the other. Drowsy, half-whispered conversations in the dark, until sleep came. It was in Lotte's bed that I heard about my mother's past. My mother the family beauty. The *femme fatale*. A man had shot himself for love of her, I was told, a very fine man, too. She nearly married a member of the Austrian royal family who wanted to start a new life with her in South America after the First World War. She was not only the most beautiful, but also the kindest, smartest, the best educated, and most fashionable woman in the entire family, said Lotte. It was surprising that I never detected the faintest trace of jealousy or hostility towards my mother from Lotte or anyone else in the family. Perhaps they all recognised the sadness, the haunting loneliness, that clung to her in spite of all her gifts.

Lotte was the one who looked after me during my visits. We would sit and talk, go shopping together, share books, share a bed until I was too old for such innocent intimacy and had to sleep in a big, lonely, silent room. It was almost, at times, as if Lotte regarded me as her own child. She seemed already to know that she would never have or want to have a child of her own.

Her brothers Karl and Arthur seemed lofty, unattainable but admirable older cousins, rarely at home, both in their final years of medical school. Earnest Karl was the cousin who sang and played the guitar and whose student microscope I inherited. Arthur, with the husky voice and big smile, was the cousin who rode a motorbike. He breezed along on this noisy, impressive contraption to a lake resort where my parents were on holiday. How I ever persuaded Mother to let me ride pillion, even for a puny hundred feet, quite escapes me. Unfortunately I burned my leg on the hot muffler of the bike which made this my last motorbike ride for twenty years.

The reasons why I was THE child at my uncle's house during the holidays might well have been that I sat still the entire length of the seder and that in fact I showed signs of interest. Years later I was told that Uncle Ignatz was kinder and had more patience with me than with his own two sons.

He and Uncle Max were the only orthodox men in the family and I, it seems, was the only child who found religion interesting. During synagogue visits, I enjoyed the spectacle, the colours and the soaring singing of the cantor. I enjoyed feeling part of a group, sharing the nods and the smiles. But before long I would get bored with the endless babble of praying voices in a language I did not understand. And when, only too soon, I had to learn Hebrew, my lack of success with it did not heighten my tolerance for incomprehensible prayer.

One thing about prayer did impress me though. The rhythmical bending forward and backward of the bearded old men in their stark black and white prayer shawls, as they mumbled their lines in a monotonous singsong. Swaying . . . now here was something for a cramped-up, pew-lamed boy. Soon I was swaying, freestyle, with the best of them. It was a hollow prayer I knew, without Hebrew, but I thought God would understand. In those days I counted God among my closest friends.

I'm sure it was largely due to Uncle Ignatz, and Hitler, that at twelve I decided to have a bar mitzvah, started to wear a yarmulke, and went so far as to remove the ham

from Mother's Hungarian noodle dish. Delicious Prague
ham. I was sure God would be pleased with me, He knew
what a sacrifice that was. My mother understood too,
alas, and made an absolutely kosher version especially for
me, with walnut, cinnamon and butter instead of ham.
This was sad, for although I would have continued to
remove the ham in utter disdain, it would at least, first,
have lent its flavour to the noodles.

So much for the angels. The black side of Charlottenburg was only a few hundred feet further along the same
street, at Krummestrasse 34, my Aunt Bertha, alias Thusnelda. Thusnelda was the name I gave her after I had
read the story of a Germanic queen who poisoned her
husband. Since Bertha was a widow and mean, the name
seemed appropriate and was soon adopted by Norbert
and Susi too. Thusnelda too had an antique furniture
store and home in the Krummestrasse, but there all comparison with her sister Cilly ended. As much as I loved
Aunt Cilly, I loathed Thusnelda. And I was the child
who loved all his uncles, aunts and cousins passionately,
indiscriminately.

Thusnelda herself kindled this hatred, nurtured and
fanned it into full flame, and I still can't say who contributed more to my abhorrence of injustice, the Nazis—or
Aunt Bertha?

Surely, I must have approached her with as much trust,
love and openness as I did the rest of the family. When
she came to visit, arriving after my mother had put the
children to bed, I would do what most children do, clamour for her to visit me. Probably, having finally managed
to get us into bed, my mother had asked her sister to
ignore us.

But I called hopefully all the same. "Tante Bertha,
Tante Bertha!"

An outraged Aunt Bertha answered through the closed
door, "Oh, you naughty boy! Your mother put you to

bed long ago and you're still up? Stop calling immediately. How can you do this to your poor mother? I certainly won't come. Certainly not, you bad boy. Why don't you obey your mother!"

Almost simultaneously I heard my sister's voice, shrill, birdlike, calling from the next room. "Tante Bertha! Tante Bertha!"

And right away my aunt crooned, "Oh my darling, oh my naughty little one . . . oh you are so naughty . . . you should be asleep my little angel. I'll come, but only just for a moment. Your mother . . ." and her voice faded as she entered my sister's bedroom. And there she stayed for quite a while.

The first time this happened I cried. The second I smouldered. The third I burst into a blue flame of anger and hatred. And I became very tired of her unrelenting and unjust interference. It was from her, and at our table, that I constantly heard "Children who talk unasked belong under the table" . . . the German equivalent of, "Children should be seen but not heard." I noticed soon enough that she said this only when I talked too much. My sister seemed to have unlimited dispensation. One day, after just one too many finger-wagging repetitions of the phrase, I took her at her word, and dived under the table. And there, succumbing to temptation, bit her leg. Quite hard.

Bertha shrieked, jumped, put her hand into the hot soup and shrieked again. My father pretended he was choking with soup and not laughter. Mother was not amused.

Eventually I fought Thusnelda in every way I could. The older I got the more I refused to obey her commands, or answer her questions. Undaunted, she went on being Thusnelda the poisoner.

She took great pleasure in pointing out to my parents what a dreadful scholar I was, asking about my grades

60

solely, I felt, so that she could boast about her own two sons.

"Tut tut," she would twitter, "*My* Alfred and *my* Rudi [if only poor rejected Rudi could have heard her], they brought home nothing but straight As. Always!"

I brought home nothing but straight Fs in languages and wasn't that hot in Maths either. But I also had thousands of As in other subjects, I argued. But that didn't interest "Die Dicke Bertha", another loving name we children had for her on account of her tubby body and its likeness to the famous World War I cannon known as "Fat Bertha".

Rudi, her older son, had far deeper wounds. I suffered her insufferable injustices only once or twice a week and had parents to blunt her cutting edge. Rudi wasn't so lucky. He fought a lonely battle. Bertha blatantly preferred her younger son, cute little Alfred. Pretty Alfred could do no wrong, angry Rudi, no right. Rudi rebelled, fought hopelessly, angrily for love, and was finally banished from the happy homestead. Sent to a boarding school, he learned to stand, firmly, on his own two feet, and just as often, on somebody else's toes.

Because she meddled and trampled where angels feared to tread, Thusnelda was not overly popular with grownups either. In fact, my mother was the only relative whose doorstep she could darken.

When visiting Aunt Cilly, I was but a few hundred feet from Bertha's lair. It never occurred to me even for one moment to go and see her. There was one unforgettable visit though, one of my mother's it's-your-own-flesh-and-blood reconciliation efforts. A reluctant Mulu, Leona and their children were invited. They had not spoken with Thusnelda for months because, as usual, she had interfered in her sister's marriage. Mulu disliked Bertha almost as much as I did and would come only if we were coming too.

The peace pipe my mother had lit went out after the first puff thanks to Bertha's unequalled stinginess.

We had come at one o'clock as appointed and found Mulu and company already there. At two-thirty we were still waiting for Sunday lunch, brunch or whatever, but there was no sign of it. Mulu was puffing his horrible cigar, my father his interminable cigarettes. Mother and Leona were exchanging troubled looks. Everybody was waiting. Everybody that is except big-bosomed Bertha. She was talking about her Alfred. Mulu ostentatiously pulled out a gold watch from his vest pocket, popped the lid open and, shaking his head thoughtfully, made clacking tongue noises. With a polite smile he kept on holding it open, the dial facing Bertha. It was unusual for him to be so restrained, I thought.

Lilian cut the Gordian knot with a shrill, "Mummy, I'm hungry!"

"Oh, . . . oh, of course, my darling," said Thusnelda jumping up, "I nearly forgot. How silly of me. We shall have some tea."

"TEA?" Everybody exclaimed at the same moment in horror, astonishment and indignation. "TEA?" A veritable Greek chorus. "But what about lunch?"

"Lunch?" said Bertha, as if "lunch" were a strange, foreign word.

"We're starving," I said, always willing to clarify matters for her.

"Oh lunch!" she exclaimed, shocked in turn, her pencilled eyebrows raised. "But didn't you have lunch before you came?"

"Bertha, are you crazy?" Mulu barked. "Didn't you invite us for one o'clock? It takes an hour and a half to get here. When the devil were we supposed to have had lunch?"

"Oh," she said, brushing this aside coyly, "I don't really know about these things. I never have lunch. I'm on a diet. But look, there's some *Baumkuchen*, surely that will please everybody." Exit Bertha, hastily—my mother and Leona following close on her heels.

When they returned there was tea and a very small pile of air-thin slices of *Baumkuchen*, a delicious, sugary cake. The only substantial offering came on a silver platter, some soggy, sad-looking *Zwieback* and a few leathery slices of Westphalian pumpernickel. Any one of us could have finished off the lot.

A scramble by the kids ensued. The parents sacrificed themselves and contented themselves with a few tiny slivers of cake. Apparently there was nothing else in the house.

When the children wanted some cake too, the dragon, standing guard, breathed a fiery, "Now children, just one slice. You know cake isn't good for you!"

Norbert and I, still hungry, decided to look around a little. Lilian followed. We wouldn't have minded including her in our explorations but she had one foot in the hostile camp and couldn't be trusted. We tried to lose her in the eleven rooms and three corridors of Bertha's big apartment, but she stuck to us like a burr. We threatened murder. We threatened to throw her out the window. Midget followed. On our way I opened a door and quickly closed it before the others could look inside, saying, "broom closet". But it was what I was looking for, the larder.

I whispered to Norbert. Lilian looked at us suspiciously, head forward, black eyes piercing. Generously we offered to play hide-and-seek with her, and hesitantly she fell for it. She was a pushover for hide-and-seek. We played it straight at first. Finally we left her counting, sneaked away, and dived into the larder. Boy oh boy, food. First we chewed some squishy dill pickles. Not ripe yet. Then there was some terrible cheese. Never. Then we managed to pry open a glass jar of home-bottled plums. Not bad.

Not bad at all. In the middle of fishing them out of the syrup with our fingers, slurping and munching, the door opened and we were caught literally red-handed by Lilian, a look of fury and triumph all over her face.

"I'm going to tell Aunt Ber . . ." I grabbed her arm and pulled her into the larder before she could finish the sentence.

"You're not!"

"Yes I am." Stamping her foot.

"I warn you!"

"Am."

So we anointed her all over with gooey gobs of the stinkiest Harzer cheese anybody had ever smelled and pushed her out howling, to do her worst. Might as well get even with her in advance.

Punishment was swift. Our pleas of starvation were allowed as mitigating circumstances in spite of Bertha's howls . . . but poor little Lilian . . . she's your little sister, she's your little cousin, Norbert. We were sentenced to solitary confinement for the remainder of the visit. Norbert in one room, I in another. It was the best thing that ever happened to me. Heaven had seen my sorrows and sent me a miraculous gift in the shape of two thin bound folders.

I had been banished to the library, a reward in itself. Passing through earlier, I had been astonished at the quantity, quality and variety of the books . . . could it be that Thusnelda had a socially redeeming feature? But no, I learned later that the books all came from her husband and it was unlikely that she had ever opened one. But I did. I opened any number of them. I was having a splendid time being punished . . . and then I hit the jackpot: two slim booklets, just hard covers with adhesive strips on the inside to which one could attach sheets of paper. These two folders had lots of papers stuck in them—and what papers. The collated, unexpurgated school reports of my much touted genius cousins Alfred and Rudi. What I saw got me into such a state that I entirely forgot my banishment and marched straight into the living room, hiding the folders behind my back. Something about the way I entered and stood there in front of Aunt Bertha must have been compelling. Conversation stopped, and everybody looked at me.

"Tante Bertha," I said as sweetly and evenly as I could. This was not easy considering that my knees were shaking and my hair standing on end.

"Yes?" asked Thusnelda.

"Tante Bertha, didn't you always tell my mummy that Alfred and Rudi had nothing but As in their school reports?"

"Oh yes, indeed, they certainly did. Certainly. Straight As." She was looking around practically delirious with motherly pride. "They were the best students in their class."

"Tante Bertha," I squeaked with excitement, "here are their report cards. There are Bs and Cs, all over the place, and look, there are even some Fs." I quickly read the worst scores, switching fast from Alfred to Rudi and back. I got in a full ten seconds before my mother found her voice and stopped me.

"All right. That's enough! Give me those folders . . . and go back into the other room."

As I left I caught Mulu's expression. I had just become his favourite nephew. Obviously Bertha had done the same number on his children. Better still, I saw my mother's reproachful look as she silently handed Thusnelda the folders.

Another thing I didn't like about Thusnelda was that she almost annihilated my entire immediate family in her Essex Super Six. She had become the proud owner of a car. Not many ordinary people had cars those days, let alone an Essex Super Six, a monstrously big American car. It said much for the integrity of my character and convictions that not even this impressive attribute could in any way soften my intense dislike of that woman. I heard with undisguised pleasure how she was repeatedly failing her driving test. She gave right turn signals and then turned left. She entered one-way streets the wrong way. She went through red lights. During her sixth test, on a hill, she had rolled back smack against the car behind her because she forgot the brake. She admitted all this, and worse, but was convinced that she was failed solely because the test drivers were anti-Semitic.

When she finally did pass, on her ninth attempt, Uncle Mulu suggested that the testers must have dreaded driving with her so much that they let her pass just to be rid of her.

Since my mother was the only relative who could tolerate Thusnelda for more than three minutes at a time, we had the exclusive privilege of being taken on little outings. We learned never to expect her when it rained. That would get the car all dirty, and it was so expensive to have it washed.

But from time to time, we would find the gleaming beauty standing at our doorstep. My mother expressed some concern about this. Everybody knew we were Jews, wouldn't it arouse the neighbours' envy to see such a car in front of our door? My father felt it didn't matter much what a Jew did, it would always be wrong. He added quickly that if it worried her, he would be perfectly happy not to go on those rides with Bertha. But one of the very few pleasures my mother still had left was to get out into the country once in a while and breathe some fresh air. Bertha was driving, Father next to her in front—as Mother insisted for good reasons—the rest of us in the back. And as the countryside rolled by, my mother's fantasies took solid shape.

They were such modest fantasies. No castles or man-sions, or elegant houses. A little cottage in the country was all she yearned for. And the peace and rural tranquillity it implied.

"Look at that house, Bertha, such a lovely, darling little house. That's all I want, just a little house like this with a little garden and I would be so happy." How I longed to give it to her . . . well I would, I decided, when I grew up.

One Sunday we wanted to go east out of Berlin for country air and to meet friends. To save Bertha the round-trip to our place in the West, we went to her apartment in Charlottenburg. It was an ideal day to stay home. Hitler was being driven through the centre of Berlin, through flag-waving roaring crowds, on his way to address a mass rally. Father expressed some doubts about going anywhere that day, but my aunt brushed them aside. No Hitler was going to make her miss visiting our friends and getting some fresh air in the country. She also dismissed my father's suggestion that she pick us up in Spandau and avoid the city by taking the peripheral route. No doubt she thought that he was just trying to con her into picking us up. So we had a tough time on buses getting to her house and then, driving, immediately found street after street blocked.

Passing through a wide avenue with big stores, we saw pavements full of people enjoying the sunshine, window-shopping on the way to see the Fuehrer. We kept to the right of the dual tram-tracks in the centre of the road. Thusnelda was crawling along in second gear, holding up traffic behind her. Perhaps she was nervous because the tram rails could make steering a little difficult at times. She went so slowly that a tram overtook us on the left even though it slowed down for the stop just ahead of us. By law, Bertha should have stopped behind the tram car to let people enter and exit. But she didn't. She crawled on until she drew level with the front entrance, and there

she stopped because she only now noticed a car parked
ten feet in front of her. There was enough room to pass
diagonally between the tram and the car, but she didn't.
She just stood there blocking the front entrance.

"People have to get in and out and there's plenty of
space to go ahead," my father pointed out quietly.

But she shook her head vehemently. Grumbling,
people had to squeeze past our car to board the trolley.
When they had gone my father gently suggested that
perhaps she might want to continue on the way—there
were still lots of people getting on and off at the back—
and if a policeman saw us blocking the entrance? . . .

"Under no circumstances," said Bertha. "That is
illegal!"

Father shrugged his shoulders and we waited and
waited. One minute. Two minutes. Suddenly Bertha
moved. So did the tram. We were just about to be crushed
between the parked car and the tram.

There was a furious clang of the trolley bell. Bertha
screamed, let go of the wheel, lifted both hands to shield
her face and slammed her foot on the accelerator. The
car surged forward, raced diagonally across the street,
towards the store, towards an oncoming tram. I saw the
big store windows coming at us as if in slow motion head-
on, the tram coming at us just to the right. Bertha, hands
to her head, was still screaming, as were people on the
sidewalk who saw us coming. Just before we could mount
the pavement, Father grabbed the wheel and wrenched it
sharply to the right. The car screamed louder than Bertha
as we were all thrown violently sideways. For a moment,
almost on top of us, was the big glass windshield of the
oncoming tram and behind it the bulging eyes and open
mouth of the frenzied driver, madly clanging his foot
bell. The tram's brakes shrieked as we recrossed its path,
missing it by inches. And now we were racing for the
right pavement, Father fighting for control with frenzied

Bertha, who with her foot still on the accelerator, had grabbed the wheel again and was wrenching it too far to the right. Kicking her foot of the accelerator, Father quickly turned off the ignition and the car came to a jarring, jolting halt, the front wheel already mounted on the right kerb.

Bertha, her face grey and ugly with fear, tried to push Father away, brushed her arms with her hands as if brushing of dirt, grabbed the wheel again and hissed, "Leave me alone, let go!"

My father held on to the wheel and told her he would drive but she wouldn't let him. Angrily, she pushed his hand off the wheel, started the car, got it off the kerb and went straight through the red light of the major crossing in front of us. Pandemonium. Honking, hooting, shouts. We were stuck in the middle. A policeman appeared out of nowhere and, holding up his arm majestically, led her out of the traffic, across to the far side.

"Ach mein Gott" said Aunt Bertha. *"Ach mein Gott."*

The officer tapped his forehead, then shook his finger at Bertha with controlled indignation, while searching for something with his other hand. Up came a little black book, and a pencil. As he lifted the pencil to write, the lights changed and the tram Thusnelda had originally refused to pass, pulled up on his far side. The driver, red in the face with bursting veins, leaned out, screaming strings of insults at Bertha past the policeman's head. Then, giving her the same you-idiot sign the policeman had just given her, but stabbing his finger practically into his forehead, he screamed that she should be locked up. A lunatic, insane, a menace. He tried to tell the officer what had happened . . . but there was so much noise now that no one could understand anything. We were blocking half the road, and traffic diverted from Hitler's route had piled up behind us and on all sides of the crossing. Honking, hooting, clanging of bells. Hell on wheels.

The policeman, his little black violations book in his left hand, gave up with a silent curse written all over his face. He commanded the tram to move. He bent down in frustration to Bertha's window and, pointing forward, roared in her ear "Go. Go—and for heaven's sake, don't ever come back this way."

My Aunt Bertha saved by Hitler.

For weeks she kept on pointing out the fading black and blue mark "where Henjou had kicked her". She would have managed perfectly well if my father had not interfered. She would have been "perfectly all right". Ironically, even if this had been true, nobody would have believed her.

Despite sisterly love, my mother was disinclined to risk her family again after this incident and the Essex Super Six disappeared out of our lives forever. At the earnest entreaty of my mother, Thusnelda once more became a pedestrian, which lengthened her life by a year or two.

OLD SPANDAU

The boycotts and frequent "Jew" graffiti on our store windows achieved their purpose, and my parents had to close before they lost everything through bankruptcy. Anyway, what was the point of being in the main street of Spandau if no one dared to enter your shop? They decided to unite store and apartment, moving everything to one location in the middle of the old town with its narrow, winding, busy commercial streets. The "busy" was perfectly all right with me. So were the big store windows. It was really very exciting. But instead of the perfume of flowering trees and the scent of freshly mowed grass we had enjoyed at our previous apartment, we now had whiffs of primitive drainage and the musty odour of old houses, not to speak of car fumes. Dingy or not, I liked the Old Spandau houses, with hidden corners and alleys that could be explored. As for nature, well, there were at least five trees sprouting in the cobble-stoned Heinrichsplatz between the Romanesque, red-brick Nikolai Church with its square, squat tower and the low little houses surrounding it.

If you left this quiet little medieval village square with its iron and glass lanterns and proceeded through a narrow passage, you found yourself in the curving, busy Havelstrasse. Our store-apartment at No 20 was right above the Odeum Cinema. A large square opening and a dark passage, just wide enough for a horse and carriage to

71

enter, led to an inner courtyard. On the left of that passage, just before the courtyard, a gloomy, angular winding
staircase took you one flight up to our apartment-store.
There was another small staircase, going up from our
landing to Mrs Hohmann's tiny Mansard apartment. On
our landing was the shared, bring-your-own-paper toilet,
not very inviting at the best of times, and a dank, drafty,
cold affair in winter.

The store was in a large rectangular room straight off
the hallway. Against one long wall, deep shelves held the
heavy rolls of suit, dress and coat fabrics. On the opposite
wall a row of windows overlooked the small courtyard.
In front of the shelves, there was a long L-shaped counter.
Add to this a few heavy-chested tailor's dummies, four
creaky wicker chairs, a wicker table, some tatty, out-of-
date fashion magazines, white lighting globes—and that
was the store.

Winter heat was provided by a high, square, white-tiled
stove that had to be lit and cleaned every day and ate
lozenge-shaped, black, pressed-coal briquettes. A similar
stove in the living area was kept going at a low setting
day and night. I got to cart the buckets of ashes down the
stairs all winter!

Looking out of the courtyard windows one could see a
sort of metal chicken ladder that climbed steeply to a
door in the middle of the blank wall. It led to the cinema's
projection room with its two gleaming, smoky, oily-smell-
ing, snarling projectors. I often saw the projectionists
standing on the staircase puffing a cigarette and cooling
off and wondered how they could possibly not be watching
the film.

A door from the store and another one from the landing
led to our four-room cold-water flat. The kitchen,
squeezed in as an afterthought, had no light or ventilation.
There was a closet that served as a larder, an ancient gas
stove, a rickety wooden table, a few shelves and cup-

boards. The deep sink and cold water tap in the store served both kitchen and cleanliness. Major laundry had to be done outside. Yes, it was definitely a comedown.

Lilian was unhappy about giving up her own bedroom. My parents were unhappy about giving up a decent kitchen, good laundry facilities, but most of all about losing the hot water bathroom. Neither Lilian nor I considered this a tragedy. Too much washing took off your skin, that was certain. And the weekly bath pilgrimage to friends or family was quite enough for us, thank you.

What I missed most was the big field in front of the town hall where you could always join a soccer game, or play war in the four-foot-high mountains at the far end.

But there was something quite wonderful near us now, the Spandau Citadel, with its round, squat, reddish-brown brick tower, its park, a bridge from which you could fish, a moat on which people skated in winter and ancient ramparts where badges, bullets, pieces of helmets, spent shells and other treasures could still be unearthed.

The Havel River with its beaches was also close and since it was May I was eagerly waiting for jump-into-the-water weather.

We were also near the cows. I was one of those lucky city kids able to verify with my own eyes that milk originates in the cow—not the carton or bottle. I even knew how they got the milk out of the cow. By pulling its teats, not by pumping its tail. I did it myself, in a cowshed which was in the courtyard of a building in the middle of Old Spandau, two minutes from the Havelstrasse.

I went there every day with my white enamel can and got the milk still warm from the cow. One late afternoon I succeeded in convincing the plump milkmaid that my school studies made it imperative for me to see how a cow is milked. She grinned, led me backstage and showed me how. Then she handed me the bucket, pointed at the stool and beckoned me to try.

"Who? Me?"

I swallowed hard, sat down on the stool, put the bucket between my knees the way she did, breathed in deeply the unique odour of cowshed . . . and looked at her for inspiration. She laughed and showed me how to get hold of the teats, move my fingers in sequence, squeeze and pull. I pushed my forehead into the side of the cow and gently got hold of the two nearest appendages. They felt warm, velvety soft in a floppy, firm way and I started squeezing. A live cow, by God, a real live cow.

Nothing came out, but at least the cow did not seem to mind. Then my right fist squeezed harder, and a little squirt of milk shot into the bucket with a plonk. Nothing from the left teat. But again something from the right. I guessed I was going to be a right-teat milker.

The teacher had to attend the counter, and as I got up she assured me that I had done very well for a first time. Out in the dusk, floating home on a cloud of happiness, I ran smack into an ambush. Before I knew what was happening, they had landed a whole series of punches and kicks, knocking me right down. There were three of them and they must have been waiting in the dark, impatient, furious because I had stayed in the cowshed so long. A welcoming committee. The local heavies had discovered that a Jew had moved into their neighbourhood.

I was so concerned about spilling the milk that I didn't protect myself well. This earned me a black eye, a bloody nose and a split lip. Stupid. They finished off by pouring the milk over my head anyway, so I should have dropped it right away and moved my back to the nearest wall.

All was not lost, however. I took a good look at my three assailants and recognised one of them from my old school. So that's how they knew.

There was something in what my father had told me. Hit back. You'll feel better, and they'll respect you more.

I hit back, and more. I remembered my assailants' faces for months on end; and when I encountered one of them alone—and he wasn't twice my size—I would move quickly. Before he knew what was happening, I hit him on the chin as hard as I could, so hard that I hurt my knuckles. The violence of the impact and the shock worked wonders. It scared and shook up some of the toughest bullies, including the former school mate involved in the cowshed ambush. Standing over this bawling hero of yesterday I hissed, quivering with knee-shaking rage:

"You rotten shit coward. Remember this the next time you attack me with two others. I'll get you on your own, no matter how long it takes. That's a promise."

I would usually clear off before my adversary could get the notion of hitting back. Skinny as a rake, I was absolutely no match for some of the toughs I walloped. It was surprise, speed—and beat it.

News of my apparent toughness and some nimble footwork in soccer got around pretty quickly and saved me quite a few beatings and taunts, at least in my immediate neighbourhood. Every so often one of my soccer friends would voice a pat anti-Semitic slogan like, "We can thank the Jews for that", then stop himself and look sheepish. I'd shrug my shoulders and ignore it, or if I felt in the mood I'd reply:

"Yes, it's all the fault of the Jews and the bicycle riders."

If they hadn't heard it before they would ask. "Why the bicycle riders?"

And I would answer, "Why the Jews?"

In June, my innocence ended abruptly when some of my classmates told me the facts of life. In the vilest way, of course.

"My parents did that? Never!"

I was so repelled, I refused to go to school the next

day. I didn't even pretend to be sick. I just didn't want to go. It was still dark in my bedroom when Mother came to sit at the edge of the bed. Eventually she got me to give her just the slightest hint of what was bothering me. She understood immediately.

"All right. You don't have to go to school today. Have your breakfast and we'll talk."

After breakfast she sat with me, spoke quietly, gently and explained things in a different, surprisingly frank, sensible way. I was still in shock but beginning to feel better. I was also curious.

"How often do people do it?"

"Oh, go on. I'll tell you on your wedding night," she replied.

I said "surprisingly frank and sensible" because today I realise how contradictory my mother had been on that subject. She had never prepared the ground. There was a marked avoidance of nudity or references to sex at our house. When it had become absolutely necessary, she had told me the basic facts, but neglected to impart some most valuable practical information. My schoolfriend Weil thought people did it once a year, and that seemed reasonable.

There were also Mother's quite absurd views on masturbation. She would point at people in wheelchairs, on crutches; point at misshapen, mongoloid or pockmarked people and tell me:

"You see what happens if you play with your menkile!"

Don't ask me where that "menkile", "menki" for short, comes from. Or where she could have acquired those weird and wonderful notions. But in those days a great many mothers seriously believed that masturbation led to hideous diseases, or at the very least to the asylum for the criminally insane.

To prevent this fate worse than death, Mother absolutely insisted on bathing me until I was nearly eleven years old. I told her that I considered it undignified. I resisted. I protested that I wasn't a baby any longer. I was not heard.

She nearly fainted one day, when she saw me, lying on my back in the tub, splashing so that the water pushed my limp penis—splash left—splash right.

"Stop it instantly!" she shouted in horror and went into her usual lurid litany.

"Mother, I wasn't even touching it!"

It was my substitute rubber duck, that's all it was. At that time I still had no idea what one could do with an erection nor did I have the foggiest notion why anybody in their right mind would want to play with their menki. Play "aiming for the sky", sure, but that was just a game among the boys as to who could pee the highest. But in any case you had to hold your menki to pee. What on earth did she want?

Not surprisingly my first major battle for independence was fought and won right there, in the bathroom. One day I simply locked her out. I rushed into the bathroom, locked the door and bathed with a beating heart while she thumped, screamed and raged outside the door. Since I emerged from that bathroom clean, neither a cripple nor an imbecile, and perhaps also because she discussed the event with my father, I was permitted to bathe solo from then on. That defiant night, my father gave me a long, amused look. He had a twinkle in his eye and an aura of secret pride that made me melt with love for him.

A bit later, when I did have some idea what masturbation was about—pure theory, of course (who would want to lose all his hair and teeth)—Mother earnestly told me that she preferred me to "go with a woman" to masturbating.

"But don't I use my menki when I go with a woman?" I asked.

Mother looked distressed. "Well, yes . . ." she hesitated, then added quickly, "but it's different," and brushed aside any further questions. Something was wrong there. Even a kid could see that.

A couple of months later, at the children's holiday home in Kolberg, I was sick and had to spend a couple of days in the "hospital room". My roommate Max was lying quietly in the bed next to mine. Not so quietly, I noticed suddenly. His blanket was moving in a strange fashion, up and down, up and down, not far from where his rear end ought to be, and he was breathing most heavily. This alarmed me . . . was he about to choke?

"Are you all right, Max?" I asked.

"Sure," he answered huskily, "sure," and I went back to my book. After an hour his bed started shaking and he was grunting strangely again . . . but, he insisted, breathlessly, that everything was quite all right. Quite all right.

A couple of hours later that whole business started all over, but this time I got up quietly, tiptoed to his bed and yanked his blanket down.

My God, he was playing with his menki!

I was stunned and tried to warn him. I pleaded with him, but he just went on doing what he was doing with a mad look in his eye. Good God, Mother was right, he was going crazy.

I ran to the nurse and asked her to save him from the wheelchair. She looked interested and asked me what I meant. I told her. She asked me what a menki was. Then she told me quite calmly that my mother must have misunderstood something; that nobody would be harmed by playing with "their little thing", as she called it. I stood there, head cocked sideways, my mouth open. She laughed, patted me on the head and told me to get back into bed at once. Standing around barefoot when I'm sick, that could land me in a wheelchair, she added with a grin. I was shocked. I was shattered. I only half believed her. On the other hand, I now only half believed my mother.

Bad Kolberg, a Spa on the Baltic Sea, evokes a kaleidoscope of colours, tastes, smells and sensations.

My first view of the sea. Waiting in the yard of the Kinderheim with a whole bunch of excited, impatient children. Finally marching straggly, out of step, lined up in threes, a long chattering column, counsellors at the back, in the middle, and leading in front. Slowly we wound our way out of the sleepy little town that smelled of brine and smoked flounder, past the well-tended flowerbeds of the little park, to the sand, the twisted pines, the dunes. Suddenly we saw the blue water through a gap in the dunes, through the branches of the pine trees. All the kids danced up and down shrieking. "The sea, the sea!" and broke out of the column, running towards that blue. I raced, sandals in hand, feet kicking up the hot, white sand, shins pricked by the tall, sharp, yellow-green beach grass, down the dune towards the blue. And there in the sun, the endless water, the endless, landless horizon. I thought my heart would burst.

Almost every day was carefree, happy. I walked along the Baltic beach, looking for amber among the seaweed, or on the wet, buff sand. What a thrill to find suspended in some glowing droplet, ancient insects or fragments of long dead plants. A boy's treasures beyond compare.

And the cry of seagulls hovering. The white beauty of their flight. The salt sea smell.

The smell of the thick, hot brine at the spa as we sat soaking, two in a tub, up to our neck in the warm brownish liquid that cures all ills, tended by a heavy, buxom maid. A Brunhilde with rolled-up sleeves.

"Come on, out you two and into the shower. No nonsense now!" And a pat on the bare behind.

Kolberg is also the memory of freshly smoked flounders bought secretly at the smokehouse down the road. Glistening, golden-skinned, greasy flounders, bought after a collection of pennies by the four inmates of my room. They were smuggled in under the shirt of our contraband runner and munched by the open window, towel-fanned by friends, so the tell-tale smell would not seep out into the corridor and reach the noses of higher authority.

The revelation at Kolberg that Mother was not always right strengthened me in the ensuing battle of the bicycle. Actually this wasn't just a battle, it was a long campaign, with many battles, feigned retreats, ambushes and sudden breakthroughs. And even this campaign was merely a part of a much bigger thing, the constant war called "Educating Mother".

It had already started way back in the Kleine Tiergarten when Papa, moved by Mama's frown, bravely tried to hold and balance me on my first bicycle. I pedalled madly and broke away to my first taste of delirious two-wheeled freedom. Although I returned without a spill, I saw the writing on my mother's face. It said, "Thou shalt not ride anywhere but in the park." And this was rigidly, relentlessly enforced. Year after year, honour bound, I had to walk my impatient bike all the way to the park and only there could I mount. By the time I was eleven this had become quite embarrassing. Helpful kids riding past me on their bikes would stop to ask whether my bike was in trouble. Did I have a flat tyre? No? Just scared . . . ha ha ha! The time had come to do something about it.

I started to ride on the rarely used road at the side of the park. Soon enough, Mother was asking the expected questions.

"Where did you go? What did you do? Whom did you see? You didn't ride anywhere except in the park, right?"

"Wellll . . . not really."

"What do you mean, not really?"

My mother had done a great job on me. Pavlovian conditioning. Reinforced above all were two things. "A

promise is a promise" and, "Lying is the worst thing you
can do. I can forgive almost anything but a lie."

When the cash register rang up either one of those two
numbers my saliva ran. Of course, there were the lies we
don't even know we utter, the ones we believe in. But
deliberate lies—those I would use only in most dire need.
This frequently left me defenceless in some trying circumstances where lying or breaking a promise would have
been perfectly appropriate. Where, in fact, it would have
been regarded as a social grace. It took me fifty years to
learn that a lie in time saves nine.

But there was one kind of lying that wasn't all that
difficult for me: telling half the truth. Where did you go?
The park. What did you do? Played football. True, all
true. But I played football for only thirty minutes and then
went swimming, which I wasn't supposed to do because of
my cold. Had she asked me whether I went swimming,
then it would have had to be the truth and nothing but
the truth. My mother relied on it . . . and for once, so
did I. I wanted to be found out.

So when she asked, "What do you mean . . . not
really?" I put on a good show:

"Wellll," hesitantly, looking at my feet and then raising
my eyes heavenwards. "Not really." Looking sideways.
"I mean I just rode a little bit on the road. Lots of kids
ride their bikes there." Pointing my hand in the general
direction of the park, "You know, that little road right
next to the park." Finally looking her in the eyes, "I was
riding on it, just a little. That road is really *in* the park,
you know. It really is!"

"*Jaj istenem!*" she wailed in her native tongue, as I
knew she would. "*Mein Gott*, what have I done to deserve
such children. Have I not told you a thousand times . . ."

I won't waste paper. It went on for about ten tiring
minutes, and the last word was the foreseen, absolute

81

prohibition of the bicycle for two weeks. Not bad, I was expecting at least three.

I sat around at home, where she could see me. I suffered, moped, trailed from room to room. I did a dying Camille and got on Mother's nerves thoroughly.

"It's a beautiful day. Go to the park," she advised.

"Can I take the bike?" eagerly.

"You know very well you can't!" firmly.

"Oh," broken-heartedly.

Standing around in the living room brooding was not easy on me either. I would much rather have sat reading in my room or in the park. I was in the middle of *Ivanhoe*, and it was really exciting . . . and a great consolation. Everybody hated us so much, it was good to learn that a brave Christian knight could be on the side of the Jews. I was dying to get back to the book . . . but I had better do what had to be done: it was in a good cause.

"Go to the park!" she said. "You look pale. Take your nice book and get into the sun."

My God, how this woman knows me, I thought. "Don't feel like it," I whimpered and concentrated on looking haggard and wasting away in front of her very eyes, driving her crazy, I hoped.

Two days later I was back in the park with my bike. Back on that prohibited little road, too. Again, truth would out, followed by her punishment for me, my punishment for her. Back to the park . . . and so on. Total war. "When the irresistible meets the immovable the immovable has to bend a little." Zeller's Third Law.

After a month the little street became part of my permitted territory. After all I'd come back alive from there so many times already.

It took another month to win the freedom of the street from our house to the park. By the end of July, I could ride the bike to the Havel swimming baths, but there the line was drawn. I withdrew behind prepared lines, waiting for reinforcements.

A year earlier I had dramatically and quickly learned to dog-paddle. The occasion was one of our family bike outings. My enthusiasm for cycling had borne fruit: my parents bought bikes themselves, and on nice summer Sundays we all went on little runs into the woods or to a lake. Mother a little wobbly, Lilian on the back of Father's bike beaming because she had her daddy all to herself and I on my best behaviour, proving to Mother what a safe rider I was. These outings were marvellous. Somehow, being together on wheels felt more together than just being in the same place at the same time.

We would picnic under the trees, usually within a short walk of a Gasthaus, where you could buy a cold beer, or hot water to make your own tea or coffee in enamelled pots brought along for that purpose. Having paid your modest way, you were usually permitted by the restaurant to use one of the big wooden tables in the shade, for bourgeois comfort and *Gemuetlichkeit*.

On one of these outings we found a delightful beach on the lake next to a steep, pine-studded hill. I watched a bunch of kids pushing their bikes up the hill and coming down wildly with clouds of dust and shrieks of delight. This appealed to me, and I pushed my bike up too. It had a good front brake and a drum brake that literally locked the rear wheel when I back-pedalled. I made two thrilling descents, slaloming between the trees and making a tight, dusty, skidding turn at the bottom of the hill where it dropped off sharply into the water. The third time I was unlucky. The front brake cable snapped. And the chain broke when I jammed on the back-pedal rear brake. So I had no brakes and one hell of a descent through a maze of pine trees, bushes and rocks . . . and at the bottom, deep water. I wailed like an air raid siren as I shot down, missing trees by inches, flattening bushes, miraculously avoiding rocks, landing with a tremendous splash in water well over my head. The bike disappeared under me. I dog-paddled and screamed between choking mouthfuls of water. Happily my father had recognised my descending wail and was already sprinting to my rescue. I was not aware of it . . . struggling blind with the fear of drowning . . . but somehow staying on the surface long enough for his arrival. He pulled me out quite a bit the worse for wear.

Since I was only an incipient dog-paddler it took a series of major battles with Mother to get permission to go bathing alone. She could not accompany me, having her hands more than full with looking after Lilian, the store, the home, my father and me. Father was staying away from home with increasing frequency and for longer periods. There had been a Gestapo daytime visit to "question" him. Luckily, he was out, and they left after asking Mother some questions about his Austrian birth certificate. Of course, when they really wanted someone they came at five in the morning. But now, whenever the heat was on and mass arrests were made or rumoured, Father spent nights at the homes of Christian friends or Jews with foreign passports.

It was a hot summer. Mother finally took pity on me and let me go bathing provided this, that and the other . . . and I had to sign a whole lot of her rules in blood. After a few rides there I decided to walk to the bath and leave my bike at home. It kept getting vandalised. Somebody was undoing the brakes, letting air out of the tyres and, once, even cut a tyre. Was it a coincidence that it usually happened when I saw Werner in the swimming baths? Werner was one of the three assailants outside the dairy with whom I later evened the score. He and his two companions smiled at me in a particularly snide way whenever I met up with them at the swimming baths. I didn't tell Mother about it. I wanted to go on swimming.

The swimming baths was bordered by long, floating beams chained together to form a huge rectangle. I would dog-paddle, letting go of the beam, advancing a few feet and grabbing the beam again until I went the full circumference, and back again. Gradually the paddle turned into a swim stroke, and then into a few strokes at a time.

I was making good progress until one day, clutching a rolled up towel, sweaty, hot from the long walk, I put my ten pfennig on the counter for an admission ticket, and froze. There was a sign nailed to the side of the wooden booth. *"Juden unerwuenscht"*, Jews not welcome. The elderly man behind the counter tore a ticket from the yellow roll and put it down in front of me. I still stood frozen. Puzzled, the man followed my stare and froze too. Looking questioningly at me he saw the answer in my eyes. After a moment's hesitation he leaned forward in an awkward, embarrassed way, picked up the ticket and held it out to me.

"Na Mensch Kleener, jeh doch schon rein" in Berlin dialect—"Oh come on kid, why don't you go in", then adding, "I didn't put that stupid sign there."

I shook my head slowly. I was thinking of Cousin Maecky and his two beatings. Thanking him I turned and left. A bit farther, I paused by the fence, looked in, watched the wet bodies and heads in the shimmering water—and hated, hated, hated.

I should have expected it, but it still came as a shock. There were plenty of those signs everywhere, but a summer without swimming? What was I going to do?

Late in the spring, the SA had started again. This time there was something different about it. It wasn't organised, orchestrated, purposeful as it had been just before and after Hitler took power, like their nationwide boycott of all the Jewish stores. This was a sporadic, spontaneous, gratuitously virulent bubbling up of widespread hatred all over Germany from small groups or individuals. Here and there a store window was broken and plundered. There were arbitrary raids on coffee houses or other meeting places frequented by Jews; door-smashing raids on individual homes; a few SA men waited at street corners to catch, beat and batter some of their victims, "arresting" others to put them into concentration camps on charges such as "spitting on the Nazi flag", or "insulting the Fuehrer".

And something else was different. Now it was no longer just the SA or the SS who were the threat. For men, women and children in general, Jew baiting had become a popular movement. I ceased to be "their" Jew to quite a few Christian friends. Norbert's close friend Ulli Grimm, whose family used to go on outings to the Grunewald with us, spat on him in public whenever they ran into each other. A good mouthful of spit. First there was a notice barring Jews here, then there, then suddenly everywhere, at cinemas, restaurants, shops, even food stores. What are we going to do if all the food stores put up these signs? Some were forced on shopkeepers by the SA; many went up because people joined the pack.

Every day there was a new story. A wealthy Jew's house in Dahlem was burned down. Another's car tyres were slashed. Near the Grenadierstrasse religious Jews were beaten up, their beards set on fire, by a bunch of jeering young kids. The Hochmann store across the street had, "The Jews are our misfortune" painted in large white letters across two windows. A trail of white drips led to a hallway two doors away. Only three people lived in that house, none of them Nazi party members. Former friends denounced Jews for listening to foreign news broadcasts, owning banned books or other such offences, offences serious enough to put them into concentration camps. But not only Jews were denounced. "Former friends" had become dangerous even to Christians, even to Nazis who, denounced, couldn't prove absolute loyalty.

We were sweating, my friend Fred Weil and I. It was the middle of the long summer holiday and we couldn't go swimming. My few remaining "Aryan" football friends told me to ignore the notice. Sure, bring your friend too. We'll protect both of you. We'll take you inside personally.

"An' if anybody don't like it we'll show 'em what!"

I discussed the matter with Weil. No. We were scared, besides, it could get our parents into trouble. Yet there had to be some way to cool off. We were brooding on a park bench looking across the water of the Citadel moat. There was plenty of water around Spandau and even places where it should be easy to get in. But who's going to take us? Who's going to keep an eye on us so we don't drown? Then one thought led to another and we had it all worked out.

We had bicycles . . . and a bicycle pump, right? For about two marks we could each buy a patched, old car inner tube and blow it up, right? If we swam on one of those it would prevent us from drowning, right? And that should satisfy our parents, if we ever were to tell, rather if we ever had to tell them that we went swimming in the open lake. And even if one of those tubes went kaputt in the water, there was always the other guy with a tube. Right? Doubly safe! That should satisfy anybody.

A simple and brilliant, a simply brilliant solution. We'd have to find an accessible hiding place for the inner tubes and we would have to swim in the buff or wear underpants and dry off in the air. No telltale wet towels or swimsuits. Those were hardly serious obstacles.

Berlin is a city of rivers, lakes and sandy pine forests. In the west, just above as well as below Spandau, the river Havel opens up into apparently endless lakes with many side arms, islands, beaches and forested shores.

Scouting on our bicycles we soon found a few hidden spots not too far from where I lived. Much too far on the bike for *my* mother, of course. Weil's mother allowed him to ride anywhere. But neither mother would ever have permitted us to swim at an unguarded, totally deserted beach.

Still, with our safety equipment, we felt we had done everything sensible that could be done under the circumstances and embarked on our career as inner-tube sailors. But since being so profoundly sensible had been such a strain, we were soon doing something profoundly silly. We went further out on the lake than anyone should, especially someones who could hardly swim.

This sunny day we were floating side by side, way out on the Tegeler Lake. My parents thought we were in the park. Well, we were in the park and would swear to it any time. Who's got to reveal that the park we went to was at the Jungfernheide and not the Citadel?

Weil was telling me a marvellous Hitler joke.

Goering and Hitler are discussing the Jews and fat Hermann says, "but I've got to hand it to them, they're smart". Hitler disagrees. They fight about it and Goering sets out to prove his point. He drags Adolf to an Aryan household store and picks out a set of china. He sets up the cups on saucers so that all the handles point right and then calls the store owner. He tells him that he likes this style but that the friends to whom he is giving the service are all left-handed. He would like a left-handed set. The owner is taken aback. He has never had that request before and would have to call the wholesaler. Would they come back tomorrow? Goering nods, grins at Hitler and leads him into a Jewish store. Goering goes through the whole thing exactly as before and then calls the owner.

"Left-handed cups," says Mr Cohen frowning, "Ah. I will check. Just one moment, please."

He takes the cups and saucers on their tray to the rear

88

Mother in 1929.

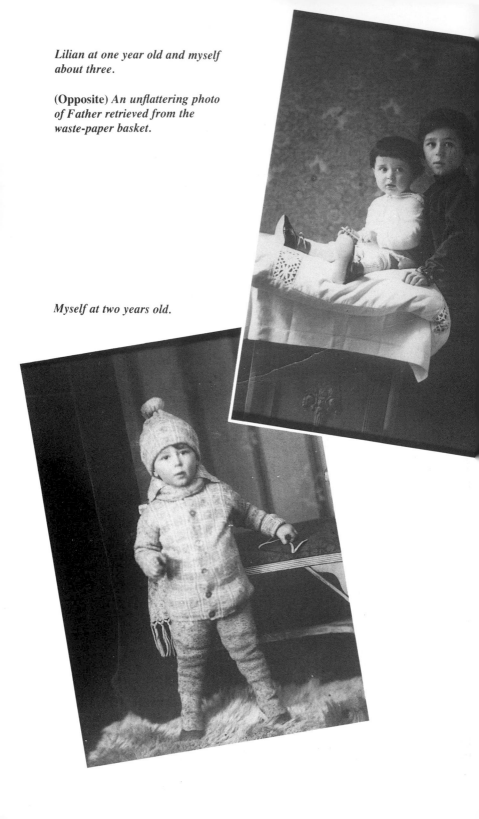

Lilian at one year old and myself about three.

(Opposite) *An unflattering photo of Father retrieved from the waste-paper basket.*

Myself at two years old.

The disappointed bar mitzvah boy.

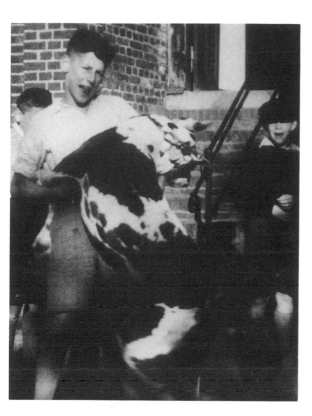

*Doing a Tarzan at
Kolberg with Kuno.*

*In the Citadel park
after the bar mitzvah
reception.* **(Left to
right)** *Ruth
Papiermeister, Lilian,
Norbert and Susi.*

Lilian a few weeks before her escape to Holland.

The last photo of Father in Berlin, spring 1939.

of the store, turns all the cups so the handles face left and returns.

"*Meine Herren*, you have no idea how lucky you are. We still have eight settings of this left-handed service. May I wrap them up for you?"

Goering beams at Hitler and is so pleased, he buys the whole service. Outside he says:

"Well, what did I tell you!"

Hitler shakes his head, "Ridiculous, this proves nothing. The Jew was lucky, he had them in stock."

We were still laughing, when we heard distant shouting and saw a short, fully clothed man walking on the water, shaking his fist at a departing sailboat. He was in the middle of the lake, miles from anywhere and from our water-level viewpoint, seemed to grow taller and shorter on the horizon as he walked. We realised that this was a tall man "in" and not "on" the water—and that he was walking on a submerged sandbank testing the depth.

Cautiously we paddled nearer. The sailboat had gone. It was a weekday, and the lake was practically deserted, except for far distant sails and two rubber-tube sailors.

The man walked up and down agitatedly, muttering to himself. Sounds of his voice echoed over the water. Now he noticed us and waved both arms imploringly for us to come nearer. But he still stood hunched up like a ferocious bull.

Hesitantly we paddled closer. A beefy, dark-blond Baltic type with a brutish face, up to his knees in water. Jabbing his thumb back over his shoulder he yelled:

"Did you see that? Did you see that bitch take off with my boat? MY boat! *Mensch*, would you believe it, with MY boat! I'm pushing it off the sandbank SHE put it on—and she tells me to go and find myself another woman—and then she just sails off. And she knows damn well I can't swim."

We didn't know what to say and looked at him from

a cautious twelve feet away. He softened his tone and asked:

"Where did you just come from?"

We pointed back.

"Is there a road?" and at our nod, "Can you help me get there?"

After a second's hesitation and a look at Weil, I told him that he could have one of our tubes to sit in and paddle. We would get into the other tube and paddle along with him.

"And you? You can swim?"

"Not that far," "Not far," we spoke simultaneously.

He grinned appreciatively, said, "You're good boys," and came cautiously towards us into deeper water. We moved towards him a little reluctantly. Normally I would only be too eager to help, but this man? He had a mean face.

We helped get the tube under his behind and our little flotilla got under way, towards the beach, a good eight hundred feet away. He wasn't talking much, obviously scared in the deep water, and he appeared very keen on having us right next to him. Every time we were separated by more than a few feet he called anxiously:

"Now, now. Let's stay together. Let's not lose each other!"

Frankly, we were just as anxious not to lose him. Taking turns inside the tube or holding on behind the tube, pushing, paddling, moving along was tiring. Weil expressed the hope that we wouldn't have a blowout. I whispered back that if that happened we'd all have to hold on to one tube.

"If he'll let us," said Weil, and I knew just why he said that.

But we made it safely to the shore. That man didn't even get his shoulders wet. On the beach he handed back our tube with a nice thank-you grin, then paused and looked at us curiously.

"You're Jews, aren't you?" he said pointing at our lower anatomy. In the excitement of the rescue we had forgotten that we were stark naked . . . and, of course, circumcised. Very few German Christians were.

We must have looked startled and frightened because he laughed, a good-natured laugh one would say if it weren't for the nasty undertone and said:

"Ah well, I suppose there have to be some good Jews."

Then, as if receiving a sharp command from above, he jumped to, pulled up his chest, clicked together the heels of his plimsolls, flung up his right arm in the Nazi salute, and shouted:

"*Heil* Hitler!"

Without further ado he turned on his heels and marched off like a soldier, one-two, one-two down the shaded lakeside road . . . plimsolls squilching water, trousers dripping and clinging to his rhythmically wobbling big behind. One-two, one-two.

When he was out of sight we went to where we had hidden and chained together our bikes, dug up the pine-needle covered knapsacks containing shorts, shirts, underpants—dressed quickly and pedalled off. This whole nonsense had made us late. But we took the long way round rather than pass old fat-arse on the road.

In September we lost Gerda, our maid. She was no longer permitted to work for us because the new Nuremberg laws prohibited German women under forty-five from working for Jews.

Another new word for my vocabulary. *Rassenschande*. Racial disgrace . . . intimate relations between Aryans and non-Aryans. Weil wondered who'd be disgraced, us or them?

Mother had her own technique in looking for a maid. According to her, the best way to find out a maid's charac-

91

ter and what kind of a worker she would be was to sit her down, put a lot of food in front of her and watch her eat. That's a real give-away, she maintained. Gerda, it seemed, was neither picky, nor greedy, ate neither too fast nor too slow, and had perfect table manners. She not only got the job, she became my mother's constant shining example of how I should sit and eat.

In spite of this, I was sad to lose Gerda. She was a gentle, quiet young woman who hardly ever spoke. Gerda with the long, straight chestnut hair, always looked so proud sitting, with hands folded in her lap, next to her man on the horse-drawn carriage, rolling through the streets of Spandau.

There were still a great many horses in Spandau, and this made a perpetual mess of my pockets. I would never dream of going anywhere without a lump or two of sugar or an off-colour carrot in my pocket, just in case I came across a starving horse. I would have brought the horses home too, just like the poor, lost, hungry dogs to whom my mother steadfastly refused refuge, but horses were usually attached to a big cart or wagon. Not that this stopped Schnapps from following me, pulling along her Schultheiss wagon loaded to the hilt with wooden beer barrels.

Schnapps was a beauty. The heaviest, biggest, roundest, most broad-chested brewery horse you've ever seen. She was so heavy that all she had to do was to lean forward slightly to make the wagon roll—or lean backwards to stop it. There was another horse next to Schnapps, a real nothing, a dumb-dumb which steadfastly ignored me and even my carrots. I made Schnapps's acquaintance one day when she was stamping her right front foot furiously, her iron shoe producing sparks on the cobblestones. A few people were standing around at a safe distance. I saw the problem right away, marched right up to her, and amid gasps among the audience, grabbed her foot, lifted it and freed her from the reins that had become tangled up around her foot and shoulder. She neighed and gave me a friendly push with her nose which nearly sent me flying. An impolite voice said loudly that someone must have dropped me on my head as a baby. That horse could have killed me, said the voice. Nonsense, I thought, a horse knows a friend when she sees one, gave her a piece of sugar and got a slobbery kiss for it. We met again, frequently. Her beat took her through the Breitestrasse regularly. And whenever we met we exchanged a piece of sugar for a nudge or a kiss. I became her sugar daddy.

This day I had something on my mind and walked right past old Schnapps. Her boss had forgotten to put on the brake and she just followed me patiently pulling the wagon, I on the pavement, she a foot or two behind me in the street. I heard a commotion behind me. A man screaming:

"Whoa! Halt! Schnapps halt! *Schnapps du verdammtes Vieh*, HALT!"

Then I heard the clippety-clop of hoofs and the squeaky groans of wooden wheels on my immediate left, stopped, turned and there was Schnapps looking at me reproachfully, but full of trust and hope.

Schnapps, so that was her name. That was nice to know, we had never been formally introduced. Now the red faced, moustachioed Schultheiss man with peaked cap and knee-long leather apron had arrived, furious, gasping, out of breath. He grabbed the greasy looking reins, saw me and speared me with his bulging grey eyes.

"Oh it's you, the brat with the sugar . . . Don't think I haven't noticed. See what happens? Don't you ever give my horse anything again, do you hear!"

"But she looked hungry," I protested.

"Hungry!" he screamed, and I thought he was having a fit. "Hungry! Have you ever seen Schnapps eat? She eats like a horse!" he bellowed, breaking into a wild, yellow-toothed laugh at his own joke.

A bystander joined in:

"How come the brake wasn't on?" she asked nicely.

"Mind your own business," said the man in the apron, giving first the old lady and then me a poisonous look. Before he could start screaming again I decided on a strategic retreat, terribly sorry about poor old Schnapps, still looking so full of hope.

The maid problem was solved. Gerda's mother, Frau Wilhelmine Schulze, safely over forty-five, came to clean in place of her daughter. Nothing much had changed. Mother always insisted that I clean my own room, keep it tidy, brush my clothes and shoes. Actually I was a little better off with Wilhelmine. She did a little tidying up for me when my mother's back was turned. And she talked to me like a grown-up, confiding in me and telling me her marital problems. Very interesting. Her estranged husband, a brute of an alcoholic, had broken her window in the middle of the night and climbed into her room on the ground floor "to get at her".

She winked and said, "If you know what I mean?"

I smiled as if I did, but I couldn't really imagine why her husband would want to "get at her", nor could I fathom why she looked half disgusted and half proud about it.

Two months later I knew the answers. Everything. My mother's gentle, ethereal explanation about how babies were made never quite took solid shape until I got under the table and played submarine.

I was sitting there, Kapitain Fred von Zeller of the U–20, at eleven, Germany's youngest U-boat captain, about to make a crash dive. My mother walked into the room. Well hidden under the table by the tablecloth, I decided to sit absolutely still. I watched and heard her

94

shoes clickety-clicking around the table. She stopped in front of my room and 'knock-knock' on the door:

"Fred?"

I almost answered involuntarily from under the table.

Satisfied that I must be out, she clickety-clicked past me again and stopped by the big sideboard with the glass vitrines, shelves and drawers full of treasures, old silver dollars, porcelain figures, Japanese vases and table silver. Peeking from under the table I watched her take one of the Japanese vases, turn it upside down and shake it. Out fell a lump of cotton wadding. Opening the lump she took something out, something very small. What on earth could that be? She opened a drawer and pulled out the little cedar box with "Jerusalem" written on it. The box I could never open because she had lost the little key. On several occasions I had offered to break it open, but she was always sure she would find the key one of these days. She opened it now . . . with the key she was supposed to have lost . . . took something out, something wrapped in cloth. I pulled my head back quickly as she started to turn. Her footsteps receded, and I saw her feet stop in front of the linen closet. The one that was always locked because of the "maid". Another one of my mother's mysteries.

"How come you lock up the linen closet but not the silver?" I asked.

I considered that to be a perfectly reasonable question, but it always annoyed her and was always brushed aside petulantly. Another thing kids couldn't understand, obviously.

I never found the key to that closet and heaven knows, I looked. My sneaky mother . . . in the un-openable box from Jerusalem!

But what could there possibly be in that closet?

Mother reappeared with sheets and put them on the chair right next to my face. I watched her wrap the big key in cloth and put it into the box. She locked the box, put the little key into the lump of wadding, stuffed the lot into the vase.

At my very first opportunity I reversed the process and there, in front of my conquistador eyes, undiscovered territory: Linen and towels. Towels and linen clear to the horizon as far as the eye could see. There was something wrong here. Where were the natives hiding the gold? I reached in behind and under the linen. Now the next shelf. And the next. A chair, quick, and now let's try the top shelf.

There it was!

Boxes, way back behind the linen. No, big books. And my sex education took a giant step forward. Eduard Fuchs's *Illustrierte Sittengeschichte*—the history of manners and morals through the ages. Privately printed, pious pornography, in several volumes, lasciviously illustrated, with a warning on the first page.

"This work may be offered only to scholars, collectors and libraries."

Since I went to school, collected books and was a member of a library, I felt qualified to read on.

Also among the linen I found van der Velde's *Ideal Marriage*—describing every position, every angle, every move in every detail. As well as how often, why, when, where, before, between and after.

Quickly I decided on a volume of Fuchs. I think the illustrations did it. Holding the book tightly under my chin I neatly restacked the others, hid them as before, got rid of the keys, fled to my room. Now what? I reversed a few books so the pages, not the backs, faced forward and slipped Fuchs in among them, reversed too.

In my subsequent scholarly study of the material, I quickly learned to read selectively, going past the author's pious disclaimers, mock horror and indignation, to the real meat. I was particularly partial to François Bouchet's

96

erotic murals for the Versailles boudoir of Madame la Marquise de Pompadour. It seemed Louis Quinze had a good thing going there. By the time I got to van der Velde I was getting quite blasé about the whole subject. But, I felt, there were some sections in that work, particularly concerning the nature of taste and smell, and how to explore, enhance, diminish and employ these senses in the service of eros that, though not exactly original, were worthy of consideration.

Simultaneously with these studies I was also doing some serious reading in the *Kinderzeitung*, a learned monthly children's paper that featured coloured comics, stories, jokes, puzzles, stamp and coin collection tips, "how to" instructions and other such serious matters. Man can't live by sex alone. I became so addicted to the journal, life did not seem worth living without it. Some of the larger stores used it as a "give-away" to attract customers with children. Not a bad gimmick; it made hundreds of children plague their parents every month to go and buy something at Lindeman-Denniger in the Breitestrasse.

The problem was that by this time my parents didn't have the money to buy anything much so I learned to live by my wits. Lindeman had several cashiers, and I would walk from department to department looking for the kindest face of the day. Putting on the most winning smile I could muster, I would ask most politely for a copy of the latest issue. On a really tough day I would resort to a desperate subterfuge. I'd work myself into a frenzy of courage, pick a suitable woman customer, follow on her heels surreptitiously but firmly and act, behind her back, as if I were her son. Exerting all my psychic power I would will her to walk past a suitable cashier. As we passed, I did a quick sidestep, snatched the *Kinderzeitung* from the pile with a smile at the cashier . . . and rushed off to catch up with "Mother". If crowned with success there would be a triumphant dash home with the journal.

When all else failed I would get out the big gun, my little sister. She was so small and had a way of looking so sad and suffering, she melted the heart of the most icy cashier.

One day it was all over. I ran home in triumph with the latest issue and the first thing I saw when I opened the pages was a comic strip showing ugly little hook-nosed Jewish brats doing mean things and getting their just desserts. I didn't take it in for a moment. I stared at the pages and started to feel all cold inside. I couldn't help turning pages and reading here and there, but I didn't know what I was reading. Nothing got through the pain.

Mussolini attacked Ethiopia. I was shocked and disappointed. I knew he was a Fascist like Hitler, but he didn't persecute the Jews. Everything I had ever heard and read about Italians made me decide I liked them even though I had never met one. Father too, who fought against them on the Austrian side at the Isonzo, said:

"The last people in the world I wanted to fight were the Italians."

And now my would-be friends were attacking a helpless, poor, practically defenceless people. An underdog myself, I was decidedly prejudiced in favour of other underdogs. Not only that, but Haile Selassie claimed his people to be one of the lost tribes of Israel. That did it. I felt it was just great that somebody wanted to be a Jew. I was proud of those brave people and daydreamed about going there and fighting heroically on their side.

When Il Duce used poison gas to win his war, my disgust turned to horror. Not just with him, or the Italians . . . with the whole of goddamn humanity. They let him do it.

Cousin Lotte Bobath and Korle Kirstein were arrested during a random SA raid on the Café Dobrin. My mother was as shocked by Lotte's going there in the first place as she was about the arrest.

"What has my poor sister done to deserve such a

child?" Mother said to Father. "Bad enough she should go out with a goy, which is against the law . . . she has to take him to a café frequented by Jews, which she knows full well has been raided several times already."

What saved Lotte was her Czechoslovak passport. She was interrogated, bullied, threatened. It was a terrifying experience, but she was released. Korle had bigger problems. Eventually they let him go, but he now was a marked man. Whether it had to do with his arrest nobody knew, but something had snapped in him. He started to lose contact with reality and became stranger and stranger. A few months later he had to be admitted to an asylum for the insane, and he died there, one of the earliest victims of Nazi euthanasia.

My mother's firm convictions and equally firm stand on how much sleep a child should have were a dreadful bore. Like so many fellow-sufferers, I tried reading under the blanket with a flashlight. Besides being very expensive, this was not easy. One can get awfully hot and cross-eyed from being so confined and so close to the print. And it affected one's choice of literature. You can't expect Nietzsche from a half-choked boy under a blanket. Karl May on the other hand, Karl May with his Wild West full of horses, cowboys and Indians was eminently suitable under-the-blanket fare. However, escape literature has certain disadvantages. I often got so excited and involved in the plot that I failed to notice the door opening and the quick, silent advance of another kind of Indian on the warpath. She would pounce and catch me bug-eyed and sweaty, the book still open, the flashlight still on.

Instant punishment. If the book was halfway decent, it would be confiscated for a week or more. If utter trash, it was promptly torn to shreds. My first intimation of the awesome power of literary criticism.

A solution had to be found—and it was. I rigged up a crystal radio consisting of a tightly wound wire coil mounted on a little box with a small glass tube in which a fine wire touched a little crystal. You wriggled the wire on the crystal until you got one or the other of the powerful local radio stations on your earphones. The thing worked without battery or power: all you needed was a reasonable antenna and a good ground. I ran a hidden wire to ground, the tap, and connected my mattress springs as antenna. It worked. Two Berlin stations came in perfectly clear. But now came the difficult part . . . training Mother.

I started pretending to sleep with my head under the blanket. It was essential to get her used to that idea. After lights out, I lay, bored to death, waiting for Mother to do one of her sneak checks. The moment the door started to open my head went under the blanket.

Aha, he's reading again.

She'd rush for the bed, pull down the blanket . . . and there lay Mother's good boy, fast asleep, angelic. Neither flashlight nor book. A yawn, a groan, a stretching, another yawn, a brave bed-creaking rise to the elbows and the sleepy question:

"Time to get up? Mummy?"

Utter confusion. Utter horror. "Oh no. No. Sorry, go back to sleep, Fred."

And after tucking in her poor exhausted child she would tiptoe out, devastated with guilt. Now it was my turn to feel guilty, but what can a poor bored boy do?

It needed quite a few repeat performances. But, knowing that being too good would make Mother suspect something wrong, I let her catch me reading a couple of times. She soon learned that when the blanket was bulging up I was reading; if it lay flat over my head, I was "sleeping"— before long with my earphones on, listening to the crystal radio.

The two Berlin stations gave me some choice of entertainment, though sometimes it might only be between Hitler hysterically addressing a mass rally or a talk about the importance of bees in the propagation of wild flowers.

Listening to Hitler was both fascinating and frightening. Absurd though the comparison might be, in some ways Hitler had much in common with an old-time Bible-thumping, soul-rousing, preacher. A preacher totally involving his congregation, speaking their language, playing on their emotions, singing out questions and listening for an answer. Working up tension, raising his voice higher and higher . . . striking with it like a hammer— making his anvil audience ring out in unison, "Hallelujah!"

Hitler had the same power, the same charismatic ability to involve and dominate his staggeringly huge audiences. And he had the advantage over the preacher in that it's always been easier to rouse people to hatred than to love. His words and images were simple and direct. And no matter how monstrous the lie, how distorted the truth, he was totally convinced and utterly convincing. He manipulated his audience, mesmerised it. Using his voice softly, firmly or harshly, making it rise from deep resonance to shrill hysteria, asking, like a preacher, perfectly timed rhetorical questions, he roused masses to sheer frenzy. One hundred thousand fanatical people would roar as if with a single voice, answering this one man on the platform.

"Do you want this?" "NO!"

"Shall we permit this?" "NO!"

"*Ein Volk*." One people. "*EIN VOLK*!"

"*Ein Reich*." One country. "*EIN REICH*!"

"*Ein Fuehrer*." One Leader. "*EIN FUEHRER*!"

Finally, wildly, jubilantly, at the end of his speech, "*Sieg Heil, Sieg Heil, Sieg Heil*" on and on and on . . . for minute after minute until the voice of the radio commentator cut in and the hysteria was slowly faded out.

101

He made them feel invincible. It filled the cemeteries of Europe to overflowing.

Lying in the dark, my chest tight with foreboding and fear, the heavy earphones hurting, I listened to the endless *"Sieg Heils"*. I tried to switch off earlier, but I couldn't.

Music, stories and plays, and even some talks, those I enjoyed. But they were a bit too big on Wagner on the radio then. Like the *"Sieg Heils,"* his stuff went on and on, and people screamed a lot and loudly, even when they were dying. Perhaps the knowledge that Wagner was anti-Semitic did influence me, I admit. But Mozart, they could give me Mozart any old time. Even his operas. His people screamed a little too, but nicely. And the tunes were really great. Bach wasn't bad either.

My listening was as indiscriminate as my reading. I was discovering good music but loved the Schlager, the hit tunes and popular songs of the day, just as much. At a pinch I even listened to chamber music. I didn't prize it then as I do now, but it was a lot less boring than just lying there in the dark. I had to be careful with it though . . . it could put me right to sleep and I didn't want to be caught napping with earphones.

Having been caught a few times reading Karl May hidden under my Hebrew text in class, I acquired the nickname *"Der Indianer"*. The redskin. I wasn't thrilled about this but decided to brazen it out. There's nothing like painting something red if you want to hide it. So, at the next fancy dress class party, I strutted around in a glorious Indian feather headgear, carrying a peace pipe, filled with real tobacco, saying, "HOUGH white man" to everybody. I called the teacher "Great White Father" and offered him a lit pipe. Damned if he didn't take a puff.

There were three prison outfits, two nurses, one chimney sweep . . . and then I saw this stunning, blonde, blue-eyed girl with the most delicate complexion. Straight out of Watteau, wearing a silver satin eye mask, she was dressed like a *gentille petite* Rococo shepherdess, white crinoline, lilac bodice, blonde curls piled high . . . Just my type, shades of Mariechen, my first love. But this love was more mature. I was devastated, in love at first sight.

I walked over to Weil, hiding behind an eyepatch and pirate's hat, and whispered:

"My God. That incredibly pretty girl with the mask? She's not from our class, surely?"

He opened his eyes wide, looked at me, looked at her and neighed like a horse. I looked at him . . . it was laughter:

"You mean you don't know?" . . . and he almost ripped my sleeve off as he pulled me over to the girl.

"He doesn't think you're in our class!" Weil brayed like a donkey. Laughter again. I could have killed him . . . but in front of her, I was crippled with shyness.

The girl, looking pleased, her blue eyes shining, broke into an utterly ravishing, wide-mouthed smile and asked:

"Really? You don't recognise me, Fred?"

I recognised the voice —and my sexual orientation did a somersault. It was Wolfgang, dressed up as a girl.

My knees were shaking, I felt sick. And I got so excited! Never will I trust appearances again. From now on it's "show me" first.

When I came home that night Mother told me that Uncle Max was going to Palestine. She was crying, saying she might never see him again. I thought this was rather odd because she had not wished to see him for all these years since their family quarrel. I was the one who had sneaked in a visit here and there. Grown-ups were rather odd.

Max heeded the writing on the wall, packed his family's bags and emigrated. He risked being considered a fool for sacrificing part of his fortune, running off to unknown hardships and uncertain economic conditions in a hot and dusty country with malaria swamps. But he went. And in 1935 he was still able to take part of his fortune with him.

What amazed him was the cold collaboration of the SS and a warm, helpful German emigration service. He couldn't get over it. The SS was icy, but polite, the emigration service, mostly older professionals, actually friendly and sympathetic.

I asked my parents why we weren't going there. Mother replied that since Uncle Max had plenty of money he and his family could live in Palestine without having to worry about finding work. What could we do there? she asked . . . there were no jobs there. I mentioned the kibbutzim, the communal settlements, and asked why we couldn't all go there. I wouldn't mind becoming a farmer. Father loved gardening and, after all, wasn't she always talking about wanting a house in the country?

"And what kind of education would you have in Palestine? And Lilian?" she asked reproachfully.

ALEXANDERPLATZ

For me, the most dramatic event of 1936 was not the fall of Addis Ababa, nor Hitler's march into the Rhineland, nor the latest persecutions . . . it wasn't even the Berlin Olympic Games! It was Mother's birthday.

One afternoon I came out of my room and there was Mother standing in front of me. The way she stood, the way she looked, I knew right away something was wrong.

"What day is it?" she asked very quietly.

Nervous, I mumbled something about Tuesday . . . Wednesday . . . but she kept looking at me with this strange expression.

"Yes, but what's the date?" and there were tears in her eyes.

Suddenly I knew. I had forgotten her birthday. I felt absolutely terrible. I ran to embrace her but she turned and, crying, walked out of my life forever . . . or so it felt. I followed her from room to room begging her to forgive me. She didn't talk to me for the rest of the day.

When I told a friend about this thirty years later, discussing the pains of childhood, he seemed amazed and shaking his head asked:

"And how do you feel about that now, today?"

"Why, terrible, of course! How could I possibly have forgotten her birthday? You know," I told him, "I felt worse . . . it hurt more than anything the Nazis had done up to that time. They hurt, and I was angry at them.

Ridiculous. As a kid, sometimes, I even felt a tiny, nagging doubt whether the Jews might, perhaps, have done something somewhere, somehow, to cause such relentless hate. But here there wasn't the faintest doubt. I forgot. I was to blame."

My friend's head kept on shaking in amazement, and I stopped.

"Kids don't remember any birthday but their own. Normally the other parent reminds the child. Did your father forget too?"

"I think he was hiding or in the hospital. He had a bad back, and something was wrong with his blood."

My friend gestured, "Well there you are," and continued, "I wonder, with your father absent so much, your mother must have felt very alone. You became a sort of . . . some kind of security, and she forgot how young you were. You know, that Nazi thing, it wasn't just suffering the persecution, it affected your whole perception of the world, your whole family life." And he kept on insisting that my mother's reaction was unreasonable.

But it took more than that friend. It took Laura Thaler and her exceptionally nice boys, seven, ten and twelve years old.

"Remember my birthday on their own?" she laughed, "You must be kidding. Know what I do the night before my birthday? I bake a cake. Then I call them all in and I tell 'em, 'It's my birthday tomorrow—and if you guys don't behave extra, super well *the whole day*, I'm going to eat that cake all on my own.' "

With Father in hiding so much, my help was needed more and more. We sold fabrics, but a customer could have a dress, a suit or a coat made up by "our" tailor . . . and a fur collar to match the coat, by "our" furrier. Mother did the measuring and fitting. And as long as we still had customers, mostly Jewish by this time, I made frequent trips to and from tailors and furriers. Each garment meant a few trips. Material to the tailor, half-finished garment back for Mother to pin and fit, back to the tailor, back once more to get the finished garment and all over again if the customer was extra fussy. A lot of travelling for a few marks, but nothing could have pleased me more. Not only did these errands give me a sense of being needed, there were some most desirable side benefits. There was a delirious sense of feeling capable and all that implied in terms of growing independence and freedom. Better still, I now had what it took to make good use of this new freedom. Money. I had found a secret way to riches. I was a professional watcher of bicycles. Taking up a position at the entrance of the post office, I would wait for a cyclist to dismount, run up to my potential client and ask eagerly but politely:

"Excuse me sir, may I watch your bicycle?"

Some people waved me away lightly, some were surly; but often enough there would be a searching look, a quick smile and a nod. "Sure, *Junge*, go ahead."

It was amazing how few cyclists had a lock and chain. Or, if they had, how few wanted the bother of using it when some kid would watch their bike for a few pennies. Sometimes, with a browbeating smile, I would be asked how much I charged. Leaning forward with maidenly modesty, hoping to put them in a generous frame of mind, I would answer that the reward was entirely up to them. Entirely, *mein Herr*.

The hourly "take" depended on weather, time, day of the week and the competition. One thing you learned bloody-nosed soon was to stake out and keep to your turf. It was permitted to cross the border if your rival already had his bike. When there were too many kids at the post office I plied my trade elsewhere. Woolworth's was a good bet, or some other big store. In a diary I proudly noted that one good afternoon I made enough to buy: a cinema ticket, two candy bars, a water-damaged

107

book and a green metal frog, made in Japan, that could jump one metre. I put the cinema ticket first, not because it necessarily ranked before the frog, but because it was symbolic of my new freedom. Gone was the sting of Mother's worst punishment, "No films for three weeks." I had finally become financially independent.

Now, since, at the tailors', I often had to wait hours before the work was ready and neither my parents nor our suppliers had a telephone, nothing was easier than to sandwich a film into the errands without anybody being the wiser for it.

The flea pits around the Alex were neither finicky about admitting possible Jews nor about demanding proof, for an adult film, that a customer was definitely, positively more than sixteen. For such entertainment I would approach the ticket booth with a nonchalant and earnest air, sure to convince anyone that I was considerably older than eleven and three-quarters. Of course, it helped that I paid an adult price for an adult film and that on weekday afternoons business was so bad that I was often the entire audience. Management obviously agreed with my mother who claimed, "Better a fly in the soup, than no meat at all."

The films were usually tired, jumpy, brittle and breakable. At adult shows especially, I hated for the house lights to come up and expose me for what I was. A wicked, underaged fraud. Should I dive under the seat? Mercifully the lights would soon dim again to safe darkness and the thrills of the flickering screen. It was thrilling. At least one dead body for every dime I paid.

As with books, my taste in films was catholic and no matter how stupid a film was, I had to see it all the way through to the end. I didn't even snub girlie shows if they had socially redeeming features, such as snappy music or dancing. Especially tap dancing. In one of those musicals I picked up a song refrain that I could never again shake out of my ears. It was an early 1930s film in which one of the ladies sang a song, in English, not dubbed, that had the mysterious refrain, "You are, Mallagista." Mallagista! What a wonderful ring that word had. I couldn't find it in the English-German dictionary. It wasn't in the Encyclopedia Brittanica at the main Berlin reference library. Mallagista. Who was Mallagista? A king? A magician? A gangster? It haunted me for decades until, knowing a trifle more English, I saw the film again. The refrain seemed to be, "You are my lucky star". Nonsense. I simply refuse to accept that and still hum—You are, Mallagista.

Another great pleasure on these business trips was the hospitality of the tailors who kept me waiting. Beside steaming samovars I learned to sip tea Russian style, through cubes of sugar clamped between my teeth. I experienced the sweet, oily joy of halva for the first time, tasted strange, garlic-blessed Polish, Russian, Latvian and Lithuanian dishes never served at home where Mother cooked in the "aristocratic" Austro-Hungarian style. Ah, the joys of cold red Russian borscht with a little white floating island of sour cream. And how your teeth cut through chewy pirogen exteriors releasing pangs of inner hidden flavour.

I marvelled at the variety of exotic Eastern-Jewish faces I encountered. I heard Yiddish spoken as a language rather than as an occasional flavourful expression. Heard sentimental Yiddish songs about love and life, quite different from the modern up-and-at-them Zionist songs I knew from school. I saw the homes of people who had so much less even than we did. The one thing they had that we didn't was bedbugs . . . and the blood stains they made on the wallpaper where people had squashed them.

The errands I ran gave me more time to experience strange streets, explore places I would not normally visit. I had leisure to study store windows, monuments, street vendors, prostitutes. I watched elaborate performances by hucksters demonstrating to little groups of drab burghers, anything from "miracle" household cleaners, "lightning-fast" vegetable slicing gadgets (the salesmen were fast, not the gadgets) to liquids that "put a layer of solid chrome over the most tarnished metal". Presiding over rickety, portable trays with merchandise, they talked a slick blue streak, bid themselves down to "ludicrously low" prices, cracked off-colour jokes, launched insults at scapegoats in the audience and performed the most fascinating choreography of footsteps, hand-gestures and body movements.

Since I was the owner of a bicycle with a most tarnished handlebar, I handed over a precious fifty pfennig to the man with the solid chrome liquid. It worked at his stall, I saw it with my own eyes. It worked when I got it home, too, for an hour or so. Then the handlebar turned black. No wonder that huckster never ran out of tarnished metal for his demonstrations.

The mime robot in one of the big store windows was something else. He wasn't selling anything, he just moved, click, click, click, his face a snow-white, frozen mask with dead eyes. Silent, rigid, dressed to perfection in evening wear, he moved with such exact, short, jerky, robot-like movements that people swore he had to be a machine. Just look at his eyes, they said, they don't blink, they're made of glass. I used to go ten blocks out of my way to catch his performances.

In February I decided that Benno Papiermeister was my very best friend. I had known him for some time because his and my parents had become close. They had much in common. The few Jews of Spandau had become increasingly isolated and dependent on each other because most of their Christian friends feared being seen with them—and their own families were starting to disperse. So the Papiermeisters became family. I had always

110

liked Benno but he was a year or so younger, too young for me, I felt, until somehow, at eleven, he seemed to have caught up with my twelve years. He lived near us, had an older brother, Josi, and a younger sister, Ruth, who was friends with my sister.

They were Latvian citizens and, for the time being, protected. Hermann Papiermeister, stocky, gentle and courageous, tried to hold a frail wing of this protection over my family too. When mass-arrests were rumoured and Father went into hiding, Hermann would leave his own "protected" family at home and spend nights on the couch in our living room. His presence made a difference on two occasions, when there were indeed dawn "visitors". The word *"Auslaender,"* foreigner, had a strange power those days. Foreigners were to be left alone. Wooed in fact. This was to convince the world that the Nazis were much maligned by Jewish hate propaganda. Even foreign Jews had to be left alone. They should have no excuse to trump up charges of maltreatment at their consulates.

To keep up their Latvian connection the Papiermeisters departed, *en masse*, every summer for a few weeks' holiday at Libau, by the Baltic Sea. I was always relieved to see them return because it was mostly to the Papiermeisters' house that the Zellers marched for their weekly hot bath. Mother had the key to the apartment and while they were away, Lilian and I were subjected to an absolutely unnatural number of baths.

Besides cleanliness, we could also thank the Papiermeisters for the telephone. There was one at their shoe shop, in the Charlottenstrasse, just around the corner from their apartment. When there was an important message for us one of their kids would come running.

Suddenly, in March, 1936, Hitler broke the Treaty of Versailles and the German army marched into the demilitarised Rhineland. Everybody seemed to hunch up and

111

hold their breath. But nothing happened. Nothing. France
and England did nothing. The press was jubilant. There
was euphoria in the streets. Strangers smiled at each
other, comrades in arms. Even anti-Nazis, friends of my
parents, now said Hitler was doing *some* good things for
Germany.

"Germany has been on her knees too long," we heard
them say, wagging a finger. "And look at unemployment . . . he's certainly doing something about that."

My parents didn't reply. I heard them say later, "He's
clearing up unemployment . . . yes, but how? The *Reichs-
arbeitsdienst*—Universal Labour Service conscription—
hard labour with practically no pay. Military service call-
up for millions. Armament production. Don't people see
where it's all going? Do they really want another war?
Are our last good Christian friends turning into Nazis
too?"

And then Father mentioned a Jewish businessman in
Spandau who said that Hitler was really doing good things
for Germany.

"He's making us strong," Herbert said. "He'd be all
right if only he didn't have this thing about the Jews."

Father caught me following the conversation, saw my
eyes widen at his saying—making "us" strong—and
smiled:

"Yes . . . the man said '*us*'."

Ten-foot-high slogans appeared at factories and work
places everywhere. They read, "We can thank our
Fuehrer for being able to work here!" Soon a little joke
went around select circles:

Everybody in the family comes home, one by one and
leaves a little note, "Sorry, won't be home for supper,"
before rushing off to their SA, Hitler Youth, or BDM
(League of German Maidens) meeting. When the family
finally gets home they find the apartment stripped by

112

thieves who have left a note of their own: "We can thank our Fuehrer for being able to work here."

People did go to all those functions and meetings. In a way, the Nazis had banished loneliness. Millions of people thought it was marvellous how many comrades they now had, how close they felt to others, how powerful this fellowship made them feel. And the best binder to keep holding people together is common enemies.

There were also any number of jokes about yet another version of Nazi camaraderie, KDF, *"Kraft durch Freude"*—"Strength through Joy". This was not just a propaganda stunt . . . enjoy your leisure so you can gain the strength to work harder for Fuehrer and Vaterland . . . it was a state-organised mass movement that sent regimented hordes of "workers of the fist and of the brain" on trips and cruises, to symphony concerts, theatre, sports events. KDF even built their own cruise ships. I got to know a little about it from two sources. The newsreels at cinemas and the Kachels. The Kachels were among the very few German friends who were really still our friends. There were the others, those who looked around quickly to all sides before nodding to us on the street and who never came to see us any more. Peter Kachel and his wife had been customers at our Breite-strasse store. It was Frau Kachel who had slipped into our store past the boycotting SA men three years earlier—and whom I saw crying in my mother's arms. That was the beginning of a friendship that lasted until my mother was arrested at her Berlin apartment and carted off to Maidanek in November 1941.

The Kachels were simple, ordinary, decent people; quiet, kind and courageous. They continued to see us when it was dangerous for them to do so. In 1936, bullet-headed, bald, slightly stooped Peter was ordered to present himself at the state employment office, "immediately". He went immediately and sat in front of two offi-

113

cers, scared and trembling, while they scanned through his "work book", the document everybody had to have, that showed his or her work record and skills. It went through Peter's mind that maybe it had something to do with having Jewish friends. But then they looked up and told him . . . they didn't ask . . . they told him:

"You will work at the such and such armament factory as a foreman at so and so much per hour. You will start there on the first of the next month. Give this notification to your present employer. *Heil* Hitler!"

Out he went, still shaking, but not with rage. He was shaking because he had been afraid they were going to accuse him of some misdeed and not because they were ordering him around like a serf. That didn't seem to bother him. My parents never quite understood why.

Peter had been a front-line soldier in the First World War and was not overly keen on getting into another war . . . but, making armaments? That's not using them, is it? Surely not even "those people" want war. Surely they're not that crazy? "Anyway," he shrugged, "I'll be too old for any war."

Something did upset him, though, about the new job. He was to have a salary that was far from generous. He had more responsibility, he was going to work longer hours and he wouldn't make any more than he was earning now. And now there were so many deductions. The Nazi party, the church, taxes, social security, compulsory health insurance. Everybody had their fingers in his pay envelope . . . and those "voluntary" contributions they asked for, the *"Winterhilfe"*, Winter Relief . . . well, you had better make them, if you knew what was good for you!

"The others at work are bitching about their salaries and deductions too!"

"Winterhilfe for the poor people. Poor people! I know

what poor people! That fat pig Goering is buying French champagne with it."

But Peter wasn't entirely discontented. He recalled bitter years of unemployment. And there was KDF, *Kraft durch Freude*, Strength through Joy. Fabulous. Fantastic. A ten-day cruise to Madeira for two for hardly more than it cost to eat out for ten days in Spandau.

"They're making up for my lousy salary," Peter beamed.

When they came back from Madeira we heard some of the details of their trip. It sounded rather like an army manoeuvre *mit Gemuetlichkeit*, discipline like in my old German school. The teacher claps his hands . . . you stand up. Another clap . . . turn left smartly. Another . . . march out, one-two, one-two. However, with KDF, as you marched in step there was music and you were permitted to shout, joke and laugh. The Kachels didn't mind the regimentation. None of them did. It was rather nice not to have to wear out your brain worrying. Everything was beautifully organised. *Und ach*, those palm trees in Madeira!

At the end of March I was exiled from home. Lilian was carrying diphtheria germs that didn't affect her but could infect others. Nothing could have pleased her more. She didn't have to go to school and had our parents all to herself. I was sent to my father's sister, Aunt Dasha, who lived near the Alexanderplatz. Nothing better could have happened to me either, I felt. I loved Dasha. Here was a woman who loved me without the silent, mysterious demands that always seemed to be at the back of my mother's sad eyes. Here was someone who was always pleased with me and appreciated every little thing I did for her. What a staggering discovery. And, of course, I loved doing things for her.

Dasha was divorced and lived with short, barrel-chested bespectacled Dresner, who always smelled of cigars, was

115

dour, distant, but vaguely tolerant of me and sometimes even reluctantly, gruffly kind. They ran a small wholesale lingerie business out of their apartment. Poor old Dresner. He hardly expected to have fatherly duties foisted upon him at this stage. But still, I came in handy. I never minded going down four flights for his cigars, or to the bar—coming up again, tenderly carrying his glass of pale yellow beer. I got my reward twice. At the bottom of the stairs, where, I felt, I had to take a good sip so as not to spill beer on the stairs. Then, of course, I was permitted a sip on delivery.

And there was Hexe, the shiny, sleek, brown, female dachshund. A dream come true. I took her on long walks, sneaked food to her under the table and permitted her to jump into my bed, where she would quickly burrow to the bottom and spend the night curled up around my toes. A furry, toe-licking foot-warmer.

After a few days at Aunt Dasha's I became concerned about my parents. How could they manage without me running their errands? I was half relieved, half peeved when they assured me that they were managing "fine". Since my parents had no telephone, they'd call twice a week at a pre-appointed hour from the Papiermeisters' store.

It was usually Mother at the receiver, with reminders, instructions and warnings. Did I bathe often enough? Were my shoes clean? What marks did I get in Hebrew?

"Don't take the dog into bed with you, it's not healthy," she admonished.

"Don't worry Mummy," I replied. "the dog has never caught anything from me yet." Mother was not amused.

After a little while I got a little bored sitting around. I had no Jewish friends near the Alex, and it wasn't safe for me to go to any park or field nearby to play with Christian kids. Sooner or later one of them would be asking what Hitler Youth troop I belonged to, or what

116

school I attended. My answer would be an instant give-away that I was Jewish, and then, more likely than not, there would be taunts, jeers or beatings. In Spandau I still had some Aryan protectors and was usually near enough to home or friends if I had to run for it.

Mother had refused to let me take my bicycle to the bustling Alexanderplatz where cars and trams lurked at every corner just waiting to run over her child. There was just one place, once a week, weather permitting, where I could still let off steam, exercise and play football: the Jewish sportsfield in the Grunewald. So I walked through the streets a lot, sniffed around, explored odd places and discovered museums.

My first one was the Post Office Museum. Columbus couldn't have been happier with the New World than I was with my discovery. There were fascinating things you could move, prod, or push. I tapped out a Morse code SOS, mounted a stage coach and operated the pneumatic postal system. After writing a note to myself, I watched my pneumatic missile whiz through glass pipes all around the huge hall and into the receiving bin, thirty feet to the right. Racing over, I triumphantly retrieved the note, read it and sent myself an answer.

And then I found out that there were other museums too! Berlin was full of them. I walked through miles and miles of hallowed halls and did more museums in one week than any American tourist on a six-week jaunt through Italy. There were a few disappointments. All those portraits of stuffy old men with white millstones around their necks, fat naked ladies and, still worse, those dead birds with bunches of flowers, grapes and apples.

But, as an ancient Greek, I climbed up and down Pergamon's temple steps, walked as an Assyrian among huge winged beasts with powerful claws and bearded human faces; and as a Chaldean among golden, glazed lions roaring on the lapis-lazuli-blue walls of Ur.

117

All those museums. In my love-hate for Berlin, there was still a great deal more love than hate. It was such an exciting city. So many wonderful places and surprises. So many beautiful buildings, parks, rivers and lakes. I loved it. It was my home town. No, it was not my home town, and I did not love it. It breathed hate, and hate is more contagious than scarlet fever. There were days when I wanted the walls to crumble and bury everybody. I hated love and tried to deny what I knew of myself, the knowledge that, were the walls to crumble, I would be the first to help dig out even my enemies.

The Jews were not the only ones who suffered. Frau Brettschneider was crying in my aunt's store. Her son, in the Hitler Youth, denounced his father to the SS for listening to foreign radio stations. Herr Brettschneider was arrested and had been missing for over two weeks. No word from him or about him. Most of the neighbours were avoiding her. And she was living in dreadful silence with her fifteen-year-old son, who was smugly proud of himself.

"I can't look at him," she cried, "I don't know what to do . . . he's my baby, my son."

Dresner, completing an order for shipment, was short of an item. He sent me to his friend Neumann to borrow the merchandise until he could replace it. Naturally, I met Neumann's new *Geschaeftsfuehrer*, his new store manager. As I was about to leave he beckoned me over with a fat finger, inspected the package I was taking, became gruffly friendly, teasing me and patting me on the head. Finally he dismissed me with a *"Na ja—gut, gut."* Back with Dresner I mentioned the nice, jovial man.

"Oh yes?" asked Dresner with a twisted smile. "Nice man. And was he wearing his uniform?"

"Uniform?"

"His SA uniform."

Neumann's *Geschaeftsfuehrer* was a *Sturmfuehrer*, a

118

local Nazi boss. He knew Neumann from the days when, before becoming a *Sturmfuehrer*, he used to accompany his wife when she shopped at the store. One day, about a month ago, without his wife but with a charming smile, the *Herr Sturmfuehrer* walked into Neumann's once more, walked past Neumann and sat down at the cash register. He was sitting there still "to protect the nice little Jew". What's more, he was even bringing in business. He encouraged his storm troopers to buy things at greatly reduced prices at his very own "special Neumann sales". Neumann was promoted to chief salesman, and, naturally, the *Herr Sturmfuehrer* kept whatever money came in. But since he was really a kind man, he gave the Jew a little pocket money.

"But it's not his store, it's not his money," I exclaimed in outrage, remembering the kids who stole my film when I was little.

Dresner looked at me for a moment as if wondering whether he wanted to tell me something, and then explained that there had been a sudden rash of such takeovers of small and even larger businesses.

"I'm afraid every day that one of my former customers might remember me and take over this store. It's a matter of luck. Simply luck."

There were instances where a substantial bribe bought off a takeover and provided temporary protection. Eventually the takeovers stopped. They stopped in small stores because, with boycotts, with "Jewpig" and other such stay-away notices all over Jewish shop windows, the pickings became so meagre that even the greediest Nazi did not want to sit all day with his fingers in an empty till. They stopped in bigger stores for less obvious reasons which soon became obvious enough. Goering and other high-ranking Nazis had first discouraged and then outlawed the practice. They felt that in such spontaneous appropriations the money went into the wrong pockets.

119

They themselves then appropriated in the grand manner, "for the common good".

In July, Lilian was finally declared safe and I was permitted to go home to parents and sibling rivalry. I had missed my sister and she jumped with joy to have me back, but it didn't last. She soon found the loss of her "only child" status intolerable.

At this time the Nuremberg Laws seemed infinitely more bearable than the constant rivalry with my sister and the way I always seemed to find myself in the wrong.

Lilian couldn't compete with my competence. But she certainly knew how to get me into trouble. I was sitting in the living room, reading. Mother, serving one of our rare customers, called me to the store to help her get down a heavy roll of cloth from a high shelf. When I returned to the living room, my book had disappeared. I asked and kept on asking Lilian to return it, but she had no idea where it could possibly be. Finally I got so mad that I threatened her. Knowing Mother had a customer, Lilian screamed bloody murder. And there came Mother flying through the door. Sister pointed her finger, "He pushed me!" All I had time to say was "But . . ." before her slap, slap, slap—a series of stinging slaps on my bare arms or knees. Soon I learned to rely not on justice but on speed. I could run around the table faster than she could.

But the worst was being given responsibility for Lilian without the authority that must go with it.

"Here, take your sister to the park . . . hold her hand all the way . . . and don't let her cross the street alone. Promise? I'm relying on you!"

But, of course, a minute later Lilian tore herself loose, ran across the street, just missed getting run over by a truck. Horrified, I caught up with her, grabbed her hand, yanked her along warning her never to do such a thing again.

Later, with the air of a much abused child, she reported to Mother how I beat her up . . . and I got punished.

"But Mother . . . I only yanked her hand . . . she ran across the street! And you told me . . ." I protested uselessly. I could not make her understand that I was only trying to do what she had asked me to do. But Mother did not hear me.

"She's only a little girl. The older and the wiser one gives in. She doesn't know any better."

Somehow this gave me the impression that my sister was the favoured child. She was always right, and her needs always came before mine. "Not at all," Lilian told me years later. "You were the wiser one, and therefore Mother's favourite. I was just a stupid little girl."

In mid-July something odd happened in Berlin. The "Jews not welcome" signs suddenly disappeared. I did not look for an explanation; it was enough for me to know that I could again go swimming at the Havel public bath. What else was important? Hermann Papiermeister came to the conclusion that it had something to do with the start of the Olympics and all those foreigners who were pouring into Berlin.

A little ditty chanted at the time by the Hitler Youth seemed to confirm Hermann's thinking.

Nach der Olympiade Schlagen wir die Juden zu Marmelade.
After the Olympic Games, we'll make marmalade out of the Jews.

The great event had come at last. I passed the Olympic construction site frequently, saw the buildings rise foot by foot and marvelled at the staggering proportions of the project. Equally staggering was the pomp and circumstance when the Olympics finally opened. The whole city was a sea of flags and decorations, music, fanfares, processions. Red, white and black, the colours of the Nazi flag, predominated.

Benno and I hung out on the Olympic grounds. It was exciting to be in this gigantic turbulent show, on this huge stage on which we too acted a part. There were so many people, so much colour, so much clamour and so many foreign faces and languages.

Our greatest moment came when a well-dressed gentleman suddenly appeared in front of us, smiling, and asked whether we had tickets for the football match between Germany and England due to start in a few minutes. We informed him, regretfully, that we had no tickets to sell.

"No, no. I wasn't asking whether you could sell me tickets, I wondered whether you had some for yourself?"

Our hearts pumped faster. We looked at him sideways and told him that, most unfortunately, we had neither tickets nor money for tickets. Most unfortunately!

Could he hear our hearts thumping with sudden hope? He grinned and just handed us two tickets. *Un miraculo*. We wanted to fall on our knees with thanks. I forcibly restrained myself from kissing his hand. This was the one football match I was dying to watch. He saw the unbelieving joy in our eyes and grinned even more widely. We squealed, stammered and gulped "thank you" over and over, and the nice man seemed most pleased as we walked off. Delirious, we raced to the stadium.

And what a stadium. Coming out of the dark access stairs and corridors we were suddenly faced with a brightly lit enormous, swaying, milling, moving mass of people— left, right, across the oval field, all around, near and far, people, people, people, completely filled our field of vision. A sea of voices larger than the ocean. We stood breathless with awe, exhilaration and fear. Someone looked at our tickets and pointed the way—and somehow we got to our seats. Almost immediately the giant 100,000-headed monster in the stadium roared and got to its feet. Like a huge flock of birds, 100,000 white hands rose and descended in the Nazi salute. The teams had entered, and their national anthems were being played. The hands rose for both the British and the German national anthems. Everybody's hand except ours. I thought people were looking at us. We glanced furtively at each other, felt conspicuous and afraid. Besides, it occurred to me, for whom were we going to cheer? I felt an acute conflict of loyalties. I looked all around me for inspiration, for divine guidance, and became aware of the huge number of swastikas that decorated the stadium . . . it was as if they were all lit up, standing out brightly against the darker mass of the people. I couldn't cheer for those, I decided. Never. I whispered to Benno and he nodded. But are we going to cheer for the English team? I looked at the audience surrounding us, tense and excited, looked down and saw a group of people who seemed to be cheering for the English. Again I whispered to Benno and we left our seats to make our way towards that group. They held little red flags quartered by a white cross. Danish. We pleaded in sign language for a little space and after a short hesitation they winked and motioned us in. They probably thought we were moving down from cheaper seats, but made room for us good-naturedly all the same.

As the game continued they gave us curious looks. They had noticed that we were cheering neither for the German nor the British team. During intermission, after attempts in Danish and English, two Danes who spoke good German, started asking us questions. It took a little time and reassurance until we trusted them sufficiently to tell them why we were not cheering "our" team. They got most interested in us and started to ask questions about things in Germany, about Jews, and how we managed. It never occurred to them that we couldn't speak freely. We answered quietly, keeping our voices down and they kept repeating questions, asking us to speak up. Some of their friends joined in, loudly. We looked around thoroughly alarmed by now to see who else was listening, clammed up—and were saved by the end of intermission. They invited us for refreshments after the game, and we smiled non-committally.

The British won. While their national anthem was being played they stood relaxed, remarkably at ease. Not sloppy, but at ease. So unlike the Germans who stood stiffly, like soldiers, chest out, heels together, one hand on the trouser seam, the other raised in the Nazi salute. Our new Danish friends renewed their invitation, but we thanked them nicely, shook our heads and rushed off to disappear in the seething river of people, glancing back uneasily to see whether we were being followed.

There was no doubt about it, Jesse Owens was the star of the Berlin Olympics. A black star, shining brightly. Not exactly what the Fuehrer had in mind when he cooked up this propaganda-laden extravaganza called "Olympiade". It wasn't just sport, it was a showcase for the new Germany. Shades of a Wagnerian Valhalla: pageantry, a million flags, twenty-foot-high swastikas at focal points all over Berlin. And wherever you went, togetherness: men, women and children showing solidarity in a multitude of Nazi uniforms. Brown-shirted storm troopers lined all the approach roads to the Olympics. Mass gymnastic spectacles displayed valiant, healthy German youth: hands, legs, bodies moving in perfect unison. A cast of millions. Benno and I included.

Until the Olympics I had only seen one or two real live blacks and perhaps an Oriental or two. People in Berlin would stop in the street, turn around and stare at such a sight. And here now, there were many such sights every day.

After seeing Owens win the 100-metre dash I heard people near me discussing the blacks: They're closer to animals, those blacks, they ventured, that's why they can jump and run so well. That's funny, I thought, so what are all those smart, superior Aryans doing out there, trying to out-animal the animals? And losing at that.

The Jews of Berlin had their Olympiade too, at least for the kids. Since Jews were not welcome on German athletic fields the Jewish schools got together and created their own in the Grunewald. Throughout the spring and autumn, my class would meet there, get sorted out, boys this way, girls that way, and the "good-for-you" body building stuff would start. I loved it in spite of its being "good-for-you". And since the subway station "Grunewald" was right next to the Avus car racing circuit, I could often watch practice runs. The scream and silver flash of those low-slung, big-wheeled racing cars were among the greatest thrills of my childhood, and at least half of my childhood heroes were racing car drivers. Names like Brauchitsch and Stuck comfortably rubbed shoulders with Einstein, Schweitzer and Tom Sawyer. I knew the features of Bugattis, Maseratis, Alfa Romeos, Auto Union and Mercedes racing cars better than the features of the Alps or Himalayas.

Each year, on our Sportsplatz, there was a mini-Olympics for Jewish schools. My thing was the 100-metre dash . . . and in 1936 I did especially well. I won that race and also helped my school win the relay race and football match. This heady triumph consoled me no end for a less than brilliant academic showing.

My mother was not consoled. She seemed to equate my lack of brilliance in French, English and Hebrew with a lack of love for her. Her belief that I could do anything I put my mind to, though flattering, was a little unrealistic and very hard to live up to. Eventually I found an answer, a little practical demonstration to remind me when needed, Mother notwithstanding, that no matter how hard I tried, there were things I simply could not do. I just stood there and flapped my arms vigorously. I never managed to fly off the ground and hit the ceiling.

My father was easier on me. He would talk to me, not man to man yet, thank heavens, but like a kind, loving, understanding father. My limitations did not seem to bother him. And he would ask me what I wanted. Mother always knew what was good for me. Cod liver oil and education were good for me.

"What you've got in your head nobody can take away from you," she would declare with ghetto wisdom.

I was not old and persecution-experienced enough then to answer: "Yes they can. They can take off your head."

It is ironic that, not many years later, her disdained views on education somehow imperceptibly became my own.

Even if I had not had other sources of information, I would have known Hitler's Olympiade was over at the end of August. The "No Jews" signs started to reappear quite promptly, and at more places than ever before. There was even one at my local tobacconist, which was a calamity since he was my source for cheap white clay pipes. Yes, one of my early vices was tobacco. Hiding from head-shaking and finger-wagging adults, Norbert and I smoked peace pipes in the bushes, cross-legged, à la Karl May's Indians. The variety of weed we smoked depended on how rich we were at the moment. When we were really destitute we used tobacco extracted from cigarette butts found on the streets. On wealthier days we smoked black, flaky bits of squashed cheap cigars. The pipe was brittle and had to be handled gently. Sitting face to face in a proud, dignified manner, we took puffs, exclaimed "Hough" looked "imperturbable" and passed on the pipe. The consequences were pretty predictable. Norbert would soon get up, whisper "good-bye", stagger to his bike, wobble half a block, hold on to a lamppost and throw up. He always inhaled, the dope. I knew better than that, but after a few puffs often I didn't feel all that great either. Yet we kept on making brave attempts to form the habit. It seemed so grown-up, and our fathers obviously enjoyed it so much.

Norbert and I still got into trouble quite frequently. Later, he claimed that I was always to blame. I led and he followed. If he followed, he certainly followed with alacrity and managed to get into quite a bit of trouble even without me. For instance, there was that unauthorised fishing expedition he led, taking along my shrimp sister. They climbed around the understructure of the bridge over the Citadel moat, sat on a beam twenty feet over deep water fishing with a bent pin, a little ball of bread and common sewing cotton, black of course. No float. Neither of them could swim. When the policeman saw them and hollered, Norbert left Lilian up there, on the beam, and came running to my house.

"And you just left her under that bridge?" Mother screamed as I shot out of the door.

When I got to the bridge, gasping, there was a small excited crowd of people looking over the parapet, laughing and giggling with joy. I looked too.

Lilian had obviously managed to get out of the beams on to firm land, and there she was, in the distance, a tiny figure bobbing up and down, emitting short piercing shrieks of terror. Close on her heels was a heavy policeman holding on to his helmet stumbling over the bumpy, lumpy field, falling, getting up, falling . . . gaining on her slowly. But, like a jack-rabbit, Lilly seemed to shoot sideways, zig-zagging, evading his grasp—combining a shriek and a hop at each zig and at each zag. People around me were howling with laughter, applauding, shouting encouragement. And now I, still fighting for breath, chased across the field after both of them. We all arrived together at the spot where the field ended at the water's edge and the policeman had Lilian by the arm. He lectured me about not looking after my little sister.

"She could have been seriously hurt," he ended, shaking his head, out of breath and full of reproach.

I saw the beads of sweat running down his face and throat and wondered whether he realised that we were Jews.

I thanked him and walked Lilian home, holding her little gritty hand in mine. For once she did not tear herself away in defiance. She glanced up at me flirtatiously and smiled.

School started in September, and I was back in full harness, doing homework, running errands, shopping, helping Mother when my father was absent and we had a customer. There weren't that many Jews in Spandau and many of them were now as poor as we were. We bartered far more than we sold; a set of dishes for a dress length; a hat for a pair of shoes.

I started to avoid the Potsdamerstrasse. One day it was a street near my house like any other, the next it became the hangout for a bunch of Hitler Youths who took great pleasure in plaguing me. They would encircle me and push me around between them. One guy would try to crouch low behind me so another could push to make me fall backwards over him. At first it was all just good, clean Nazi fun, but gradually they became meaner and meaner, jabbing elbows into my stomach and bloodying my nose. And they had a prize selection of little verses, like:

"Jude Itzig, Nase spitzig. Kinder eckich, Aschloch dreckich."
Jew Ikey, nose spiky. Children irky, arsehole dirty.

At first I defended myself. It didn't do much good, but occasionally I could land a good punch or give one of them a bloody nose, and that made me feel better. Then I thought of taking them on one by one, like in the good

128

old days, a year ago, but there were too many of them now . . . and it was getting too dangerous. These attacks were no longer kids' games. So I avoided the street.

On a business trip, waiting for one of our tailors to finish some work, I got hungry and went round the corner towards the Alexanderplatz. That's where one of my favourite places was, Aschinger, a fast food place with branches all over Berlin except, alas, in Spandau. Imagine, for pennies one could buy a simply delicious pair of steaming hot dogs and get, free, absolutely free, all the crisp, tasty rolls one could eat. On this occasion, as usual, I stood in line, got my sausages and mustard, took the golden rolls out of the big wicker basket, and hurried to an empty table. As I munched I suddenly became aware of a boy of about seventeen at the next table —and felt a wave of hot and cold fear that made my scalp tingle. That boy-man was staring at me with such vicious, violent hatred that I feared he would get up and attack me right then. For a moment I sat paralysed. I avoided looking in his direction, forced myself to eat calmly, but finally got up with food still in my hand. Anticipating a blow to the back of my head, I set out slowly towards the revolving door, listening for footsteps behind me. Outside, I glanced back quickly to see whether he was following, ready to run if I had to, but he didn't come after me. Then it caught my eye: the notice at the door that said, "Jews not welcome". Yes, the Olympics were well and truly over, and all the foreigners had gone.

But there was at least one foreigner left. During one of my errands, I noticed a little crowd in the Alexanderstrasse and joined it. There was a tall, big-chinned, stupid looking SA man leaning over a chubby, swarthy, middle-aged man who was bleeding from the mouth.

"No Jew, me . . . *Italiano*, me, *Heil* . . ." said the little

man, pointing at himself vigorously. But he was not permitted to finish.

The brown shirt smashed his big fist into the man's
face. The Italian went down. I expected him to stay down
after such a blow, but, with his fine business suit all
rumpled and dirty, he got up protesting, gesticulating with
both hands.

"No, no," he said, pointing at himself again with a
pudgy index finger. "*Italiano, fascisti.*" Drawing himself
up in dark-suited, dazed dignity, he gave the Nazi salute
and shouted, "*Heil* Hitler!"

"*Judenschwein,*" growled the Nazi, looking around
him, tipsy, smug, and knocked the Italian down again.
Nudging the prone man contemptuously with his boot, he
turned round and left him lying on the ground, moaning
quietly. The audience stayed utterly silent. I looked up at
their faces. No one was looking back at me. No one was
looking at anyone else.

How did the storm trooper decide the man was Jewish?
It sufficed that you did not look German. All you needed
was dark brown hair, brown eyes, a nose a fraction longer
than medium and a stupid storm trooper. There were
times when I went unrecognised. And there were times
when I was asked whether I was a Jew and would not
deny it, even though it might mean a beating. I still don't
know whether that was heroism or insanity.

I risked trouble and sneaked into cinemas even when
they had "The Sign" up. One day I saw Remarque's *All
Quiet on the Western Front*. Some of the finer points might
have been a little beyond me then, but the film affected
me profoundly. With the constant talk of rearmament and
the Glory of the Reich, I could not understand how an
anti-war film could ever be permitted a showing,
especially at a place as "official" as the Berlin Planetarium. This had become a favourite haunt for me. There,
for the same money, you could see celestial stars as well

as film stars on the curved screen of the domed roof. There you found the oblong, humming, turning, double-globed machine with hundreds of blind eyes that sent light rays through the dark and transformed the ceiling into the Milky Way. And there, too, was the fascinating man at the dimly lit lectern who explained everything and made arrows appear in the enormous sky using a flashlight pointer. The Planetarium showed quality movies as well as documentary films about the cosmos, earth, nature, animals and peoples from different countries. It was all fascinating and hopeful, too, because more convincingly than all my books, the documentaries showed that there were other, less frightening, less hateful worlds and millions of people beyond the German borders.

If *All Quiet on the Western Front* surprised me, another film I saw, by mistake, at about the same time, dumb-founded me. It made me doubt my sanity. I saw it by mistake because I went to see a cowboy film that had finished the day before. The film called *Hitlerjunge Quex* lit up the screen instead. Would I stay to see a movie about the heroic Hitler Youth? Of course. Having spent my hard-earned pennies to get in, I wasn't about to leave just like that.

That was crazy to start with. By then, I had experienced quite a few beatings from little gangs of Hitler Youths or "Pimpfs", the pre-adolescent version of the Hitler Youth. Stonings or beatings were hard to avoid, especially when they were waiting for you outside school or in front of your house. You were lucky if you had a friend or two around, so you didn't get all the attention yourself. If you just happened upon them you had a better chance. There were two golden rules. One. Walk with your eyes wide open, always. Two. When you see a bunch of Hitler Youths loitering in the distance, not on duty, not standing at attention or performing some other military drill, do suddenly remember something you just left behind, turn

131

on your heel and go back the way you came. Look back as little as possible, but listen for quick footsteps behind you. If you hear some, run like hell.

And there, in that fleapit, I was sitting watching *Hitlerjunge Quex*, an out-and-out Nazi propaganda film, about a blond, cute, heroic Hitler Youth who got himself killed by a bunch of pimply, slimy Communist brats. Involuntarily I found myself routing for Quex, hating the vile Communist girls who betrayed him, despising the slimy criminals who hunted him, fearing for his life. The last scene was set in a dark, deserted fairground. Quex is hiding from his pursuers in the tent of a shooting gallery. They get closer and closer. A giant moving shadow is thrown against the tent fabric by one of his pursuers and Quex, backing up in fear, touches the trigger of a life-sized metal target figure holding a tin drum. My heart practically stopped. At his touch the dummy drummer sets of an explosively loud drum roll and I gasped. Quex is caught and knifed to death. I was heartbroken. As I left the theatre, tears were rolling down my cheeks. Out, in the daylight, I scratched my head and asked myself, "Am I sane?"

CITADEL

"You will *never* learn English," said Fraulein Jarislovsky, the teacher, "and you are a disturbing influence in the class." I reluctantly agreed with her on both counts. The reluctance came less from being kicked out of the English class than from having to face my mother who had volunteered me for this extra-curricular course. But England had shown no signs of wanting any part of me or my family, and I saw no purpose in wasting my time on a language I would *never* use. Instead I was drawing and passing around caricatures of my classmates and Fraulein Jarislovsky.

When I told my mother that I would never know English she was unreasonably upset, just as I had expected. But who wants to sit at home chewing grammar, mumbling hour after hour to no one in particular, "*Je soois, tu ess*" or, "zee cat is black; I like zee cat"? No, language was not my thing.

This probably dates back to an early, unhappy experience with a foreign language. My mother spoke Hungarian to her sisters whenever something was discussed that "children were too young to understand". I bore this with fortitude until, aged nine, I had been the subject of these secretive exchanges just once too often. Quite determined to break the code, I listened most carefully and transcribed several sentences phonetically. Over the next few weeks I painstakingly and discreetly asked Mother and her sisters the meaning of every single word until I had a complete translation. What they had said about me and about others was so dull, so dreary and so ordinary, I concluded that there was absolutely nothing to be gained from learning a foreign language.

Mrs Millicinsky, who taught Hebrew, which, unlike English, was obligatory, would also have loved to throw me out of her class. I was not only the worst student, I also made beastly drawings of her spidery shape and her myopic squint behind thick glasses. I whispered to neighbours, teased girls, read books hidden under the desk and plagued her endlessly with inattention.

She did obtain a mild measure of satisfaction from writing nasty little notes to my parents. These had to be signed by either parent and shown to her at the next lesson. Had she suspected how painful it was for me to get those notes signed, she might have felt more than mild satisfaction. My problem was that her little notes were not the only ones.

"Instead of paying attention during his French class, your son made ink blobs in his exercise book . . ." etc.

This was unfair. They were not ink blobs, they were drawings of black beetles with white eyes and hairy legs.

What I considered even more unfair was that no teacher ever gave me a little note to be signed when I was good. A note like, "Dear Mr and Mrs Zeller, your son behaved extraordinarily well in my class today. He knew how to conjugate *être* faultlessly, and did not draw a single caricature during my entire lesson. Yours sincerely . . ."

The notes were hard on me, not just because I feared punishment. My parents had enough to worry about without my causing them grief. I postponed getting their signature until the last moment. And every minute of that time, the note was there, a hollow pain at the back of my mind. I became extraordinarily helpful in fetching, carrying, cleaning. I said "yes" to almost anything my mother demanded but avoided eye contact. She had a knack for sensing trouble. On one occasion I was so ashamed I became a criminal; a vile forger. After several hours of practising my father's signature, I signed on his behalf. But as I presented this travesty to the teacher I was so petrified, expecting to be unmasked as a villain in front of the entire class that I didn't have the courage to be a forger again.

But one day Hebrew sneaked up on me. It was 1937, my bar mitzvah beckoned, and I was getting religion.

What I knew of religion came largely from the Jewish holiday visits to the Bobaths in Charlottenburg—unless one can count my parents' perfunctory, once-a-year visit to the local synagogue during the High Holidays. Quite fittingly it was uncle Ignatz who said one day:

"Of course, you'll be having your bar mitzvah next May."

And I answered, "Of course," and told my mother.

I wanted a bar mitzvah because I believed in God, but there were other reasons as well. My eyes had finally been opened about the Jews. There was constant proof in the newspapers and on the radio, every day. Millions of good, stolid burghers were accepting it. It was written in black on white and there just had to be something to it. Jews were filthy-rich Bolshevik-Capitalist, hook-nosed scum. They were powerful beyond words and ready to dominate Germany and the world from Moscow. I didn't want to go to Moscow, but can anyone blame me if I wanted to declare my allegiance to such a rich and powerful people?

Perhaps still more important, a bar mitzvah was an official recognition that I was no longer a child. Being a child hadn't been all that much fun—with everybody always telling you what you want, or ought to want, and what was good for you.

When I say that I saw the light about greedy, ruthless, Bolshevik-Capitalist Jew exploiters, I wasn't being

135

entirely satirical. I knew my parents and close family had
no hooked noses, were far from wealthy, and had no
intentions of dominating the world. It was obvious that
something was very wrong somewhere—that I was being
told absurd lies. But why? And what was the truth? Later,
as an adult, I marvelled at how so many millions of people
could have swallowed such a silly hogwash of hate. Such
stupid lies. And then I discovered that I myself had swallowed some of that hogwash, that I too had become a
victim of Dr Goebbels' hate propaganda. It had influ-
enced most of my life. I avoided trading as if it were dirty.
I rejected many good opportunities, insisting on working
for others rather than going into my own business. I
wanted to be a renter rather than a landlord. For I did
not want to be one of THOSE Jews. "Exploiters. Cheats.
Getting rich on the backs of the poor. Parasites who never
got their hands dirty."

What was stranger still was that this state of mind contradicted my entire intellectual attitude. I tried so hard to
free myself from chauvinism and prejudice. So if I didn't
believe in "Jews", why did I have to prove that they could
be decent too?

It was simpler in 1937. I wanted to be a Jew because
they said I was a Jew. I couldn't understand why they
hated me but I believed in God and I thought He knew
what He was doing. Nor did I just want to do a "short-
cut" bar mitzvah; sing just a couple of prayers before and
after the cantor chants the appropriate passage from the
Torah scroll. I wanted to go the whole hog, even though
it meant months of preparation and . . . Hebrew. When
I saw a reproduction of Michelangelo's Sistine Yehova
pointing his finger at Adam I knew what he meant
instantly. He was telling Adam to wake up and have a
proper bar mitzvah.

Missing soccer games and skating, braving ice and
snow, I became a martyr to my faith. I suffered almost

136

silently through Cheder, and Hebrew, and fearfully followed the private musical reciting technique and moral
Judaic teachings of the Herr Rabbiner Doktor Loewenstamm, alias Haeppchen. His weighty title, his direct
access to God and his strict demeanour gave him, in my
eyes, a stature at least six feet in height and four feet
wide. No other teacher ever loomed as large and impos-
ingly over my life. Even the origin of his nickname
"Haeppchen" did nothing to dispel this awe.

The Cheder, in this case a Sunday morning course of
religious and historical instruction, usually ended with a
sweet bribe, or consolation prize of honey cake, cookies
or other goodies.

"Have another little piece . . . *ein Haeppchen,*" the
Herr Rabbiner Doktor Loewenstamm would say. "Go
on. Take another *Haeppchen!*" He smiled through his
beard . . . but it was a slightly lopsided, sinister smile.

Ten years later, having discovered him safe in London,
I called on him, and we slowly walked around Hampstead
Heath. He was a frail, gentle, lonely, old man who barely
came up to my shoulder. I went to him in need. Perhaps
he could help me patch up the faith in God which hung
around me in tatters. I missed believing—and still thought
life would be easier if I could believe.

We walked slowly, arm in arm, for a long time. It was
autumn. Misty. Sweet-smelling leaves were falling, and
there was sadness in the air. We talked. I tried not to let
him see that he was not able to help me. I took him, my
Herr Rabbiner Doktor Loewenstamm, back to his front
doorstep, hesitated for a moment, reached out and
embraced him, my childhood's six-foot-high and four-
foot-wide illusion.

The bar mitzvah at the end of May '37 turned out to
be a decidedly humid affair. Everybody cried. And each
for a different reason. Mother cried with sadness when
she heard the clear, unbroken voice of her child at the

altar. Her little boy was growing up. My father cried with pride. His son was becoming a man. My sister cried because she wasn't a boy and would not have a bar mitzvah. The aunts cried because it was an emotionally charged family occasion. And because times were bad— and this could be the last big family occasion. I cried because I did not get a piece of the *Nusstorte*, Mother's famous ground-walnut cake, made with love and fourteen eggs. I had worked hard to help her make it, cracking pounds of walnuts, grinding, mixing them with a wooden pestle into the other ingredients in the heavy, earthenware bowl. Then the smell of the baking and of the finished masterpiece sweetly permeated the whole flat for days before my bar mitzvah. I couldn't wait to get my teeth into that cake.

Finally my great moment had come. I was standing at the altar, wearing my first pair of long trousers. First darkly, with shaking knees, then brightly, in a strange trance of heightened awareness, I sang my heart out. Suddenly, it was all over. The cantor took my place at the altar, Doktor Loewenstamm smiled his lopsided smile from the pulpit. Later, on the street after the service, I suffered congratulations, head patting, wet sloppy kisses—and oblivion. Everybody got very busy with one another. Dozens of people I knew well trundled in little groups through the Breitestrasse to our flat. My elation had gone, and I felt strangely let down. All the guests seemed to have forgotten my existence. At our flat, too, they sat at the laden table, talking loudly, totally ignoring me. I didn't even get a seat, never mind the seat of honour.

"Whose bar mitzvah is this, Goddammit!" I asked myself.

Standing at the end of the table, I was feeling very low and lonely, when the cake came. I started to feel better. With a chorus of ah's and oh's everybody fell on it—

gobbling it up right in front of my eyes. Anxious to preserve my dignity as a new adult, I did not climb over their heads to get at the cake. I asked politely whether they would please pass along a piece, but it was noisy and they were too busy stuffing themselves to hear me. They didn't leave me a crumb. Not even a crumb, and I was the bar mitzvah boy. Hurt and outraged, I ran to my room, threw myself on the bed and cried. A year or two later, Lilian stuck her head into the door and said:

"Oh, there you are! We were wondering . . ."

She stopped in surprise at my tears and ran away like a startled rabbit. Almost immediately my father, Uncle Mulu and Norbert came running.

"What's the matter?" everybody was asking at the same time.

I told them very exactly what was the matter and they dragged me back to the table, where suddenly everybody made a big fuss over me. The men were drinking to the bar mitzvah boy. The women were smiling sweet encouragement. The kids were smirking. I was embarrassed. It wouldn't bring back the *Nusstorte*, I thought, with a pang of anger. Somebody made me drink some terrible stuff, made from plums, that burned a hole inside me, all the way down to the stomach. More head patting. I escaped with the kids to the Citadel park and by the time we got back it was nearly dark and everything was just about over.

My parents must have made considerable sacrifices for that bar mitzvah. They had become very poor. Only an occasional customer would dare enter a Jewish store. Somebody like Gotthard Blenn, the son of the minister of the Nikolai Church right around the corner. Ironically, he came to buy material for his black corduroy Christian Hitler Youth shorts. He was sent to buy from us, probably by his father who preached against racism and hatred, was denounced, arrested, released and began to preach

139

tolerance again, this time quoting the words of Christ instead of using his own. Gotthard, a year or so older than I, became the one remaining young Christian friend who smiled and waved openly when we passed on the street.

But an occasional customer was not enough. And borrowing from friends and family became more and more difficult, too. What was happening to us was also happening to them. Things were just as bad among the professionals. By the middle of 1937, nearly every Jewish professional my parents knew was out of work. Teachers, scientists, accountants, film and stage professionals, musicians, doctors, lawyers.

One day my mother did not have enough money to buy us the next meal. She was crying in a gloomy corner of the kitchen and when I finally got her to tell me why, I was deeply shocked. I had no idea that things had become that bad. And I remembered how I had scorned the inevitable *"Knochensupper"*, a vegetable soup enriched by stock and marrow bones. It was the most nourishing thing you could buy for pennies.

I went into my room, got out my hoard of secretly earned bicycle-watching money and gave it to her. She was taken aback. I saw her lips parting to ask where I got the money, but she stopped herself. Her face turned pale, then she blushed, and her eyes showed a quick succession of feelings. Shame, relief and then a flood of tenderness. She held my hand for a minute then asked me to shop for some food. I think this was the closest I ever felt to my mother. Strange that it should be when I gave her something.

But the bar mitzvah was much more than just a financial burden. With Father frequently in hiding or sick, she was now on her own for long periods. I helped her whenever I could, after school, at weekends and during holidays, but the load she carried must have been overwhelming.

140

It was also the time of Goering's "Guns before Butter" campaign, the wrong time to cater a bar mitzvah. There was no butter. No cream. There were all kinds of food shortages. It was the beginning of "ersatz"—substitutes. Ersatz butter. Ersatz gasoline. Ersatz rubber. Ersatz fabrics. People talked about clothing woven with yarn that was made from wood. They joked about dresses that would sprout green leaves; about branches growing out of men's suits. They smiled about "petrol" trailers, the strange, smelly coal-gas contraptions pulled on two wheels behind cars and trucks. Yet "Guns before Butter" brought about an important victory for me, that led to greater freedom and self-reliance and ultimately to my being allowed to flee to Holland on my own a year and a half later.

One Sunday, Mother discovered that she had run out of butter. I offered to go to Aunt Leona's, but, after a hesitation, she told me that trains were slow on Sunday and that lunch would be ready in an hour.

Aunt Leona was our butter lifeline. She had "connections". One of her former customers and admirers owned a grocery shop. Now a Nazi, he still had a soft spot for blonde, blue-eyed Leona. He permitted her to enter his store in spite of the "No Jews" sign—and graciously sold her black market butter at steep prices.

I calculated. The train would take two hours, but by bicycle I'd make it in less than an hour. Well, well. Here was a way to take another decisive step in "bringing up Mother". I would defy the limits she set *and* be a good boy in the bargain. So I rode the bike halfway across forbidden Berlin and back, returning sweatily triumphant, holding out a pound of butter. Can you beat up a kid returning from a mission of love? Of course she remonstrated, but I pointed out to her once again that Aunt Leona permitted Norbert to visit us on his bike. And was Norbert smarter than I? And was he a better cyclist than

141

I? Was I not old enough? Her last resistance finally crumbled, and I was permitted free daytime use of the bicycle.

An unexpected consequence of my bar mitzvah was another summer holiday at Bad Kolberg. Since I was tall and skinny and since there had been more tuberculosis in the family than was absolutely necessary, my mother was forever carting me off for X-rays and chest pounding. Sending me to the sea for my health seemed imperative to her. But how? We no longer had the means. Enter the Herr Rabbiner Dr Loewenstamm. I was his bar mitzvah boy, and he convinced the little Spandau congregation that my family deserved help.

So once more I was in Kolberg, which had become even more exciting because of Kuno, the Great Dane. He was tied up in the yard and had a chesty bark that was almost strong enough to push people over. He barked at everybody and only his keeper would go anywhere near him. With my extensive experience of dogs, horses and a carp, I just knew that Kuno was barking out of sheer loneliness. Talking calmly, in a soothing fashion, I slowly but confidently approached the monster. Nothing impresses a dog more than confidence. I stopped a foot outside the reach of his teeth and held out the back of my hand to let him sniff it—real doggie stuff, this. He was enchanted. Rearing up on his hind legs, he managed to put his long front paws on my shoulders and when I moved closer I received a wet, sloppy, passionate kiss. It was the beginning of a short but intense relationship. Every day I saved him little goodies from the dining table, and he soon drooled and licked his lips whenever he saw me coming. In next to no time I was able to make him sit, stop barking and shake paws with me.

My ability to handle Kuno was most useful the day he got off the chain and cornered little Margot Rosenthal. Rescuing the damsel in distress was no problem. I grabbed

Kuno by the collar, yanked him back to his customary place, made him sit down and chained him up again. He offered me his paw.

Margot, decidedly impressed, made appropriate little cooing noises and flashed her eyes. She had lovely eyes—and altogether I thought her uncommonly pretty. I didn't tell her that she had been on my mind a great deal, that I had been too shy to approach her and that, with a sudden blast of inspiration, I had undone Kuno's chain when I saw her coming into the yard.

I rescued her again a few days later, this time from a fat boy. I was quite sure he was pestering her. Even though he was heavier than I, I told him I'd knock off his block if he didn't leave her alone instantly, which he did. On the strength of those two heroic acts I won her heart completely; we swore eternal love and promised to write faithfully when we parted. She came from Eisleben, a hundred miles from Berlin. Amazingly enough, we did write to each other for more than a year, hiding little love notes in the coloured tissue linings of the two-layer envelopes common in those days. We had a secret postage stamp code too. Sticking it upside down on the envelope meant, "I love you", mounting it diagonally, "I miss you"—and so on. We stayed in touch, and it was to visit Margot that I ran—or rather cycled—away from home a year later. Another stepping-stone to Holland.

There was one shocking letter from Margot waiting for me one day when I came home from school. Written in variously coloured crayons, it was monstrously senti-mental, hideously tacky. And those red hearts pierced by green arrows. I was devastated. Could I love a woman with such bad taste? I sat and sat, staring dumbly at the letter, and then I gasped. There was something wrong here. Although the stamp had been franked, there was no trace of the round imprint where it should have con-tinued on the envelope. I got out a previous letter from

Margot and a magnifying glass, looked at the stamp and compared the writing. It was obvious that the envelope had never gone through the post and that the writing did not match. It was equally obvious where I should look for the perpetrator. I marched into her room and there she was; there they were. Lilian and plump, short Ruth Papiermeister—all wide-eyed, smirky girlish innocence. As soon as they began to shriek and just in the nick of time, Mother came to the rescue before I could strangle them both.

On one of my business trips near the Alex I ran into Hans, an old school friend. I hardly recognised him. His face was covered with scabby lacerations, he had a black eye, a gauze pad covered his nose, and his right arm, in a sling, was bandaged.

"What's the other guy look like?" I joked.

"Other guys," he answered quietly, "and they look fine. Hitler Youth. They lashed me with their leather belts, metal buckle forward. Three of them."

"They nearly got your eye."

"Yeah, I was lucky," he said, gently touching the gauze pad with his finger. I felt a twinge of horror. To be blind!

But, it seemed, the beating wasn't the worst of his troubles. He and his brother Joachim were staying with an aunt who hated kids. His father had been missing for nearly two weeks; everybody suspected he was in Schutzhaft, "protective custody", at the Oranienburg or Dachau concentration camp along with other people from the last wave of arrests. And then his mother had gone into a hospital with a nervous breakdown.

"Oh shit!" I said to Hans. "Oh shit!" What else was there to say?

"With all these terrible things going on," people ask, forty-five years and a few thousand miles removed, "why didn't your parents just leave Germany?"

144

"To go where?" Or to put it even more succinctly, "Who wanted Jews, especially poor Jews?"

The mark wasn't worth much outside Germany, and there were tremendous obstacles to transfering money legally out of Germany. If you did so illegally, you risked the concentration camp. Some loopholes, some complex transfers were possible for a while. But by 1935 Jews could leave Germany with only a very modest amount of portable personal property—no valuables such as jewellery or art—and ten marks, less than the price of a cheap meal.

A deadly trap. Get out, said the Nazis and then made it impossible for anyone to go. In the spring of 1938 there were nearly half a million German and Austrian Jews with nowhere to go unless they could find help from abroad. And my parents had no one who could or would shelter, feed and clothe a family of four.

Surely, Americans will say, you can find work? Hardly. Which country would permit a foreigner to work? And what work would an impoverished businessman be qualified to do? In the 1930s, with severe unemployment everywhere, there was an absolute prohibition throughout most of the world against employing foreigners. Here and there, rare exceptions were made, if no local labour could be found. England didn't mind taking a few domestic servants; Brazil could find a spot for road engineers. Even the United States, often open and generous to immigrants, erected formidable barriers. You were permitted to work, yes—if you could find work. In the meanwhile, to guarantee an immigrant would not become a burden to the taxpayer, he or she had to bring a considerable amount of money into the country or find a sponsor who would provide an affidavit of financial support.

Not one single country modified its visa restrictions to help rescue a few Jews except Great Britain, briefly, late in 1938, after Munich.

There were single people or childless couples desperate
enough to creep past armed border patrols on both sides.
Then they would hide in Brussels, Amsterdam or Paris,
work "black" for nickels and dimes, beg, starve, live in
constant fear of arrest and deportation, only to be caught
again by the invading Germans in 1940.

Leave everything behind? Become a domestic servant?
Hide and starve with your children? Such considerations
explain why, as late as 1938, my mother could still say:
"*Ohne Alles koennen wir jederzeit.*" "Penniless, we can
go at any old time."

You were wrong, dear Mother, terribly wrong. But
who, even as late as 1938, bad as things were, could even
in their worst nightmares have dreamed the dream of the
gas chamber?

We had been trying for years to go almost anywhere
"reasonable" while it was still possible to take a little
money out of Germany. Canada was reasonable, Chile
was reasonable. Uganda was not. After 1936, almost any
country where my family could earn a scant living was
reasonable. Even Uganda. Like so many others, my
father was "learning a trade" in a hurry. He was taking
lessons from the projectionist of the cinema on the ground
floor of our building. It was a skill that might gain us a
visa to Columbia, Panama or heaven knows where.

I have vivid memories of trailing from consulate to
consulate, collecting information and questionnaires
about job openings or other "opportunities" abroad, and
then returning to hand back slightly crumpled, inky sheets
to bored-looking staff members with strange accents and
fascinating skin colouration, from lightest yellow to deepest brown. My prowess in geography may well derive
from these visits to foreign soil in Berlin. I became a
vicarious globetrotter. Before I went to any consulate I
would check the location of the country, who ran it, flora,
fauna and whether it was the sort of place to which I

wanted my parents to take me. I leaned heavily towards any place that offered American Indians or live volcanoes. Guatemala was on the top of my list. Every so often a friend or family member called with a red hot news flash.

"Peru is taking electrical engineers."

My father, having served in a searchlight company of the Austrian army and being very handy with fixing electrical gadgets, was fully qualified, I felt, as I dashed to the Peruvian Consulate for forms. More often than not, however, the quota had already been filled, or there had never been such an offer.

There were a few "opportunities" my parents were glad to have missed. The consul of a large South American Republic sold visas. They cost several thousand marks and were absolutely genuine, on the right kind of paper, with all the correct rubber stamps. It was said they were so expensive because a lot of big and little wheels had to be greased. Well, at least they weren't worthless, like those other, cheaper visas, sold by the consular underlings of various remote Republics.

For a while, quite a few families managed to enter the country with the good, expensive visas. Then its Immigration Authorities became suspicious and sealed the border again. The consul disappeared without being able to deliver the last thousand or so visas for which he had already been paid. The general feeling was that the man was mercenary, yes, but also that he was a decent man, had really wanted to help, had greased the wheels and would have delivered the visas if he could have done so.

Apart from learning a little geography, it soon became apparent that these consular jaunts were mostly an exercise in futility. I'm sure many of the completed forms landed up in a Berlin waste-paper basket rather than one in Bogota or Buenos Aires.

There were moments when I wished I had taken my English lessons a little more seriously. Having no one

147

anywhere who would help us, I started to send letters to a dozen or so famous millionaires in America. Henry Ford. Rockefeller. Charlie Chaplin.

Fired by a news story about a boy in need of life-saving surgery who wrote to and got help from a Chicago multi-millionaire, I set out to get my parents a visa to the USA. All it took for an affidavit, I knew, was just one kind multi-millionaire. Just one single multi-millionaire. We would never become a burden to him. Never. "America is a wonderful country," I wrote to our would-be benefactor. "In America you can work, and everybody in my family would work very hard." I never got an answer. Perhaps, my English wasn't good enough, I thought.

All that foreign correspondence reminded me of my stamp collection. I had been too busy that autumn of 1937 to do the usual sorting and mounting. Just before Christmas I pulled out my album and all the other paraphernalia. I started to mount the Dutch stamps . . . but . . . but that's funny, where was the triangular, maroon stamp I got in my last swap? And the Dutch envelope felt so thin . . . I thought I had just gained a whole lot of Dutch stamps. I picked up the envelope with Egyptian stamps, and that was practically empty—and where . . . I got hot under the collar. Perspiration tingled on my forehead. It just couldn't be . . . but there were hundreds of stamps missing.

With my heart pounding I marched into Lilian's room and asked her whether she had any ideas on the subject.

I could tell right away she did; she couldn't look me in the eye. She shrieked innocence at the top of her voice, and I wanted to kill her. But Mother came running through the door and wouldn't let me. Instead she made it an informal lecture on brotherly love and forgiveness. No, it wasn't right, but a little girl doesn't know any better, and an older and wiser brother must forgive her.

"You see, she is sorry, aren't you, Lilly?"

She had stolen my stamps to give them away and curry favour with her teachers and class mates. But there were also several visits to our home by detectives who had caught her stealing really silly things at their store. Just sibling rivalry? A bid for love, for attention? A loss of family?

We weren't a cohesive family any more. No more bicycle trips, *en famille*, to the country, or outings in the Tiergarten. No father for weeks at a time. Mother too burdened to have time for the children other than to supply their most immediate physical needs. Our family had started to disperse more rapidly, and there were fewer visits from uncles, aunts or cousins. The fabric of our childhood changed.

Towards the end of 1937, despairing of being able to find a way to emigrate together, my parents finally took steps to try first to send their children to safety. With the children taken care of, they could attempt to get out themselves. This was a decision made together with Norbert and Susi's parents. They registered us for "children transports" to England or the US, where Refugee Committees were trying to raise funds to save the children. There was a deluge of applications; at the rate things were going, the four of us would still be waiting today for a posthumous visa.

The mothers held their breath, hoping for and dreading the "good news". We children waited impatiently, discussing the toys, games and items of clothing we must not forget to pack. I pulled all the remaining stamps out of my album and, for portability, put them into envelopes. I was also most seriously contemplating setting aside an hour or two for the study of English. But with the skating season getting into full swing, I was unfortunately quite unable to follow up on this resolve.

The moat of the Spandau Citadel was a magical place in winter, a man-made, zig-zagging, circular frozen river

149

with steep, wooden banks. On one side of the moat was a park, on the other, rising above the banks, the massive walls of the fort with its Juliusturm, the medieval-looking round tower. Evenings and weekends there were lights among the trees, where stalls served steaming, sizzling, tantalising sausages on rolls, mulled wine and Grog— hot tea spiked with rum. Loudspeakers played music for skaters.

One late afternoon in January 1938, I was on the ice with Lilian, having been entrusted, once more, with her health, well-being and safety. We did feel pretty safe, all wrapped up in scarves and hats, hard to recognise in the dark. Kids ice-skating at the beginning of the season are too busy to look for Jews. I was surprised and very happy that they still had no "Jews keep out" notices posted at the Citadel. I was expecting them any day and always looked carefully. It was not a good idea to ignore them nowadays, especially at places where people knew you.

I had just finished warning Lilian to be more careful on her skates or she would fall and get hurt, when I hit a bump, tripped, flew through the air with the greatest of ease, and crash-landed with a thump on my hands and knees. I chose my landing area unwisely, a razor-sharp groove in the ice, hacked open with the back of a skate by some unkind fellow skater. When I got up, there was a sizeable hole in my ski pants and an even greater one in my knee. A thick, dangling lump of flesh was still just about attached to the knee and blood ran hotly down my leg. I limped shakily to the nearest bench under a lamp and tried to take off my skates without bending my bad knee too much. My sister, seeing something was wrong, followed and helped me. I decided not to show her my wound. It had nearly made me sick to look at it and I was a *man*. Instead, I asked her to run ahead and get my father.

She did, and I limped along after her through the lamp-lit streets. There was a feathery fall of snow through the yellow light of the street lanterns, a faintly acrid odour of coal-burning stoves in the misty air. The wound hurt ferociously. But having read all about brave soldiers—and what boy had not, in Germany—I was determined not to cry. My father and sister came hurrying towards me. He led me to a nearby lantern, made me lean against it, and gently pulled up my trouser-leg until he could see the wound. He looked up. His face was calm but I saw pain in his eyes. I also saw my pain in his eyes.

"Not too good," he said, "but you'll be all right. It hurts, doesn't it?"

I nodded and he continued, "We must . . . I think it would be a good idea if we went to Doctor Kallner right away." Again I nodded.

"Can you walk?" And once more I nodded, afraid that if I opened my mouth and said a single word I would burst into tears.

He seemed to understand and looked as if he wanted to pick me up and carry me like a little boy. And for a moment I wanted to be carried like a little boy, but instead I reached out and put my right arm around his shoulder. He turned to Lilian, thanked her, and sent her home with a message for my mother. Then in a half-embrace he gripped me across the back and with his hand under my arm, walked me the long blocks to the doctor. My lovely, wonderful father.

"We'll soon fix that," said Dr Kallner, alias Yehova. He smiled reassuringly through his silver and black beard, but I could tell that he didn't like what he saw.

"I think we'll use staples. Stitches might not hold . . . you see it's here, where the knee bends the most." He gently washed around the wound, produced a wide-necked bottle, dipped a spoon into it and came up with a heap of mustard-yellow powder.

"Hold tight!" he said as he tipped the powder under

151

the wound flap. It seared like a burn. I groaned and, with tears in my eyes, clutched my father's wrist. Involuntarily he put his hand over mine and gripped hard too.

"It's all right to cry," he said, relaxing his grip. But I shook my head.

There were six more "Hold tights", as the doctor crimped six silver staples over the edges of the wound with what looked suspiciously like a car mechanic's pair of pliers. Each time he had to hurt me, he gave me a quick glance of concern over his gold-rimmed glasses. Little did we know that this was the last time we would see each other. A few months later, he and all other Jewish physicians were forbidden to practice. He would not be allowed to see German patients at all, or even to treat Jews without special permission, and then only as the orderly of an Aryan doctor.

"There, my brave young man," he said. "That will soon be healed as good as new."

THE BATTLE OF LEIPZIG

It was raining books. Books flooded the shelves, tables and basements of booksellers. Books were spilling over my shelves, too, as our family disintegrated. One by one, those who could escape left, with a minimum of impedimenta. Rather than sell, for pennies, the books they could not take, our relatives showered them on me. And like a little old lady with twenty-seven cats, I didn't have the heart to turn away a single, little lost book. I took pity even on Cousin Karl's medical tomes with all those awful pictures of diseases.

Some books captivated me by their mere appearance or scent. I would sniff leather-bound volumes with reverence, trace embossed patterns with gentle finger tips, admire typography and layout. Art books were my favourites. Then came deluxe classics, especially those with engravings, etchings or woodcuts. I remember my first encounter with Gustave Dor. How I shuddered with uneasy delight at his eerie knights, riding through Balzac's *Contes Drolatiques*, through dark forests of spiky pines or needle-sharp medieval spires. And other knights, palely loitering in the dark, under their beloved's window, suddenly having their head chopped off, or body sliced into halves by an unseen rival's sword.

Even if I never read some of my gift books—I wasn't big on Hegel—I enjoyed seeing them all lined up neatly. Not only the proud, colourful sets of gold-tooled volumes.

I loved even my neat rows of ordinary-looking books by unfamiliar authors; unfamiliar to me, at least. They were a motley crew. But it was among that motley crew that I found my most delightful surprises.

I would pick out a book at random, glance at it and leaf idly through its pages, reading a sentence here or there. I'd do the same with the next book. And the next. Then something might catch me, reach right out of the book and bind me. Later, much later, becoming aware that I was still standing there, reading, in front of the shelves, I would go and sit down, turn back to the beginning and enter the book's world.

Perhaps the rewards that came from having books handy turned me into a confirmed collector of just about anything. I have certainly kept every little diary I wrote since I was eleven, every letter my family and close friends ever wrote to me, every document that labelled me since I was born. By looking at my old passports I can tell very exactly, for instance, what day and where I crossed national borders.

That early book collection climbed up the walls faster and thicker than ivy. And the books kept on coming in such quantity that even I had to get fussy. Or perhaps it would be more accurate to say that even my book-approving mother got fussy.

"As of now, for every new book you accept you must get rid of another," she proclaimed.

Of course, I got rid of Karl's medical tomes first. But then, what an agony. It drove me crazy. The little old lady having to cast her waifs out on the street. I turned into a thirteen-year-old loon talking to himself, walking around a new batch of books, gesticulating, muttering.

"I'll keep the Duerer drawings, and the book about the Aztecs, and (hand to head theatrically) oh no, not another *Collected Works of Schiller*. No way. I must get rid of that. Oh, but it's so nicely bound. No. Out! Out to Gotthard."

154

Soon, even Gotthard could no longer find a single deserving Christian in his father's church who would offer a decent home to a well-behaved, house-trained set of Schiller's collected works. I left it sadly, pretty face showing, partly bundled up like a baby, on the steps of the Nikolai Church, hoping that some erudite person would pick it up.

In the spring of 1938, two odd events followed each other in quick succession. In March, Hitler annexed Austria. Almost immediately we lost our Austrian citizenship and became stateless. It was not that being Austrian had afforded us much protection. But to have a nationality one day and none the next felt decidedly strange.

The second event, in April, was more painful. Mother's ambitions for me knew no bounds. In mid-term she switched me from the Theodor Herzl "middle" school to a "higher" institute of learning, the Adas Jisroel Ober-Realgymnasium. Just to say, "Adass Jisroel Ober-Realgymnasium", seemed a bit much. I remember a triangular conversation during which I most strongly defended the value of less work and less education. My father listened and asked me sympathetically what I wanted to become. But Mother knew what was good for me and that was that. Perhaps it was really a question of finances. Perhaps my parents could no longer pay for the Theodor Herzl school and, with the help of our good old Rabbi Dr Loewenstamm, were able to obtain free schooling for me at the Adass. We were in such bad shape by this time, that when the new laws requiring Jews to report in detail all their property in Germany or abroad—and Goering was taking steps to confiscate all Jewish shops and property—my father just laughed bitterly and said:

"They sure can have ours. They'll soon be glad to give it back to us." But he looked worried all the same. After all, it was all we had.

There was one thing I did like about my mother's insistence on the Adass school: the seagulls. They were always hanging in midair over the Charlotten bridge where the Havel and Spree rivers merged. Attending the Adass meant taking the S-Bahn and crossing the bridge twice a day on the way to and from the station. I used to stand for hours throwing little pieces of bread into the air and watching the swift gulls swoop-catch them in mid-flight. Nothing in the world seemed more graceful and accomplished.

But the price of seagulls was high. The new school meant not only heavier studies in general, but also an enormous amount of work just to catch up with the others. And I was far from thrilled with the feel of the place. For one thing, it was heavily orthodox and, just eight months after my bar mitzvah, I was already becoming disillusioned with Yehova. He wasn't exactly doing a great job looking after his chosen people, was he? For another, the Adass was almost as bad as my old German school. It was a huge, dreary brick building, with tall echoing halls and reverberating staircases. Everything looked, smelled and felt institutional. Girls had separate classes. Back to Prussian discipline too—standing to attention with heel-clicking obedience, tyrannical teachers—like old Buxbaum who taught French. Nasty, bald and round-headed, he looked like a proper Prussian and acted like one too. As punishment for the slightest offence he would make us stand for half an hour facing into a corner like naughty little boys in kindergarten. Easily roused to roaring rage, he would spit at the class, *"Na ja, eine richtige Judenschule!"* That's what this is, a real Jew-school. Jew-school? Where had I heard that before? Right, from Herr Schroeder, that Nazi teacher at my old school in Spandau who sneered in front of the grinning class that a Jew couldn't possibly be named Zeller.

Once, however, the whole class got even with Bux-

156

baum. When we entered our room after break one day we found an announcement chalked on the blackboard:

"For exchange. Comb and hairbrush for wax and polishing cloth. Signed: Baldy Buxbaum."

Our Prussian, lecturing with his back to the blackboard, didn't notice it for a while. We bit our thumbs to stop ourselves from going into hysterics, seeing the writing just above his bald pate. At long last he turned to write on the blackboard. Deadly silence. And then it came. He whipped around, eyes bulging, face distorted—and then a deafening detonation. His bellowing was audible over the roar of forty boys' laughter. Totally out of control, his pate purple with rage, Buxy stormed out of the room. There were still gusts of giggling when he returned a few minutes later followed by the principal who, facing us from the podium, spoke more in sorrow than in anger.

"Aren't things bad enough without your causing even more problems?" He reproached us, and then, leaning over, whispered to Buxbaum, like a consulting doctor to his colleague at a patient's bedside. After a pained look that took us all in, he left the room.

"Who wrote that?" demanded Buxbaum, his voice coldly quiet, once more master of the situation, but jabbing his finger like a knife at the writing on the blackboard.

No one answered. Nor did anyone snitch when he threatened to punish the entire class if the guilty person did not come forward or was not delivered to him immediately. After a five-minute ultimatum, during which he left the classroom, he condemned us all to stay in the room for two hours after school. He himself would stay to make sure no one left, absolutely no one. A boy raised his hand and at once received permission to speak. Buxbaum had a snide grin on his face. Aha!

But instead of a confession or betrayal, the boy complained:

"My parents will worry that something has happened to me."

A chorus of other voices joined in, "Yes, so will mine!" "Sir, I'm never that late!" "They'll think that something bad has happened to me! Sir."

"You should have thought of that before," blasted Buxbaum, once more furious.

Nothing of the sort had been planned. No one gave a signal. But suddenly the whole class got to its feet. Someone started to stamp on the floor and instantly we all followed his lead, stamping in unison. Slow, slow stamp, stamp; faster stamp, stamp . . . the thunder of eighty rhythmic feet on the stone floor. The whole building resounded and shook, and we did not stop until the principal came running in again, holding up his hands in despair, listening to our pleas and sending us home— again more in sorrow than in anger. As we left, shuffling out of the door quietly, we saw him standing there shaking his head sadly.

He recognised and approved the concern about our parents, but I think now that he also understood something we might not have been conscious of ourselves— that we were venting our rage at the Nazis we could not fight on the Nazis we could.

No, I was not crazy about this school, I decided, and could hardly wait for summer vacation. Both as a bribe and as a reward for the extra-hard school work, Mother gave me permission to go on a mammoth cycling-tour with my new schoolmate Schimmel. All the way to Leipzig! I couldn't believe it when she said "yes" and looked away quickly. I forced myself to act nonchalant and normal when, inside, I was hopping up and down. Had she caught my look of bug-eyed surprise and dotty joy, it would have made her wonder whether she had not, perhaps, made a mistake. Leipzig. Not only would that be the longest bike trip I had ever made, but I would also be able to visit my one-and-only true love, Margot, in Eisleben. Five days, over two hundred and fifty miles, Margot . . . and Mother had said yes!

Schimmel's purpose in making the trip was to attend a congress of the Betar, a right-wing Zionist organisation often called "the Jewish Nazis". Schimmel rarely did anything that did not have "a purpose". He was the most purposeful thirteen-year-old I had ever met. He was devoted to "the Cause" and quite determined to become "a great Jewish politician of the right". And he made it quite clear to me that as a politician he had absolutely no room for women. They always got into a man's way. Well yes, he would accompany me to Eisleben, it was on the way back, I was his good friend, but he had absolutely no intention of meeting Margot. No, not even for a few minutes. What would be the purpose of such a meeting?

I often wondered, did Schimmel have a mother? He never admitted to one and always refused to answer discreet enquiries on that subject. Perhaps, I thought, amused, he had never had a mother and was conceived miraculously by his moon-faced father, a bumbling, pudgy, nice little man—but singularly silly. Whenever I went to visit Schimmel, Papa would hover about for the longest time, silly-talking to me, reversing first letters in two-word combinations.

"Hi, Zred Feller. How about tome sea? Sith wugar?" Like a dog retrieving a stick, he thought it devastatingly amusing, and never tired of it.

Suddenly, just after my birthday in May, a number of my parents' friends who had been arrested before were rounded up again and disappeared. Cousin Lotte Bobath, who had been arrested at a café with her Christian boyfriend Korle, interrogated and finally released thanks to her Czechoslovak passport, was frightened and rarely slept at home any more. That and the steadily worsening

Sudeten crisis, had the Bobaths packing their bags, getting ready to flee at a moment's notice.

Father again stayed away from home. For a few nights Mr Papiermeister slept at our house. In the middle of his second night with us, Mother woke me. Someone was banging on the door furiously. How could I have slept through that? Mother sent me to find out who it might be: the way they were banging it didn't sound like a relative. If it was the enemy, perhaps a child's voice would soften their hearts?

"But don't open the door," she whispered. I looked at her reproachfully.

When I got to the door and asked who was there, someone shouted:

"*Aufmachen! Polizei.*" Open up, Police. When I asked what they wanted, they told me they would break down the door if I didn't open up immediately. Mother waved me to open, and two plain-clothes men marched in. Gestapo. They demanded to see my father.

"Not here? Then who is this man?" Papiermeister showed them his Latvian passport. They exchanged a quick glance, became perfectly polite and left without even searching our apartment. How I wished we had a foreign passport too. It worked. My God, it really worked. And we would be able to leave and take some of our belongings with us. How come Papiermeister hadn't left already?

Even now there were still Jews who had no intention of leaving. The tiny Jewish Congregation of Spandau was electing officers. It is said that when three Jews come together you get four opinions. In Spandau you had just two, two diametrically opposed factions at each others' throats. On one side the German-first Jews, on the other those who intended to emigrate, called "Zionists", regardless of whether they wanted to go to Haifa or Helsinki.

160

Having been told for five of my thirteen years in Berlin that I didn't belong, I concluded, "Right, I don't belong". Not the German-first Jews. Their heads were still embedded firmly in German sand as late as 1938. Perhaps it was more difficult for people who had lived there for fifty years to accept a denial of their "birthright". But wasn't it obvious to them that the Nazis went far beyond hatred, that Hitler's threats of annihilation were well on the way to being realised? That, madman or not, a very considerable majority of Germans backed him?

Any kid could see that, surely. And here I was, standing in front of the synagogue, at election time, with a placard round my neck that read, "Next year in Jerusalem. Vote List B." My very own choice of sentiment, text, calligraphy and art. A green palm tree against a blue sky, grey mountains, dark blue sea and a piece of the wailing wall.

Next year in Jerusalem? Well yes, that was the Jews' centuries old prayer—spoken only half-seriously most of the time. Until now, that is. Until any time persecution grew beyond endurance.

Suddenly, without warning, a normally perfectly polite and friendly doddery old man, quite crimson in the face, started screaming at me:

"All right. Go, go to Jerusalem. *Geh schon.* Go to the devil. But don't make it worse for us who are Germans, with all your clamouring and nonsense. It's Jews like you who create anti-Semitism."

But in spite of such loyal "Germans", the exodus gathered momentum. It turned into a flood with the emigration of professionals who could no longer work in Germany and had skills that were needed elsewhere. Physicians, for instance. There were quite a few of them in my family. The first to leave was Cousin Karl Bobath. With his romantic boxer's nose, his guitar strumming and deep-voiced ballad singing, I thought he was just wonderful. I wanted to become a doctor because of him. He had qualified as a physician just as Hitler came to power and was assisting Professor Gurband at the Urban Hospital. An excellent teacher. A promising future. A great hospital—and one of the first to fire all its Jewish doctors. Karl was among the few people who, right from the start, neither took the Nazis lightly nor expected them to disappear shortly. Though born in Berlin he had claims to a Czechoslovakian passport because of his parents and promptly set off for Prague to duplicate his medical degree there, in Czech, of which he did not know a single word. Miraculously, within a year he was a qualified Czech physician, practicing medicine in Brno.

The second to leave was Uncle Max, who went to Palestine with his wife and two children, Heini and Sigi. He left early enough to transfer a large part of his capital and possessions to Haifa.

Karl's sister Nina left next. Pretty, charming, delightful Nina, on whom I had a childhood crush. Having studied specialised pediatric nursing, she finally went to Moscow to join Erwin Schey, another physician. Erwin had emigrated to the Soviet Union in 1934 and, by 1936, felt sufficiently established to send for Nina. Aunt Cilly had strongly discouraged Nina from marrying him before she left for Moscow. Erwin was German, and Nina would have lost her Czech nationality. Erwin disappeared in one of Stalin's purges and for the next seven years Nina lived a Tolstoyan war-and-peace saga.

Then it was Cousin Alfred's turn to flee to Belgium where he joined his brother Rudi, who was already established there. His mother, my least-loved aunt Bertha, was not ready to leave yet. She still had her huge apartment, her belongings and large antique store to keep her in Berlin until after the Crystal Night.

Arthur Bobath, Karl's and Nina's brother, yet another physician, remembering that some not-so-rich relatives of his father were living somewhere in America, went with

Aunt Cilly to the Berlin Chamber of Commerce and dug up some dusty New York City telephone directories. There they found "the Soblers". Arthur wrote to all of them, asking whether they might be relatives of his father. He got two affirmative replies, and best of all, one of them was willing to give him an affidavit. It was going to be a very weak affidavit, hardly able to stand on its own feet, but an affidavit all the same. Arthur hoped it would be sufficient to get him to America. Waiting to go with him, was the woman he would marry, Erika Schey, sister of the physician Nina joined in Moscow. She had studied nursing, a profession likely to earn a US visa. They waited and waited. But the US was in no hurry.

The secret visits of our German friends, the Kachels, continued. And through their eyes we saw a little of the other Germany. They had discovered another boon, almost as good as their fabulous KDF Madeira trip. They put their name down for a car, a Volkswagen, the brain-child of the Fuehrer himself. A latter-day Henry Ford, Adolf declared that every German should be able to afford a car. Now, along with millions of other Germans, the Kachels were paying five marks a week in anticipation of a car to be built one day, when the factory was built. Well, the factory was built by 1939—and it made Volks-wagens for the German armies, who felt they needed them more than the Kachels. Of course, neither the Kach-els nor anyone else ever got their car, or their money back. The Brooklyn Bridge was never sold on a grander scale.

Just before the summer holiday started, Mother changed her mind.

"You can take day-trips, yes. But five nights away, NO!"

And she told me all kinds of horror stories about Jewish children beaten almost to death, especially in villages or little towns in rural areas.

163

"Because everybody knows they are Jewish," I countered. "In those little villages everybody knows everybody else. Schimmel looks like a perfect goy . . . and most people don't think I'm Jewish. Besides, I can get beaten up right here in Berlin just as easily. You know perfectly well that it's happened to me here, right here in Spandau."

She waved this aside with, "I want to know where you are at night!" And nothing could budge her, not even an absolutely positive promise to telephone her every night.

So much for her "A promise is a promise", I thought and brooded darkly. We had already planned everything, made all the preparations. Margot was waiting for me. Schimmel had promised to attend his conference. He did not want to make that trip all alone.

"It's not fair. She's not fair at all. And if she's not fair why should I be fair? Damn right, why should I!"

Being "fair" (used and pronounced in German as in English) had become a fundamental issue with me, a cause, a religion, probably dating back to Aunt Bertha's outrageous preference for my sister. I told Schimmel that under the circumstances I would be perfectly justified in running away from home—well, at least temporarily. He was delighted, agreed with me absolutely, and we plotted the escape in every detail. If you do something, do it right, my mother taught me.

All right. We would go for day trips taking a blanket, towel, food, canteen, even a little primus stove and cooking-gear. That would get Mother used to our taking a lot of stuff. On the morning of the escape I would forget—accidentally on purpose, on the kitchen table—my inner-tube repair kit. Just before nightfall we would call the Papiermeisters from far away, distraught, regretful: "Alas, we had a blowout, and my repair kit can't be found. No, Schimmel doesn't have one either, and we had to walk six miles to the nearest village. It's getting dark and raining a little. Schimmel's bike has no lights and we can't possibly come home tonight. It would be dangerous. Not to worry though! Everything is fine. There's a nice Jewish couple by the name of Cohen in this village who will put us up, and in the morning we can buy a patching outfit and repair the tyre. Where did we find this Cohen? In the telephone directory, of course. Not to worry, Mrs Papiermeister, please give this message to my mother."

Playing Mrs Papiermeister, Schimmel went over the whole thing with me several times and in several variations until I was well-rehearsed and thoroughly convincing. Luckily, since my parents had no telephone, I would have to deal only with Mr or Mrs Papiermeister. I wasn't at all sure that I would have been able to negate a direct command by Mother.

"If they get difficult," suggested Schimmel, "just shout 'hello, . . . hello, hello . . .' make some clicking sounds, and then shout, 'I can't hear you, hello, hello' and hang up." We were both grinning from ear to ear. I was thoroughly enjoying being a bad, bad boy.

We went over the financial aspects of the venture. Schimmel's savings weren't great, but they would do. My parents would not be financing me, and I counted out only about three marks, barely enough for the long-distance call. I'd have to work watching bicycles every spare minute until our departure in eight days.

Next, trusting in the future, I blew nearly all my money on a bunch of those cheap postcards that have the stamp and a small picturesque scene printed on the address side, a blank space on the other. With my bedroom door locked to keep Lilian out, I filled in the blanks with fictitious descriptions and loving greetings. When you are cycling at all hours you have other things on your mind than writing home. So I prefabricated. I invented convincing travel stories, wrote them in sequence on the cards and dated them appropriately. Like "The twenty-third, Leipzig, admiring the big battle monument. So stark. It's hot here and . . ." and so on. Everything was ready for the pillar box so that Mother would have one postcard in the morning post, another in the afternoon, every single day.

As we were still hatching details of the plot, I realised that this would be the most blatant, most outright defiance of Mother ever. A declaration of independence, just about. For a brief pang I felt that perhaps I really didn't want to be so totally independent and grown-up. Schimmel interrupted my train of thought.

"Have you heard about the new Jewish name laws?"

"Who hasn't!"

"Well, what do you think?"

"Too hot to think."

"Come on. It's important. From January on you'll be Fred Israel Zeller and your mother will be called Fanny Sarah Zeller and your sister Lilian Sarah Zeller."

"And you'll be Israel Schimmel. Stupid. Absolutely stupid."

"Not stupid. It's going to be on any identification you carry. Your subway pass. Your student card. Your passport. It's like having 'Jew' written on your forehead."

"I see," I replied. "You're right, it's serious. It never occurred to me." Looking at the still only half-healed skating scar on my right knee, I continued, "Another thing that's serious is this new law about Jewish physicians. Doctor Kallner, my doctor, isn't allowed to treat anybody now. Not even me. Suppose this gets worse through the trip?" I said, pointing to my sore knee.

Schimmel shrugged his shoulder as if to say "Don't be such a ninny!" Actually I was less concerned with myself than with what my mother would say if I came back with a really screwed-up knee.

The morning came. Wednesday, the last day of August,

166

only five more days and school would start again. I got up exceptionally early so I could steal as much bread and other food as I dared. I put out my tyre-patching kit where they couldn't miss seeing it. I munched a roll, swallowed a glass of milk, and alert to the slightest sound in the house, hurriedly bundled my loot into the blanket together with the other stuff one doesn't need for a day trip, like flashlight, soap and toothpaste. I had just finished strapping my big bundle on to the bicycle carrier when there was a shuffling sound and my father trundled in, unshaven, sleepy and smiling. I was sure I looked like a thief caught in the act, startled and wide-eyed.

"Here, let me take your bike down. It looks heavy."

"Oh no, Dad! Oh NO!" I squealed in horror, wanting to prevent him from carrying it down the steep staircase. This was a nightmare. He never got up this early. He hadn't carried down my bike in years—and now, when I was committing the crime of the century, he lovingly insisted on aiding and abetting me, bumping down the stairs, bike and loot on his shoulder.

I was a step behind him, trembling with fear and guilt: fear that he might ask me why my bundle was so big and heavy, and guilt for making him an accessory to my crime. Endless stairs, but finally we reached the bottom step. When he put down the bike I embraced him passionately and wanted to blurt out the truth. Instead, I jumped on the bike and pedalled away furiously, but not quickly enough to escape my bad conscience.

I pedalled across Berlin in the bright early morning sun. The colours were vivid, the shadows deep and dark; it was still cool and I felt strangely elated; felt a mixture of fear and amazing happiness. My heart was beating ge-plonck, ge-plonck, ge-plonck.

By the time I rang Schimmel's bell I had calmed down a bit. Lo and behold, Schimmel's father appeared pushing the loaded bike. Like my father, he had carried it down the stairs; like my father, he had never done it before either. What was the matter with these fathers today?

"Hello Zed Freller," he beamed.

I disdainfully refused to recognise this utterly new twist to his usual, brilliant "Zred Feller" although he was looking at me with childlike expectancy. We hurried our goodbyes and Schimmel Sr, the unrecognised genius, looked sad as we pedalled off.

We rode single file until we were out of the city traffic and could ride side by side and talk. Schimmel had something to tell me. There was a slight change in our plans. His Leipzig party comrades had originally agreed to put us up Thursday and Friday nights. But now they only had room for us on Friday. Not even the kitchen floor was free Thursday night. No one else could put us up either. There weren't that many Jewish Fascists in Leipzig.

"OK," I said, "we're going to sleep in a barn or a field tonight, so why not tomorrow as well."

Since the change of plans gave us more time, we decided to go out of our way a little and take a look at Potsdam. Schimmel was a great admirer of Frederick the Great and considered him a perfect example of the intelligent, benevolent autocrat. Potsdam was Frederick's town. As we entered I remembered to post my first postcard so Mother would have it first thing the next morning. Of course she'd know from the cancellation mark, which gave the time of day, that we had been lying and had posted it before the fake *afternoon* flat tyre . . . but, I figured, who knows, perhaps she won't look that closely, or the postmark will get smudged. Oh well.

Because of the Potsdam tour, we missed the midday sun, but it was still quite hot when we got back on the dusty country road. It stretched behind and in front of us forever, traversing hilly terrain with few trees to give us shade. We were well over thirty miles out of Berlin, in the middle of nowhere, no traffic at all, not a house or

168

farm for miles, when pffff—I had a flat tyre. Further along the road we found a tree and leaned the bikes against it. Schimmel began rummaging around for his patching kit. In my mind's eye I saw mine still on our kitchen table in Spandau.

Schimmel looked up at me with an embarrassed, silly smile that reminded me of his father. The repair kit was still on his desk in Berlin. He could have sworn he packed it!

We pushed our bikes a few hundred yards, to the next high hill. Schimmel, too ashamed to ride his bike, walked alongside me. The view from the top revealed nice, open countryside but no sign of life. Nothing. With a sigh I pumped up the tyre, jumped on the bike, pedalled madly to go as far as I could before the tyre was down again. Once more. And again. Then it was Schimmel's turn to pump and run. Well, at least I'd be telling the truth when I telephoned my parents.

One hour and a few miles later, totally out of breath, we collapsed under a tree. We came to when we saw, way in the distance behind us, a slowly moving dust cloud. Traffic! Maybe a truck, or a farm cart? Would they stop and take us to the next village? We jumped to our feet. The cloud came nearer slowly, too slowly for it to be a truck. And then we saw little brilliant flashes of light coming out of the dust cloud; sun reflections from chrome handle bars. Cyclists! Oh boy, were we in luck . . . they're bound to have a patching kit . . . and cyclists help each other. No, we were not in luck. As the cloud drew closer, we saw that we were faced with a troop of Hitler Youth. More than a dozen.

We took one look at each other, retreated to the tree and put our backs to it. Almost immediately the first flashing bikes zapped past us and it looked as if they would keep on going when someone shouted "Halt!" Brakes screeched, more dust rose, and on our right, a dozen bent backs, a bunch of behinds over wheels. Then their faces turned back towards us. Three guys detached themselves from the group, jauntily wheeling their bikes towards us.

Here goes. We stayed with our backs to the tree, apparently calm and relaxed, waiting for the attack. We moved slightly so the afternoon sun would stay in their eyes.

They lined up in front of us and one of them said hesitantly, squinting:

"That you, Fred?"

"Good God? Horst! I can't believe it!" It was one of my old football buddies from Spandau, a decent guy. I hadn't recognised him in his Nazi uniform. For a moment we stood awkwardly. We had both realised immediately that I couldn't return a "*Heil* Hitler" salute; nor could we shake hands without calling attention to the omission. He recovered more quickly than I did and roared:

"*Na Mensch*. Man, what the hell are you doing here?"

I told him and the others who joined us now, how I had run away from home, about the patching kits, the "pump and jump" and had them all in stitches. An odd picture. Two Jewish kids in shorts and shirts surrounded by a potentially dangerous gang of Hitler Youth in full uniform, all laughing together. Horst was patting me proudly on the back. Not everybody's friend ran away from home. I didn't introduce Schimmel for fear that it would provoke the old salute. Horst knew, but I don't think the others suspected. Would Horst have anything to do with a Jew? Of course not.

Ten minutes later they had fixed my flat, left me a patching kit for which I insisted on paying, with my bicycle-watching earnings, and departed after a massive "*Heil* Hitler" and raising of hands. We raised our hands too, waving a languid goodbye that looked almost like the salute. They were off to Treuenbrietzen and invited us to ride with them, but we said we needed a little rest. Having a Hitler Youth escort was an interesting idea, but, we felt, tempting fate too much.

We delayed a little, got to Treuenbrietzen and found a public telephone. As anticipated, Frau Papiermeister was outraged. How could I do this to my poor mother? Patiently, politely I described our "pump and run" ordeal, explained that we were exhausted, had no lights, that it was raining and that a nice Mr and Mrs Cohen were willing to put us up . . . to no avail. I had to do the, "Hello, hello . . . click, click, I can't hear you" bit and cut myself off.

Sitting on a bench under a street lantern we ate our economy supper, *Schiebewurst*, push-sausage. It consisted of a large, thick slice of wholesome peasant bread smeared with a little salted lard, with a single medium-thick slice of salami sausage covering about one fifth of the bread. You positioned the sausage right where your first bite would go, under your nose, for aroma. But as you took each bite, you pushed the sausage forward with your teeth, all the way to the very end where you were finally rewarded with the real thing. The other courses consisted of a few swigs of water from our canteens and a sour apple we had stolen from a roadside tree.

Switching on our lights, we rode to the southern end of Treuenbrietzen and asked a lady whether there might be some farms with a barn further along the road. She asked why we needed a barn, and when we told her we needed a place to sleep she shook her head several times:

"Oh no, you don't need a barn. There's a Hitler Youth camp just a few miles out of the village, over that way." She was sure we would be most welcome there. We thanked her profusely, set off in the direction she pointed and quietly detoured back to the Leipzig road, leaving behind the lights of Treuenbrietzen.

It's one thing to ride through the night when you have a destination, a shelter, a bed. It's something else alto-

171

gether just going into the night. We pedalled wordlessly, side by side, two small beams lighting the road, tyres crunching on gravel, and the eerie trill of a thousand crickets all around us. Not another soul on the road. After riding a few miles into the moonless, starlit night we noticed some other illumination in the distance: the lights of a small factory, looking lonely in so much darkness. Two stubby chimneys trailed streaks of white smoke that disappeared quickly into the night, and there was a continuous hum of machinery. Noise and light, what better reassurance for a couple of city kids. We pushed our bikes away from the light and sound, but not too far, across a newly harvested field with neat, long rows of stacked sheaves, small pyramids left out to dry in the air. We hid our bikes in two of them and snake-crawled, rolled into blankets, into a third one. Lying huddled close for warmth and security in a womb of straw, we stared at the star-brimming black, black sky through an opening in the sheaves. All those stars up there; the world seemed such a huge place.

"Good night, Schimmel."

"Good night, Fred."

We woke with the sun, got the straw out of our hair and clothing, got the bikes out of the sheaves and postponing breakfast, set off before anybody could catch us trespassing. At noon, by the River Mulde, near Dueben, we found a nice place to swim. We decided to spend the rest of the day here, but not until we had found a barn where we could sleep that night.

There was a barn, and we talked to the farmer who wanted to know where we came from and where we were going.

"*Berliner Grosschnauzen*, eh?" Berlin big-mouths, he snorted, then relented, saying, "Sure, you can sleep in my barn. But let me ask you this, how would you like to earn a few marks, get some supper tonight and breakfast tomorrow and sleep in a proper bed?"

"What do we have to do," asked Schimmel, "kill somebody?"

The farmer roared and slapped his thighs. "Kill somebody, that's good. No. You look like good, strong, willing lads . . . I need help picking plums, now is the time. Give you each a mark per hour—and the rest just as I said."

We shook hands on the deal, put our bikes in the yard and instead of going back to the Mulde to swim we bathed in our own sweat, picking plums. The farmer's wife, a pretty daughter our age and a younger son were working along with us, and we had a great time cracking jokes and flirting with the daughter. Schimmel cracked the jokes and I did the flirting. He never even looked at the girl and she looked at him all the time, wondering why he didn't.

We ate supper together, and I got a great laugh when I showed them how we ate push-sausage. "You won't have to do that again this trip," grinned the farmer, and handed us a great chunk of salami. That, six marks each, bed and breakfast, and we rolled into Leipzig in high spirits. They were dampened somewhat when we arrived at our Betar host's apartment. It was a tiny, smelly, terrible hole inhabited by five people. Our bed really would be the kitchen floor.

Schimmel went off to his conference and I got out of that place as fast as I could. There were some terrific, old houses in Leipzig and I "did" the Voelkerschlachtdenkmal—the monument celebrating the 1813 battle in which Napoleon was defeated by the combined armies of several nations. I was impressed. It was the most massive monument I had ever seen, and man, I was from Berlin. Nearly three hundred feet high, a Mayan-baroque-like pyramid topped by a huge masonry edifice resembling a medieval castle-keep, the whole complex guarded by the grim stone

173

St Michael in medieval armour that towered thirty-five feet up into the air. There was something quite brutal and harsh about it all, and I shuddered to think of the blood-soaked ground on which I was standing and the mutilated bodies in torn uniforms that must have lain here. I remembered *All Quiet on the Western Front* and wondered whether the designers of this monument built it in praise of victory or in condemnation of war.

As arranged, I met Schimmel and a bunch of his Betar buddies in the early evening, and we all trooped off to somebody's house where we were fed by someone's mother and entertained by a wind-up gramophone. Then all the buddies started to argue with each other, or rather, not at all with each other. They were all declaiming, making speeches. How they'd run Palestine. I left them to it and wandered around the house until I discovered a room full of books.

"This is better," I thought. I must have said it out aloud because a girlish voice responded out of nowhere asking: "What's better?"

Then I saw him, behind a pile of books. A pale, skinny little boy of about ten, wearing large eyeglasses that made him look a bit like a blond grasshopper.

"This is," I said waving my arms at all the shelves full of books.

"Aren't you with them?" he asked pointing in the direction of the distant voices.

"Only in body, not in spirit," I replied and explained how I got into this whole thing. He was amused, smiled shyly and warmed up to me. Then, seeing my interest, he became my guide through a fabulous collection of books. He knew where everything was and had read more than I; at ten, for heaven's sake. We had a great time together until Schimmel finally found me and dragged me off to our unwholesome kitchen bed.

It was nearly midnight; we were dead tired and sank

174

to the floor. I was out like a light. Up like a shot a few hours later, still in total darkness, I cracked my head against the table, my body stinging and burning. Things were crawling all over me: I was being attacked and bitten everywhere. Close by, Schimmel, too, was slapping, grunting and cursing. There was a crash as he hit some piece of furniture. I found the light switch and for a moment we were blinded. Then we saw them, creeping, crawling by the dozen: bedbugs. I was covered with them. Nearly throwing up in horror and disgust, I frantically started to beat them to death on my body. They stank as I squashed them, but I didn't care. I pulled off my underwear and slapped, mashed, beat, brushed them off, stomped on them. Schimmel was doing the same. Then we picked them off each other, checked our clothing, washed our bodies in the kitchen sink to get rid of the stench. We were both covered with hard, yellow-looking welts, larger than pennies. We didn't have to consult each other. We dressed quickly and cleared out of there, cleared out of Leipzig altogether, routed in this Leipzig battle more decisively than any Napoleon.

When we saw a lighted church clock we realised it was only three in the morning. As soon as we were out of the town and saw the first freshly mown field with pyramids of sheaves, we fell into them and zonked out. But I kept waking up to scratch, as well as when I felt Schimmel scratching. It was not a good night, and in the bright light of day our welts didn't look exactly appetising. Thank God they didn't get me in the face too much, I thought, I'm seeing Margot today.

Somehow we had instinctively taken the right road out of Leipzig, the road to Halle and Eisleben. On the way we spent precious cash on ointment for our bitten bodies. The itching subsided, and the bumps started to go down visibly. By the time I got to the street where Margot's parents had their shop, I was feeling fine. Schimmel still absolutely refused to complicate his life with women, so we arranged to meet at the main post office. Walking out of the sun into the dark store I found and politely asked Mr and Mrs Rosenthal whether they were perhaps Mr and Mrs Rosenthal.

They were delighted to meet me and told me, "Margot's upstairs in the flat, waiting for you. The name's on the door, why don't you go up."

Smilingly shyly, she opened the door. We solemnly shook hands and sat down to talk. I could see that she was immensely pleased that I had gone through such trials and had come so far just for her. I was pretty pleased about it myself, felt like a medieval knight or a troubadour, until she got so damn curious about Schimmel. She asked so many questions about him that I grew quite tired of it. What's with women? First the farmer's daughter and now Margot. Why were women so impressed with men who don't want anything to do with them? I asked her that, and she hastened to reassure me that it was me she loved and no one else. Consoled, and so happy she had said that she loved me, I even volunteered to look out of the window with her to see whether I could point out Schimmel. We were both leaning out of the narrow window when I felt her body against mine, caught a whiff of her scent and experienced an incredibly sweet excitement, different from anything I had ever experienced before. It was really turning my head. She looked back towards me and caught the expression in my eyes. There was a heart-catching moment of mutual recognition. My shyness disappeared. I turned her to face me and holding her against me gently, tenderly, just for a moment, kissed her and said my goodbyes. Our two hours had passed so quickly.

Schimmel noted that I was four minutes late. I replied that I had enjoyed every single one of them and we angrily pedalled out of Eisleben. It had become oppressively hot, the road was hilly, we hadn't had enough sleep the night before, and the journey was complicated. We had to find our way through little side roads, cross-country, to get back to the main Berlin road.

"Have you eaten?" I asked.

"No. Haven't you?"

"No."

"You mean she didn't even offer you some food?"

"She did, but I said I'd wait to eat with you."

This seemed to cheer up Schimmel, and we took our lunch break in the shade of a tree. The sun was misting over, but it didn't seem to make the heat more tolerable. As we pedalled onwards, the sky got stranger and stranger. It was turning yellow. Heavy, ominous thunder clouds formed, billowed to all sides and darkness came on fast. We were in the middle of the countryside, there was no shelter in sight, lightning flashed, distant thunder, and we pedalled as hard as we could. Surely we couldn't be far from Dessau? Whether it was Dessau or not I will never know, but miraculously a village appeared out of the gloom just as the lightning and thunder exploded. Just as miraculously, we reached a huddle of modern four-storey buildings at the moment the cool wind rushed at us and the first heavy drops splashed down on the dusty road. Hastily chaining our bikes to a fence, we grabbed our blanket-wrapped gear and rushed into the entrance of the nearest building. The door was open and, taking off our shoes, we tiptoed up the four flights as quietly as we could. Now if we're lucky? We tried the handle and beamed at each other. The door to the laundry loft wasn't locked. It squeaked a little as we slid in, but that was all. We looked around: rough wooden floor, a sloping roof, broken by three small dormer windows. On the left stood the cube-like brick box that housed the large copper cauldron in which you boiled the laundry for hours, stirring it like spaghetti with a big wooden spoon. Next to this cooking arrangement, we saw a wide, stone-slabbed cold-

177

water sink, a wooden roller wringer, and on the right, a large space with washing lines strung beneath the roof.

Home. At least for tonight. It was nice and dry too. Outside, torrents were drumming upon the roof in ascending and descending waves. Lightning flashed through the dormer windows, and the thunder made the wooden floor vibrate. We wondered whether the lightning would strike us if we looked out of the windows, and finally dared, risking instant incineration. Most satisfied with our lot, we stood by the window watching the show, munching rye bread with thick slices of the nice farmer's salami. A few minutes later we were fast asleep on the wooden floor.

The next morning the sun was shining gloriously. But not in my heart. This was the day I had to face Mother. And it was also the last day of the summer holiday. I had managed to shut out these unpleasant thoughts utterly and totally until this very morning. Schimmel looked unhappy too.

After a quick wash we crept out of the building as quietly as we had entered. The air smelled fresh, sweet with the faint scent of autumn. It must have rained for a long time. There were still big puddles everywhere; beads of rain clung to the chrome of the handle-bars; the bicycle seats were soaking wet, but we mounted and rode in silence. At least the sun was shining. I had prayed for sunshine. For tactical reasons I had planned to return at four o'clock in the afternoon. At that time, on a nice Sunday afternoon, my mother would most certainly be in the park with Lilian, and Father would be home, reading the Sunday paper . . . unless he was in hiding again. I wanted to square him away first and then face Mother. She'd assume I'd already been dealt with by Father and wouldn't enlist him for additional thunder. One thing at a time, if you please.

Everything went smoothly, and we arrived at the outskirts of Berlin right on time. Schimmel went northeast, I veered to the west. It was exactly ten to four as, with fear and trepidation, I crossed the Charlotten bridge into Spandau. Instantly I encountered trouble. A strident voice on my right pierced the sunshine and my eardrums:

"Fred!"

I jammed on the brakes and crash-stopped without even thinking.

And there was Frau Papiermeister, tiny Frau Papiermeister who never raised her voice, gesticulating, hopping up and down, and screaming like a bunch of seagulls:

"How could you?" Shriek, shriek . . . "poor mother." Shriek . . . "couldn't sleep", shriek, shriek . . . "worried sick. Don't want you . . . my house. Won't allow Benno to ever see you again!"

People stopped and stared. It was all most embarrassing. I had thought I'd just have to cope with Mother. Downcast, I remounted and cycled slowly along the Breitestrasse and into the Havelstrasse. Even more slowly, with a beating heart, I lugged the bike up the stairs, shoved it into the store, and took a deep breath. Shouting a breezy "It's me" I marched through the apartment and into the living room where Father, as expected, was lying on the sofa, reading the Sunday paper. Walking over to him as if nothing had happened, as if I had just returned from a little ride in the park, I bent down and kissed him lightly. Lightly, like on any ordinary day. And then I had the chutzpah, to ask him if there was any soda in the house. Just like that. Soda was not a common, everyday commodity in the Zeller household. It was a treat. A privilege. My father appreciated my surprise tactics and with a wry grin, and a very slight shaking of the head in wonder, said:

"Look, I don't think what you did was right. I understand why you did it, but it was not right. Your mother was extremely worried about you and very upset. We

179

both were. That's all I'm going to say, but your mother will have a lot more to say about this matter when she comes back, I'm sure. There's some money on the sideboard, so get us a bottle of seltzer."

This time I gave him a passionate hug and kiss, grabbed the money and ran.

I had anticipated that he would be lenient with me because he would have allowed me to go in the first place. But he could not be disloyal to my very cautious mother. I think my father knew that the faster I learned to cope with the world the safer I was. Too much caution can kill as surely as too little. Ask any survivor. Mother still wanted, needed, to protect her little boy. Lilian told me later that Father had paraded around proud as a peacock, boasting to anyone who would listen how well his son was managing. Naughty, yes, but a good boy too, who sent postcards twice a day so his parents would worry less.

I was in the middle of telling him my adventures when Lilian came hopping and skipping into the apartment, entered the living room, saw me and ran back screaming: "Mummy, Fred is back, Fred is back!"

I hardly had time to think that her shrieking reminded me of Frau Papiermeister's when my mother burst into the room. There was such a to-do that I got ready to run around the table. But she didn't want to slap me this time. She was madder than hell but desperately relieved to see me back alive and in one piece. Actually I looked better than when I had left, and my knee was completely healed.

The Leipzig jaunt achieved something most important. It proved to my parents that I could fend for myself. Just three months later they would let me cross the border illegally into Holland, taking along Norbert and Susi. Lilian would follow me a month later, without their blessing. Taking a leaf out of my book, she would run away from home.

180

KRISTALLNACHT

I had to go back to school the morning after my return from Leipzig. Something had changed drastically. The disciplined academic atmosphere had gone, and we all found it difficult to concentrate on anything but the discussions before and after classes and during break. There was excitement and fear about the Sudeten crisis, about war with Czechoslovakia, England and France. The papers were full of horror stories of Czechs raping, killing, plundering and burning down the homes of helpless Sudeten Germans.

"Are the Czechs crazy?" asked some of my classmates. "No, you are," replied others, pointing a finger at their forehead. "You must be out of your mind to believe this rubbish!" Nevertheless, a lot of boys found it hard to believe that there wasn't something to it.

"All those papers can't be lying, can they? It's on the radio too, every day."

One boy whispered that his parents had been listening illegally to some foreign stations and that even they were reporting unrest and street fights.

"And who do you think is setting that up?" demanded Schimmel. "Who is agitating against whom? The Czechs against the Sudeten Germans or the other way round? Are Sudeten Nazis any better than German Nazis? All that stuff about Czechs raping innocent, blonde Aryan women—isn't that what they've been saying about the

Jews, you dumb twits? Remember what Goebbels said? The bigger the lie the more believable it is."

Schimmel was right, I was sure, but still, it was confusing. However, it occurred to me that if there were a war against all those countries, Germany would be bound to lose—and that would be the end of Hitler, wouldn't it?

By mid-September the Sudeten crisis escalated to a point where it was no longer advisable for the remaining Bobaths to sit around in Berlin wondering what would happen to Czechoslovak Jews living in Germany if the two countries were at war. Aunt Cilly, Uncle Ignatz and Lotte did their final packing in a hurry. With a few trunks full of their most precious portable belongings, they fled to Prague, leaving behind an apartment, an antique store, almost everything they owned.

Arthur Bobath, still waiting in Berlin for his US affidavit, hastily obtained a visitor's visa to Denmark. Czech passports still counted. Once there, however, he had difficulty repeatedly renewing his Danish visa, as he held on in Copenhagen, waiting, waiting and wearing out the carpets at the US consulate.

Karl Bobath, who was still practising medicine in the Sudetenland, heard the radio newscast from Munich announcing Chamberlain's betrayal of Czechoslavakia. He packed his bags and fled to Prague just before the Nazis marched into Brno. I should have said just before the Germans marched into Brno. Judging by the jubilation and smiling faces all around Berlin, it wasn't just the Nazis who loved to march and conquer.

What a terrifying triumph for Hitler. Even as a boy, I felt its impact. Another hope had been crushed, another prop removed from under us. If those powerful countries would not stand up to Hitler, if they could betray their friends and allies, what hope was there for us. Until now, somehow, I had felt that if things really became absolutely desperate, those decent nations out there would intervene and protect us. Or take us.

We had started to feel some doubts about England and France when Hitler marched into the Rhineland. They could have squashed Hitler like a bedbug, but they let it happen. Then there was Mussolini's conquest of Ethiopia. Next came the Spanish Civil War, where Hitler's and Mussolini's planes and tanks played a crucial part in crushing the Spanish people. France and England let it happen. And now Czechoslovakia.

The Nazi victories had their effect on the uncertain Germans; the majority. They became polarised and decided that Hitler wasn't such a bad thing after all.

For the Jews it became an all out, "*Sauve qui peut*", and once more I envied those with foreign passports. They could just get up and go, even take some of their belongings with them. Not money, of course. Not even Aryans could take money out of the country. No doubt, the very rich had been able to swing a deal or two to get a part of their capital out of Germany. But most capital belonging to Jewish emigrants stayed in blocked accounts that would, before long, be appropriated by the German government, along with all other Jewish property.

Even if my parents should risk capture and concentration camp to smuggle a few marks out of the country, they would have little left. The mark lost nine-tenths of its value abroad.

For a while it was possible to go to Palestine and transfer money there. My Uncle Max, for example, had made use of the so-called Haavara agreement, a strange, complicated deal made among the Nazis, who wanted to export German goods, the Jewish Agency for Palestine and the British Home Office. But before long, immigration to Palestine was severely restricted; and, in any-case, we had no money left to transfer.

Uncles, aunts, cousins, friends disappeared out of my

life. Everybody else was leaving, it seemed. Not really. The poor, the "little" people, the vast majority of German and Austrian Jews, were still trapped.

I soon found out that a foreign passport wasn't always such a good thing to have. My father, born in Vienna, was Austrian; his brother Mulu, born in Sanok, a Polish citizen. On 28 October, 1938, at dawn, the Gestapo came for Mulu. They gave him five minutes to dress, pack a little suitcase and kiss his wife and children good-bye, Leona wept and wanted to go too but couldn't because of the children—even if they had let her go. She watched her husband being pushed into a military truck already jammed with other Polish Jews. They were taken to the railway station and transported for several days and nights in cattle trucks, packed together worse than cattle, tens of thousands of men. Finally they were dumped into "camps" in a no-man's land near the Polish border, where conditions were even worse than appalling. The semi-Fascist Polish government had invalidated the citizenship of all Polish Jews resident in Germany, making them stateless overnight. And Hitler flung them at Poland like a gauntlet.

Aunt Leona was numb with grief; Susi and Norbert in a state of shock. As were we all. It was this new disaster that finally jolted the sisters into action to try and get their children out at any cost.

In addition to her concern about her children's safety, Aunt Leona had another reason to get Norbert and Susi out of the country. She was still passionately in love with her husband and wanted to follow him to the camp. She decided to make use of a potentially dangerous method which she had known about for some time; talked to my mother about it and got in touch with a friend. The friend belonged to a large family that had been quietly sending small, illegal transports of children across the border into Holland. After escorting five to nine children to the

Havelstrasse 20.
Our four windows
above the Real
supermarket,
formerly the Odeum
Cinema.

(Left and overleaf)
Typical pages from
my May 1939 diary
with sketches of life
in Spandau and in
the Rotterdam
camp.

At the entrance of the camp, the only place we were allowed near the fence. Norbert, Fred, Lilian and police dog.

Photos of Lilian and myself taken at the camp in Rotterdam, for British visas.

Uncle Mulu on his way to Bolivia, visiting newly arrived Norbert in London.

Aunt Cilly and Lotte with her husband Louis, the Dane who saved them.

Freek Adriaans (left) with the Papiermeisters on their way to America, spring 1939.

The last family group, Berlin 1939: **(left to right)** *Father, Mina Zeller (Monio's German wife), Mother, Freek Adriaans and Peter Kachel.*

border, the adult "guide", who was not permitted to enter Holland, would return to repeat the procedure a few days later.

Yes, because Leona was a good friend, they would take the Zeller children. The cost per child was one hundred marks plus train fare. That paid for the guide's expenses, nothing else. There was no guarantee of success or safety, and we had to keep everything very secret. So far, the Dutch had accepted the children. But, warned the woman, tell too many people about it and soon everybody will rush to the border and stop it all. Naturally, we would have to await our turn. They still had quite a few of their own children waiting to go.

"Why don't you come back in a week?"

Our contact lived near Uncle Mulu's flat in the Turmstrasse. They had no telephone, or perhaps they had and were afraid of being overheard or called too often. So Susi and I walked there after school. We tried a week after the first contact and were told come back the next week. Then next Tuesday. Next Friday. Next Thursday. A whole month went by like this. Too many children in this family, I felt.

Through these anxious excursions, Susi and I drew closer. She was a couple of years older than I, but the difference mattered less and less the older we became. Norbert was still a special playmate, but I was beginning to have a lot more in common with Susi and less and less with him. Susi was interested in things and read a lot, unlike Norbert, the lovable, lazy clown. Neither of them were street-smart or world-wise. If we ever got off on this journey I'd feel secure with Susi, she was bright and listened but Norbert?

My family hardly had enough time to adjust to Uncle Mulu's sudden deportation when the Kristallnacht happened. That mass deportation and the Kristallnacht weren't entirely unrelated. The young Jewish Polish student Grynszpan who shot the German diplomat in Paris did so because his parents were among those carried off to the Polish border camps.

It soon became perfectly obvious that the Kristallnacht and the nightmares that followed had been waiting to happen, Grynszpan or no Grynszpan. Preparations had been made long ago. Every SA Headquarters had the address of each synagogue and Jewish organisation in its district. The lists of individual Jews and their property were complete too. The targets were set up. Every Jewish shop was marked as clearly as if it were wearing a yellow star. By law it had to display, painted on its windows, the name of the owner in white letters of a given type-face, a given size, at a given distance from the ground. Sitting in a slow-moving vehicle even the stupidest storm trooper could spot any Jewish shop along any street. Except ours. Unhappily in general, but happily in this instance, we had no street windows to lure customers into our shop. The Zeller store "window" was a barely visible, small, glass showcase inside the tunnel-like entrance to the courtyard of our building.

It all started quietly enough. A radio announcement late on Monday, 7 November, informed us that a Herr vom Rath, a minor Nazi embassy official, had been shot and wounded in Paris. The headlines on Tuesday announced that a cowardly young Polish Jew had shot a valiant German diplomat. We talked about it at school, but not all that much. We discussed it on Wednesday too. Vom Rath was still alive. "Too bad," said some "Dumb. What's shooting one Nazi going to solve?" said the others.

Early that evening, vom Rath died of his wounds. My father decided this could mean trouble and went to spend the night at the Kachels. Oh hell, just one more scare, I thought, the world's full of them; and went to bed as usual. I didn't even listen to the news on my crystal detector radio.

Mother woke me quietly. The room was still very dark and chilly. Half asleep, I heard her say calmly:

"Dress quickly and come to the window."

Almost at the same moment I heard a tremendous crash and shattering of glass in the street below and woke up instantly. My mind flashed back to that shopping expedition with my mother, the SA raid and the man thrown out through a shop window, lying prone on the pavement in the glass, all bloody. I jumped out of bed, ran to the window and wanted to pull aside the curtains. Quickly grabbing my hand, she told me to look through a small opening only.

"I don't want them to see us."

Now I saw them. On the other side of our narrow, curving street. The open truck. Nearly a dozen storm troopers, some of them in the truck hauling big cobble-stones over the side, down to others in the street. Almost simultaneously several men turned, staggered clumsily in an uneven row, the heavy cobblestone against their chests. They hobbled the few steps to the remaining two big windows of the Hochmann store and heaved the stones right through the plate glass. There was a quick series of crashes that sounded like explosions. Large chunks and hundreds of small pieces of glass shattered, fell and slithered over each other partly on to the pave-ment, partly into the store. Like an after-quake, there was a second fall of jagged glass. The empty, lamp-lit street looked like a stage set; the stationary truck, the slowly moving, robot-like, uniformed men, seen from above, the glittering, shimmering glass all over the pave-ment . . . it all seemed unreal.

Then the engine revved up, the truck ground forward and the men in the street crossed over to our side. For a minute we stood tight with fear, listening. I heard my mother hold her breath and then sigh with relief when we heard the shattering of windows farther down the street.

187

They'd missed our little showcase, they were not coming up the stairs. A male voice on the other side of the street, roared:

"The devil take you! Stop making that racket! I'm a working man . . . let me sleep, you arseholes. Leave me in peace!" The voice echoed through the empty street.

More quietly, a woman's voice behind him called anxiously, "*Na* Franz, *lass schon* . . . come back, come, go to sleep," and a window closed abruptly.

Mother grabbed my wrist. The Nazi couple across the street who, last year, painted anti-Semitic slogans on Mrs Hochmann's store windows appeared in their dressing gown. They looked left and right, then treading carefully, in slippers, over the carpet of glass, looked into the broken windows. Bending over large, sharp fragments, they reached in and hauled out ladies' nightgowns and underwear, hastily stuffing them under their dressing gowns. Outraged, my mother abruptly and vigorously rapped on our window. I flinched. She stopped instantly.

"My God, what am I doing?" escaped her as she moved back and tried to pull me away from the window. The moment she rapped I knew that if those people looked up, we would be in trouble. But they didn't, and I saw them jump in surprise and scurry back into their house, ludicrously stuffed and dangling with ladies' underwear.

"The Papiermeisters," said my mother. "We must warn the Papiermeisters!"

"Right," I quickly finished dressing, put on a pair of plimsols and flew out of the house into the night. I forced myself to walk in a relaxed, normal way, but was ready to shoot off at the slightest sign of danger. My whole being was alive with suppressed energy, as if I were waiting for the starting pistol of the 100-metre dash. There were already more people in the streets now, probably on their way to or from work. Or perhaps they were looters? I noticed an overpowering smell of burning as I turned right into the Breitestrasse. Someone's chimney on fire? But then I saw the red glow in the sky, over to the left. As I passed the Kammerstrasse I noticed, towards the end of the street, a blazing building.

"Oh no!" I forgot all about walking in a relaxed manner and sprinted to the corner of the Linden Ufer. Our synagogue was on fire. For an insane moment I wanted to rush in and get Dr Loewenstamm out of the building. Then I realised, with relief, that he didn't live there. I thought of the Torah scrolls inside, of the eternal light, and couldn't believe what was happening. They were defying God, they were burning Him.

There were a couple of fire engines standing by. Small groups of firemen stood at ease, watching the fire, their hoses ready—in case a neighbouring house caught fire. "That's what we're here for," one of the firemen was telling a bystander. There were a dozen or so silent spectators, some in dressing gowns over pyjamas. No need to worry about catching cold, I wanted to scream, there's a nice fire to keep you warm, but I didn't and just looked at the flame-lit faces. No one was gloating. I heard a sudden groaning and crunching from inside the building and a heavy thud. Something had collapsed, and the flames shot out even higher over the roof, shot right over the onion-shaped tower. A barrage of sparks flew high out of the flames and died in the dark. A woman's voice on my right said suddenly, indignantly:

"Why don't you put out the fire? Isn't that your duty? This is a house of God."

The fireman standing in front of her shrugged his shoulders without even turning to see who was talking.

Her voice jolted me out of my daze, and I remembered my errand. I ran back to the Fischerstrasse, turned left to number 3–4, bolted up the stairs and knocked at the Papiermeisters' door. Silence. I knocked again, and again, quietly, so the neighbours wouldn't wake up. Finally I heard Hermann's deep, sleepy voice on the other side. He opened the door and stood looking at me anxiously. Something had to be very wrong for me to call at Gestapo hour; five in the morning. I told him the news, and while he was dressing ran down and around the corner to the Charlottenstrasse. I rushed back immediately to tell him to hurry, because people were reaching into his store windows and helping themselves to shoes. He was already coming out of the house with his sons Joseph and Benno. The looters ran when they saw us turn the corner, dropping shoes along the way. Benno ran to pick them up while we quickly emptied the windows. But a lot of shoes were already gone.

"It won't do them much good," said Hermann, "but it's going to hurt me. No shoe store puts pairs into the windows, only singles, either right or left shoes."

When he reopened the store, a few days later, a number of the looters, laden with single shoes, came back to bargain with him. They offered anything from five to ten singles for each complete pair. A few of the thieves even brought single shoes that didn't come from the Papiermeister store. Probably from "Schwarz Shoes" farther down the street.

There were a number of other shopowners, friends, I would have liked to warn, but I didn't know where they lived. Mother was relieved to see me back, but tears were running down her cheeks.

"They're looting the Hochmann store. They have no shame. The poor woman will have nothing left, and things are terrible enough for her."

"Yes, I just saw them. I'll empty her window and take the stuff to the back, if there's anything left."

"Be careful!"

"Sure." I ran down, crossed the street, interrupted a woman in the process of putting her hand into the window and saying "Please", climbed over the glass remnants into the narrow window space. The woman pulled her arm back hastily, looked embarrassed, then huffed, then ran. I kicked open the little door that connected the window to the store and started moving the merchandise back. A lot was gone, the rest was full of glass splinters. Now that I stood in the display window, slightly above ground, I saw more clearly the big, jagged spikes of plate glass overhead, precariously suspended in the upper window frame. Guillotine knives . . . anybody reaching in could have had a hand chopped off. Shit. I had climbed in underneath that.

The second window I cleared was the same. If anything, the dangling glass guillotines were even larger, but this time I was able to enter from the store side. People stopped and watched me curiously. It must have seemed strange; a thin, gangling kid clearing the window all on his own. Some people looked sulky, others sad or shocked. And there were those who gloated. What hateful faces. Suddenly I became aware of a thin, tall, grey-haired man wearing gold-rimmed glasses, outside the window, a foot below me. He was screaming. He was screaming at me, and in such a rage, I could hardly understand a word. What had I done? I wondered. Had I dropped some glass on him? Then a few words stood out:

"Jewpigs . . . murderers . . . filthy cowards . . . killed . . . good German!"

And all the while he was holding, with both hands, a shabby, leather briefcase, folded in two—threatening to smash it into the large jagged glass spikes next to and above my head. In utter rage he stepped closer, and held the case way back over his shoulder so as to strike forward with full force. I know that if I showed fear, flinched, or jumped back, he would strike. I knew this for sure, just as I knew that there was not enough space to jump clear of the glass. My senses seemed to dovetail together into a nightmare juxtaposition of images, sounds, suspended

191

action and slowed-down movement. At the same time I saw my mother's face at the second floor window across the street, both her hands to her mouth as if to hold in a scream. I saw the hate-distorted face of the man with the gold-rimmed glasses, the raised briefcase, the person next to him, companion or bystander, intercepting him in slow motion. And I heard the words floating out of his mouth, one by one, slowly:

"*Lass . . . doch, . . . das . . . ist . . . ja . . . nur . . . ein . . . Kind!*" "Stop it, he's only a child." I felt my face freeze into non-expression. I emptied myself of fear. Turning, turning away from the window, turning my back to the threat. Turning my back to him. Bending down. Starting to work again, emptying the window. Numb. I felt nothing.

Mother told me later that when I turned my back the man had stood transfixed, briefcase still raised but no longer way back over his shoulder. He had stood like that until the other man physically dragged him away. Even then he still tried twice to go back to the window, held back both times by his companion.

When I finally did turn to see whether the man had gone, I found myself looking straight into the icy eyes of a fat policeman, bull-necked, chin forward, hands on hips.

"Raus! Sofort! Out! Get out of there at once and clean up this mess!" he barked, pointing at the glass-strewn pavement. "Out!" he screamed again and put his hands back on his hips, elbows spread wide. A picture of indignation.

For a moment I was tempted to scream back that it was neither my store nor was I exactly responsible for this goddam mess, but the moment passed and I bit down my rage. It occurred to me that he might arrest me for stealing if I told him this wasn't my store. That, in fact, he could arrest me for no reason at all. I assured him that I would look immediately for a broom and shovel in the store,

192

and he waved me on sternly. It took me forever to find a light switch and even longer to unearth the broom, a dustpan, and some empty cartons. By the time I got back to the street, the cop had gone. Rotten bastard. Nevertheless, I cleaned up, and my mere presence in front of the store seemed to discourage looters. Three hours later, when I was nearly through, Mrs Hochmann arrived and took over. She was crying and kept on kissing and thanking me on the street in front of everybody and I was embarrassed. I was dead tired too and my knees were shaking. Half-heartedly I offered to help her but caught sight of Mother at the window waving that I should come up. She'd been watching from up there all this time. God she must have been scared for me . . . and I felt a wave of love for her. When I got upstairs there was hot cocoa and buttered rolls waiting for me. Funny, I had forgotten about breakfast. I chewed and drank with my eyes half closed, and my legs felt weak. God had I been scared. I got up in the middle of eating, walked into my room and, falling on the bed fully clothed, plimsols and all, was asleep one second later.

Early in the afternoon I heard a male voice in the living room and became alert instantly. But it was only Mr Papiermeister, and I got up to join him and Mother. He had had a phone call from Father asking about us and had advised him to stay put at the Kachels.

"They're out everywhere looking for Jews, going to their stores, arresting and beating them half to death," Hermann explained, adding that he'd had several phone calls from friends warning him not to leave the house. The same thing was happening all over Germany. Every synagogue had been burned down, all the Jewish shops smashed and looted.

I noticed that my mother was no longer asking, "Where are the police?" It also dawned on me that I hadn't gone to school. Maybe I wouldn't have to go to school tomorrow either. Now that was a pleasant thought.

"You shouldn't have come," said Mother to Hermann.

He smiled and pulled his passport out of his overcoat pocket.

"I have this ready to pull out quickly. They're not touching foreigners, not even foreign Jews. Yet," he added quietly.

"But they smashed and looted your windows."

"Yes," says Mr Papiermeister, "But windows don't carry passports. They should have thought of that when they made me paint my name in white on the windows. Yes, I was wondering what they're going to do about the windows? And the stolen shoes. I've tried all morning to get the Latvian consul, but the line was busy. I tried my insurance company and couldn't get through to them either. I'm sure those swine are going to claim that they had no control over this 'popular demonstration', even though it was obviously organised in every way. They'll say that a few patriots just happened to pick up thousands of cobblestones on their way home from church at three in the morning. Even though the SA did it all quite blatantly . . . in full uniform."

What concerned him most at this moment was the security at his store. He had boarded up his windows as best he could (it was hard to find boards right now), but without windows anybody could just push their way in. We wondered what the others were doing. Was there to be a night of mass looting?

After a while he went home, promising to return in the evening. Nobody knew what would happen next, what the Nazis would do next. Luckily, his wife had a separate Latvian passport to protect her and the children at home. He would try to use his for our protection.

I went out with him because I had to go and shop. Mother wasn't happy about that, but we needed food and

194

even some extra supplies in case we might not be able to go out for days. She didn't have enough money, and I emptied my piggy bank. I didn't have much either. I had been too busy trying to keep up with school and running errands to earn money watching bicycles. Hermann lent us twenty marks.

On the way to the market we passed a few Jewish stores. What a mess: boarded up or empty, wide-open windows, and in front of most of them heaps of glass and debris swept into piles that blocked half the pavement. Where the pavement was cleared, it glittered with fine glass powder. I said good-bye to Hermann, turned right, and saw Mr Schwarz, his face bleeding, sweeping up in front of his shoe store, under the supervision of the same bull-necked policeman who had yelled at me earlier. As before, he had his hands on his hips, his chin pushed forward belligerently. I wondered whether he went to bed like that and woke up like that too, and hurried past, acknowledging neither Mr Schwarz nor the cop. On the way back with my bundles, I saw that the policeman had gone, and greeted Mr Schwarz. He had put all the heavy chunks of glass into boxes. Only the glittering on the pavement remained. And the cuts and blood all over his face. I asked him about that.

"They got my phone number and made me come all the way here. My wife said don't go, but they said they'd fine me a thousand marks and put me in jail if I didn't clean up immediately. So I came and cleaned up. People stood around and watched me. I was bending down to pick up some big glass pieces and somebody kicked me from behind and I fell right into the pile of glass."

He held out his hands and I saw they were lacerated even worse than his face.

"They all laughed when I got kicked into the glass. They were all standing around watching me get kicked, and when I got up they laughed again."

195

I saw that Mr Schwarz was crying. The tears were
running down his face, wetting the half dried blood. He
hadn't been crying before, but now he was, as he told me
what had happened. I saw it wasn't only because of the
cuts; I thought it was perhaps because they laughed, and
I didn't know what to do. Maybe I should put my arm
around him and hold him? But somehow I couldn't do it,
it felt funny. He was so much older, I didn't know him
very well and had never really liked him all that much.
But still, it was terrible to see a grown-up cry.

I hurried home, and for the rest of the afternoon we
just sat around waiting. I had no idea what we were
waiting for, but we were waiting all right. Even my sister
was quiet and just sat still. It got dark soon. We pulled the
curtains and Mother, Lilian and I ate supper in silence.

As we listened to the evening news, with the radio
turned low, there was a loud knocking at the door. We
all jumped and then sat still. Mother turned off the radio
completely, and we listened. There was another knock
and then Papiermeister's voice:

"It's me, Hermann!"

I ran to the door and let him in. He told us that something really strange had been happening all over, but
particularly at the bigger, more elegant Jewish stores
around the Kurfuerstendamm. The SS were arresting
store owners by the dozen—but both the SS and the police
stood guard at the stores.

"They stopped the looters, would you believe?"

We believed . . . later. It made perfect sense as it
turned out. The store owners were beaten and black-
mailed. And the stores were looted legally, appropriated
by decree of the state.

My bedtime came, and Lilian's had long since gone,
but we were still all sitting in the living room. Mother
seemed to have forgotten about our bedtimes. Suddenly
someone was banging against our door again. We sat

196

absolutely still, not talking, hoping they'd think no one was home. But the banging went on, urgently.

"Maybe it's Aunt Bertha? Or Leona?" Mother wondered, and I got up and walked silently to the door. We didn't have a peephole to see who might be outside. I put my ear to the door trying to listen to the breathing. Then I clearly heard a woman shouting and a man's slurred voice answering. The woman sounded more distant. The man's voice was just outside the door. Frau Hofmann, that was her voice. The lady from upstairs. Funny lady, never friendly. Mother and Mr Papiermeister and Lilian had followed me to the door. We all listened to Mrs Hofmann, nearer now, telling someone off:

"Haven't you done enough already. Get out of here . . . leave these people alone . . . they're decent people!"

An indignant male voice answered, "But I'm here to guard 'em. I'm telling 'em, I wan' to tell 'em, I'm here to guard. Thass what I wan' to tell 'em. Mother sen' me to . . . to guard 'em."

The banging on the door started again and the voice close to the door yelled, "*Frau Zeller, zu Befehl, Guenther Wallner, Wallner*, W . . . A . . . L . . . L . . . N . . . E . . . R, Frau Wallner's son. You hear me?"

I looked at my mother and saw her nod. Leaving the chain on, I opened the door a crack and a face under a storm trooper's hat squeezed itself into the opening between the door and the door frame. A round, flushed, sweaty face with a stupid, drunken grin. "*Heil* Hitler! My mother sen' me. Understan'? I sit with you an' watch you all night. Good people, she says. *Anstaendige Leute*. Guard ' em all night, understan', you understan'?"

"Leave them alone," came Frau Hofmann's voice from above, "and let them sleep in peace. Haven't you done enough already?"

"I habn't done nothin' to no Jews in Spandau. We

197

wasn't in Spandau. They sent us to the Tiergarten, we did the Jews in Tiergarten. Nothin' wrong with our Jews, 'n Spandau. Good people, Zellers, Mother say, you watch 'em, she say."

Mother thanked him and tried to get rid of him. But he wouldn't leave. He kept on insisting that he must watch over us or his mother would kill him. My mother borrowed ten marks from Hermann, gave it to our would-be protector and told him to go and have a little drink. He smiled in besotted gratefulness, pocketed the money and insisted on staying. But he agreed to stay outside, sitting on the stairs.

Reluctantly, we left him there and eventually bunked down on our beds, fully dressed, to try and get some rest. It seemed I had only just dozed off when there was a tremendous commotion at our door. It sounded as if someone was kicking it in. We all moved into the lobby, heard our drunken protector's voice protesting. Frau Hofmann's outraged voice, and a male voice shouting while banging at the door.

"Police, open up immediately!"

They were kicking the door so furiously, we feared it wouldn't hold. I looked at Mother, at shirtsleeved Mr Papiermeister who was standing behind my mother—Lilian must have been asleep—and opened the door. I forgot to undo the chain, and the door opened only narrowly. They didn't give me time to close the door again to undo the chain. I had to jump back as they rushed the door and snapped the chain.

Two SS men moved in swiftly. The shorter one stayed by the door, while the other pushed me aside and stood over Hermann Papiermeister.

"You're under arrest, Zeller. Put on your clothes and come along. Get going."

Papiermeister was ready. With remarkable calm and dignity he slowly raised his hand holding the passport and

198

said, "My name is Hermann Papiermeister, I am a Latvian citizen, and I protest over this outrageous disturbance in the middle of the night. I will complain to my consul in the morning."

For a moment, the SS officer stood taken aback. But only for a moment. Holding out a gloved hand for the passport, he examined it impassively, turned the pages, leisurely compared the photograph with the man in front of him and returned the document.

"What are you doing here?"

"Are there special restrictions or rules where Latvian citizens may or may not go or stay?"

Icy, with venomous politeness, "You may go wherever you wish, *mein Herr*. Where is Heinrich Zeller?"

"Not here."

"Where is Heinrich Zeller?"

"We have no idea. He was probably arrested. He has not been home for days."

The tall SS officer turned to the one by the door and waved him on, wordlessly, to search the apartment. A minute later he returned, with a slight shake of the head, and both men left silently. There was something incredibly sinister and deadly about the smooth way they moved, about their black uniform with skull and crossbones, about their hard, keen, pitiless faces.

We stood still for what felt like ages before my mother started to sob on Hermann Papiermeister's shoulder.

"Thank you, thank you, Hermann. You were wonderful. I don't know what we would have done without you. My God, I'm so glad Henjou wasn't here. Those dreadful men. Those terrible men." And then we saw Mrs Hofmann still standing in front of our open door, looking at us, her face drawn and white. She wanted to say something, raised her hands, lowered them again hopelessly, choked on the words, turned and ran upstairs. The hallway was again empty. Our drunken protector had disappeared.

I did not have to go to school the next day. Or the day after. Or ever again in Germany. Mr Papiermeister stayed for two more nights, but the SS didn't come back. It was a month of terror, of mass arrests, murder and blackmail. Every concentration camp—and there were dozens now—every jail and police cell was jammed to capacity.

Whereas before the "No Jews" notices had been "voluntary", they now became law. No Jews were permitted at public places—theatres, beaches, resorts, sports events, railway sleeping-cars.

Just about everything owned by Jews was confiscated. Laws were passed that legitimised such robbery. Every day brought a new nightmare. Jewish men kept disappearing and were never heard from again. For three weeks my father hardly dared go out on the street.

The Jews were assessed a penalty of one billion marks for their "hostile attitude towards the German people and the Reich—as shown by the dastardly murder of vom Rath." Most of the Jews, like us, were already desperately poor. But there were those blocked accounts, weren't there?

Papiermeister finally got through to his insurance company and they paid for the Kristallnacht damage—to maintain credibility, insurance companies had to pay all the Jews—but the money was immediately confiscated by the government. Hermann, like all other Jews, was made responsible for the losses and repairs.

Even the faces of the German-first Jews were now grey with despair. They explained that the Kristallnacht, everything, all of it, was all organised by the Nazis. Anybody could see that it was not the German people. They were against it. But the fires of their indignant outrage had burned out. These patriots without a patria now spoke quietly, earnestly, almost to themselves. Numb with pain, they did not expect to be believed. And many of them now tried to leave too.

Aunt Bertha appeared at our doorstep on Friday, 11 November, clutching a small suitcase. That was all she had left of her big apartment and furniture store. She had come to say goodbye to her sister, and I was appointed to take her to the railway station after dark. She was escaping to Belgium, to her unfavourite son Rudi. It was a misty and dank November evening as we walked over the Charlotten bridge to the S-Bahn. Formidable Thusnelda had shrunk into this grey, haggard-looking woman clutching my arm, who looked around her constantly as we walked through the dusk.

During the Kristallnacht she had hidden in her apartment just above the antique store while the storm troopers smashed her windows below. From behind the curtains, she had watched them throw chairs and other smaller pieces of furniture into the street through the broken windows.

"My most expensive chairs," she told Mother, "I heard them shouting, screaming and laughing, the animals, the drunken pigs. I heard them smashing furniture and glass . . . and expected them to come breaking through my door at any moment. I thought I'd run to Cilly's but remembered she was already in Prague, and besides, they were probably smashing her store too. It was dangerous to go out. I wanted to come here, Fanny, but people in the Krummestrasse know me, and I was afraid those pigs would kill me, and Spandau was so far to go alone. I just sat there all night and the next day, and I didn't have anything to eat in the house. I just sat there. I didn't even put the lights on at night.

"Finally I called the Papiermeisters, but nobody answered at the store. So I just came. Thank God you're all right. They killed Konrad, you know. They threw him

201

out of his fourth floor window. They did it in front of his wife!"

"Who's Konrad?" I asked.

"Nobody you know," she snapped.

And then she was sobbing, *"Unmenschen, Unmenschen!* How can people be so devoid of humanity?" But as she asked this question I heard no anger, not even indignation, just the voice of utter exhaustion, of defeat and despair.

In the rattling, noisy S-Bahn, she still held on to my arm, even after we were seated. She clutched it so hard, that it hurt. I was relieved when I could finally put her on the train. At the last minute she broke down and started to cry again:

"I'm leaving with nothing . . . look, nothing!" she sobbed, pointing at her small suitcase. Forgetting even to say goodbye, she climbed into the train absorbed in her own world of pain. She didn't look out of the window either. She sat there, sunk into herself, quite unaware of my presence, utterly drained. As the train started to move, I turned and left the dim, deserted platform, fighting down tears. I, Fred, touched by Thusnelda . . . bane of my childhood?

Shortly after I got home, my father suddenly appeared at the flat—simply to see us, he said. There was a round of hugging and kissing. For the second time that night I wanted to cry. He looked terribly ill and worried.

"Did you hear?" he said. "They are fining us one billion marks—and they're closing all Jewish shops. There's no way we can make a living. What are we to do?"

For a crazy moment I thought I could help. I could watch bicycles. But then I realised with a pang that those days were over. I would be in real danger if I did. There was nothing I could do.

I caught my mother looking at me, then looking at my father. Then they both looked at Lilian and me and at

202

each other. They'd discussed something without speaking. A decision had been made. I thought, perhaps we'll leave now . . . we'll leave without anything. We must leave! Why don't they say so?

"We'll talk later, Henjou, tomorrow," said Mother, "Now you must go, quickly!"

THE CHILDREN'S RAILWAY

My parents' unspoken decision was to get the children out. Whatever else had to be done, that was the first and most important thing. The subject was discussed openly when Father moved back into the house. Word was out that the arrests had stopped because prisons and concentration camps were jammed beyond capacity with the tens of thousands who had been arrested haphazardly during and after the Kristallnacht. I clamoured for us all to go together, I would go to all the consulates again, I would find a way. Why couldn't we go illegally, all four of us? But they said it wasn't that simple, that I was too young to understand the problems involved. They were right, of course. Quite apart from the high visibility of four people trying to cross the border illegally and then living in hiding on the other side, how could my parents, penniless, feed and shelter us and, at least as important to my mother, educate us? By sending us out illegally, alone, they were forcing our would-be hosts to provide for us, educate us— or send us back to hell.

At the end of 1938 the Dutch seemed to be the only people in the world decent enough not to do that.

Our visits to Frau Kranz became more frequent and more urgent. Until the Kristallnacht, I had been the prime mover in trying to get us into one of her illegal children's transports to Holland. Now Aunt Leona took the lead. She was frantic to get her children to safety, but also, against all advice, she wanted to join her husband in Poland as soon as he got out of the camp. She even spoke of joining him in the camp.

Instead, of "Don't bother Frau Kranz so soon, Fred," Leona was urging. "Why don't you go and see her again today? Yes, yes, she said not until Wednesday, but you never know, someone may have cancelled." Before the Kristallnacht I could sense the terrible ambivalence my mother and Aunt Leona felt about sending their children to "God knows where". There was no ambivalence now.

Frau Kranz showed no irritation with our frequent calls. She understood, smiled patiently, yet never invited us into the apartment. Her answer was always the same:

"Sorry. Not yet. Try again in a day or two. Come during the morning."

Now we could do just that . . . school was over for us. That was hardly a hardship for me, but it felt strange all the same. For the first time in my life there was no regular routine, no focal point, no tomorrow. There was only fear. Everyone was bent on escape, on being anywhere but here, with no thought about what came next.

Frau Kranz wanted us to call in the morning in order to give us as much notice as possible. She would not know until the last moment when a transport was due to go and whether there would be room for more children.

"Be ready. Keep your bags packed . . . *very* small bags . . . and no passports or documents of any kind. Remember this Susi—and make sure your brother knows it too—you must never let on that your father has a Polish passport, or that he's in Poland. The Dutch take only children who have nowhere else to go. And remind your parents we will not take you if you come with a large suitcase. At the border it must look as if you're just going to school or work on the other side. You must not draw attention to yourselves and endanger the others."

On 13 December, at ten in the morning, she told us

the bad news. I know the date exactly because of what happened next, I started a new diary. My escape diary. And on 13 December Frau Kranz said at her door:

"We're not sending any more children to Holland."

At our look of shocked disbelief, she added: "Haven't you heard? Everybody seems to know about it. The last transport was turned back by the Dutch. They put all the kids on the train back to Germany, and at the border they were arrested by the SS. They spent a night at the police jail in Kleve and then they were all sent back to where they came from. There were a lot of kids from other places, Duesseldorf, Frankfurt, from all over. Our nine kids got back to Berlin, very late last night. Right away the SS started to give the Jewish congregation in Berlin and everywhere hell about it."

She talked about punitive fines. About forcing the Berlin Jewish Congregation to cancel the legal transport registration of all the children who had been in that illegal transport. The Nazis were furious because it had shown them up badly. It was written up in all the Dutch papers and even got on Dutch radio.

Susi and I stood there numb with shock. Suddenly I had an idea.

"Do you know any of the children they sent back?" I asked.

"Of course. At least the ones from Berlin—most of them are family. Why?"

"I would like to talk to one of them. To find out just exactly what happened."

"But I just told you."

I shook my head. "No. I would like to find out why they were sent back."

She looked at me thoughtfully and then nodded. "Go and see my niece Lore, I don't think she'll mind. She might still be sleeping now. She's about your age, Susi. Wait. I'll write down her address."

206

Back in the street we counted our money. It was enough for the fares.

"There's time before lunch . . . let's go."

"But she might still be asleep."

"Right," I said. "Let's go." I had a hunch that we had no time to waste.

Having walked up five flights of stairs in the dingy apartment house, we stood facing the Silbers' door. A look at Susi, a deep breath and I knocked. We waited and waited, and I knocked again. Then, hearing someone moving quietly behind the door, I leaned forward and whispered:

"Lore, Frau Kranz sent us!"

Slowly the door, still chained, opened an inch. It wasn't Lore; it was her mother. We explained in whispers who we were and what we wanted, and she asked us to step inside. The conspiratorial atmosphere felt like something out of my spy novels.

"Lore might still be asleep," said Frau Silber in a low voice. "They arrived in the middle of the night and didn't sleep much the night before. Let me go and look." A minute later she returned and beckoned us to follow.

"Lore's awake and wants to see you. I don't suppose you mind that she's still in bed."

We sat in our overcoats on the crumpled bed, Susi on one side, I on the other. Between us, in her nightgown, this slim, pale girl with matted black hair told us her story.

"There were thirty-two children. Thirty-two, my God. Only about nine from our group, the others had come on the train at Krefeld and at Kleve, singly or in little groups. There were far too many of us. Worse still, some parents had insisted that their kids take along a hidden passport.

"Hidden!" the girl snorted. "In the tiny travel bags they took along. Real hard to find! And of course, some of those passports were Polish, or Czech or Lithuanian— and the Dutch were only taking German children, or stateless, or Austrian. Not only did those passports give away a kid's nationality, they also showed the age. Some of those kids were seventeen or eighteen or even more, dressed to look real young because the Dutch only take children under sixteen."

So they were all held for hours at the Dutch passport control near the border while a lot of telephoning went on. Finally, sadly and with many apologies, someone explained that Holland was only a very small country, that they could not absorb an unlimited number of refugees. They had already allowed thousands of children to enter, but it was turning into a flood. "Some of you have foreign passports, some are over sixteen. We can't separate you and just take this one or that one, so with much regret we must send you all back over the border."

Then they were escorted to the last train back into Germany that night and handed over to the waiting SS border control who marched them on foot through Kleve, all the way to the police station where they spent the night.

I asked whether they were locked up in cells.

"Oh no, actually the police weren't bad. The SS were nasty, but some of the police were even friendly. They didn't have enough room for thirty-two people, or food. Oh yes. You must take some food, just in case. We were starving. Some of us slept on the floor, some on benches, in offices, in storage rooms. The lucky ones got a bunk, in a cell. They didn't lock it."

"Could you have run away?"

"Oh, easily. We walked around, to go to the bathroom, or to stretch our legs. After a while they didn't even look up as we passed. I could easily have sneaked out."

"So why didn't you?"

"Where to? I had no money. We only had ten marks to start with and they took that away along with all our belongings."

"How did the whole thing start in the first place? From Berlin, I mean. Who led you? How did you cross the border?"

"Uncle Monik took us all to Kleve. We arrived in the late afternoon, then we waited around at the station and he just put us on another train, the one that goes into Holland. Uncle Monik went to some hotel in Kleve, Jewish, Hotel Verwein, he said, I think. From Kleve it's just a short ride to Holland."

"But what were you going to do in Holland, I mean, how were you going to get in?" I asked.

"Oh, we were supposed to go and give ourselves up at the pass-control in Nijmegen and ask for any of these people . . ." She pointed at her handbag on the sideboard. "Could you give me that bag, please?" She pulled out a piece of paper and handed it to me. "You can have these names. I've got another copy in my suitcase. Here, these are people from the refugee committee in Nijmegen, and these two are from Amsterdam or something."

"Thanks, that's terrific . . . but please go on . . . you were at Kleve."

"Yes. There are these workmen's trains in the morning and evening, going across the border and back all the time. And that's where all those other kids got on, at Kleve. Our secret way—everybody knows it now."

I was looking at Susi, my heart beating faster. My voice seemed to jump out of my throat, dry and raw, "We're going to Holland tomorrow morning, just the two of us," I said.

Susi looked startled. "But how can we, they'll send us back!"

"That's exactly what everybody is thinking. There won't be thirty-two children tomorrow, or for the next few days. Remember Frau Kranz was surprised that we hadn't heard all about it? I bet every Jew in Germany already knows or will know about it by tonight. This is it, our best chance! But I don't want to take Norbert or Lilly. I don't want any deadweights. We might have to try a second time—if they send us back. We'll hide some money in Kleve somewhere. Right at the railway station, somewhere. In the toilet, maybe. Enough for another train ticket and some food." I wasn't really talking to anyone, I was thinking out loud.

Lore broke in, "Yes, yes, I was thinking the same. I'm definitely going to try again. But not right away. I'm still very tired and shaky. I must admit, we were all terribly scared. But I'll try again in a couple of days, alone. Who needs a grown-up just to put you on a train? When we were in trouble he wasn't even there . . . and even if he had been, what could he have done, except get himself into even worse trouble than we did. You know, hiding some money, that's a great idea."

Now for Aunt Leona. I told Susi that if we could persuade her mother she would persuade mine. "But we must get her on her own, where Norbert can't hear us or he'll make a scene."

"But why can't he come?"

"Susi, I love Norbert, but he . . . he's a real baby, and he doesn't listen. Nor does Lilian. They could screw up everything."

I continued this argument with Aunt Leona in one of the bedrooms out of Norbert's hearing, or so we thought. Our conspiratorial air must have made him suspicious. He had crept into a cupboard and followed our discussion with considerable interest.

"No, I won't take Lilian either. Susi and I will pave the way and if we get through we'll write back exactly how it was done, and then they can follow us."

At this point Norbert could contain himself no longer and came out of the cupboard howling with outrage.

210

There were tears, tantrums and entreaties. Rosa was appealed to by both parties. Having brought up quite a few of the Gottesmann and Zeller children, she had become an "adopted" relative rather than just a maid. Rosa supported my argument, her opinion carried weight, and I won the round.

Aunt Leona now called the Papiermeisters and asked them to call my mother to the telephone.

In the meantime, while Norbert sat in a sulk on the floor and refused to get up, we discussed a plan I had formulated. Rather than go straight across the border to a Dutch railway station, like the other group, we would first spend the night at that Verwein hotel in Kleve. We would look up Jewish names in the telephone directory and call them . . . no, they might be suspicious if we just called . . . better to go to their house so they could see who we are. People at the border knew things we didn't know in Berlin, right?, such as where or how it might be possible to cross the border safely. Day or night, ride, walk, alone or with a guide. If we had no luck in Kleve, we could take the train the next morning, like the other group.

Aunt Leona aired an idea of her own. She wanted Rosa to go with us because we were only children.

"Children?" I shrieked, "I'm fourteen . . . besides, I have plenty of experience. I've travelled for days all on my own."

"The less said about that, the better," replied Leona with a dark look.

"*Na Mensch*! What could Rosa do for us?" I protested. "Keep an eye on us for just one single day longer? Hold our hands on the train, maybe, so we won't cry? She couldn't cross the border with us, could she? If she tried they'd send us all back, for sure. And do you have all the extra money it would cost to send Rosa along? For no real purpose!"

211

We argued until the phone rang. Then there was an endless conversation in Hungarian. Finally she hung up, burst into tears, pulled herself together and said brusquely:

"All right, you two will go tomorrow. I'll find out about the early trains and let you know about them later through the Papiermeisters. Fred, go right home, your mother is packing a suitcase for you. I told her you wanted to take some emergency food. Come early tomorrow morning to take Susi to the Charlottenburg station. Your mother will meet you there close to departure time."

"Oh no! Didn't you tell her we don't want anyone coming to the station? It's dangerous. And she's going to cry, I know she is. I'm sure they're watching the stations now. She must not call attention to us!"

Leona shrugged her shoulders as if to say "I told her".

I knew it. I just knew it. All the way home on the S-Bahn, I was preparing for battle. I rehearsed my speeches, my irrefutable arguments. In vain. My father listened and agreed to say goodbye at home. But Mother not only insisted on going to the station, she was going to drag Lilian along too. I couldn't believe it. How could she? Not only was it dangerous, I wanted to avoid a terrible farewell scene. She would cry and run after the train. I was absolutely sure of it.

My sister's little suitcase, measuring twelve inches by sixteen, was standing there open, already packed, on my bed. Some underwear, a sweater, two shirts, socks, handkerchiefs, a packet of figs, a bar of chocolate, a package of Petit Beurre biscuits and, right, fountain pen, ink, envelopes and writing pad. Smart woman, my mother, she would give me no excuse not to write home. No books though . . . God, my books. Now I *really* knew that I was leaving all my wonderful books behind. I had, sort of, known about it all along, but never really allowed myself to feel it. For a moment I paused and wondered

whether I really wanted to go. Again I disallowed feeling
and pushed aside anxiety.

I looked at the envelopes containing my remaining postage stamps, the ones I pulled out of the album months
ago to be ready for this occasion. But no, I wouldn't risk
taking them. Perhaps they would consider them valuables
at the border, confiscate them, and arrest me. It would
be safer to ask Mother to send them by post, with a fake
return address. If I lose them, I lose them.

It felt very strange, this moment, now that it had finally
come. I had a terrible sense of loss; a heady sensation of
excitement together with a gnawing in the stomach, little
stirrings of nausea and tight pangs of fear.

I looked around my room, at my miniature racing cars,
the electric trains, the microscope, Stabilo construction
set, my rows and rows of books. Shit! I'm never going to
see this stuff again.

Mother knocked and opened the door. "I'm going over
to the Papiermeisters. It's nearly eight and Aunt Leona
will be calling about the trains. Better go to sleep now,
you'll have to get up very early if you're picking up Susi.
Don't worry, I'll wake you." And she bent forward to
kiss me goodnight. She held me against her for a moment.

I didn't resist going to bed, for once. I was feeling
quite worn out. It's been quite a day, I told myself, and
tomorrow; well tomorrow . . .

Mother left and I walked around once more, looking
at everything, to take it with me, in my head. There
wouldn't be time for looking around tomorrow. I picked
up a deck of miniature playing cards and squeezed it into
the suitcase. Might come in handy. I picked up *Tom
Sawyer* and felt tempted to squeeze that into the suitcase
too. No. No books. Must travel light, might have to run
for it. I squeezed *Tom Sawyer* into the suitcase, he's
coming with me. Do I drop the case if I'm chased? For a
moment I thought about that rather hard and that made

me wonder whether I would leave Susi behind if we had to run for it? Never! But that's silly. What would be the point of both of us getting caught. But could I just leave her behind? And then with relief I decided that there was no need to be concerned. The best solution would certainly be to split up and run in different directions if we were chased by a cop. One of us would have a chance to get away. And he'd probably be a gentleman and chase the boy.

I turned out the ceiling light after lighting the bedside lamp and lay down. There was a knock at the door; my father entered and sat with me. I offered my hand, he took it and held it. My heart was thumping—I don't want to feel, please, I won't want to feel. A terrifying thought had come to me: would I ever see him again? See *them* again? Of course I would. Once we kids were out they'd be able to get out too, easily.

"You'll make it," Father said quietly. "I'm quite sure you'll make it."

I nodded. I knew I would, but I couldn't talk, I was all choked up. He bent forward and embraced me. I held on to him terribly, terribly tightly for a few seconds.

"Good night, sleep well." His face was wet. He turned the light out and left quickly. And in the dark I felt my hot tears wetting the pillow and I wanted to scream with rage, and hate, and love.

I heard my mother return later and ask Father whether I was asleep. She opened the door quietly and looked in. I kept my eyes closed and pretended to sleep, but she stood there for a very long time. I never heard the door close. The next thing I knew, she was waking me. The room was dark and cold. Something glistened white on the window ledge. The first snow, I thought, and suddenly I was aware that this was the day.

I jumped into the clothes I had laid out the night before, my best things, of course, since that's all the clothing I

214

was taking. Mother reminded me to wash my hands and face. Father was standing about in his dressing gown and they both watched me swallow some cocoa and down a roll with butter and jam. Lilian was still asleep.

"The train leaves Charlottenburg at 9:16 a.m., arrives 4:40 at Krefeld. From there you take the train to Kleve which leaves only five minutes later, so don't waste any time! You'll be in Kleve at six. Here, I've written it all down for you."

I wondered why she was giving me all those details when she had them written down, looked up at her and saw the desperation in her eyes.

"Call the Papiermeisters when you get to the hotel."

"Mummy, please, I might not be able to. Please don't worry if I don't phone right away. We won't have much time. I'll call or telegraph as soon as I can, I promise."

I got up and put on my overcoat. Mother tied a woollen scarf round my neck and made me wear a cap. She hadn't done that for years. I tried to look unconcerned and nonchalant as I walked over to my father and kissed him goodbye. There was the scent of tobacco on his breath. His unshaven face prickled.

"*Auf Wiedersehn, Pappi.* See you later Mummy." Grabbing my gloves and suitcase I quickly ran out of the house and down the stairs into the cold.

It was still dark and snowing lightly as I waited at the Breitestrasse for the 55 tram to Moabit. Other people came to wait, and I looked at them sideways, wondering whether they realised what I was up to. No, of course not. The wait was endless, but finally the tram squealed to a halt and I climbed up and paid a schoolboy's fare— even though I'm no longer a schoolboy, I thought.

When I got to the Turmstrasse, I was horrified to find them all still asleep. And then: outrage. Aunt Leona had changed her mind about everything. She wouldn't let Susi go without Norbert. Rosa would accompany us to the

215

border and Leona, too, was coming to the railroad station to see us off. I raged, ranted, screamed, and danced like a dervish, but to no avail. Instead I was sent to buy them breakfast rolls. I went and got them their damned rolls or we would never have gotten out of Germany at all. But I was not through yet. I still had a trump card to play, at the right moment.

Of course, they had not finished packing, and by the time we were ready to start I was ready to commit a brutal murder or two. We got to the station late, met my mother and sister in front of the ticket counter, and I only had a few seconds to play my trump card.

"Halt!" I said and stopped everybody in their tracks. Pulling out the fifty marks my mother had given me for travel and hotel I flashed it about. Then I stepped three feet away from them.

"OK, here is money, more than enough for my train ticket. Now you all know that I have run away from home before. I'm ready to run right now, hide, and go to Holland alone. I will take Norbert if he promises to listen and do as I say without question, but I will not tag along with Rosa." I looked at Aunt Leona very hard and continued quietly. "Your choice, Aunt Leona, you can send Norbert and Susi with Rosa *or* with me. I will not follow Rosa."

I liked Rosa. But she was overly cautious and more of an innocent abroad than both of my cousins put together. She wasn't bright and would insist on doing it all her way.

The sisters looked at each other, at me, already five feet away, ready to bolt, and capitulated. We got our three tickets and rushed to the platform just a few minutes before departure time. As we were climbing into the train I noticed a small, bedraggled group of children our age walking hesitantly along the platform. Four hunched up boys in their dark Sunday clothes, crowned by a cap, conspicuous in the way they were trying to be inconspicu-

216

ous. Their clothes were of poor quality, and they carried the most primitive pieces of luggage. A cloth bundle, a brown paper package tied with string, a tiny rucksack and a shabby, cracked leather attaché case. They noticed us, recognised us, and quickly looked away. Instinctive disassociation on both sides. Had they not heard about that transport or had they come to the same now-or-never conclusion as we had? Were they going to cross tonight? At Kleve? Maybe they're going somewhere else. There must be other places to cross. We must stay apart, mustn't become a big group. Mother caught sight of them too and looked at me questioningly. So did Susi.

"Later!" I whispered to Susi and gave my mother a "don't worry" sign as we entered the train. We walked through the corridors of the practically empty train and found a compartment all to ourselves. After dumping our three little pieces of luggage, we went back into the corridor, and opened a couple of windows to the platform. Leaning out, all three of us, we saw our family come running towards us. Almost instantly the whistle blew, the stationmaster raised the wand with the green disc pointing towards the engine, the steam whistle of the locomotive responded, there was a whooomffff, and we clanged and lurched forward to a slow start. Too late to change your mind now, Mother, I thought as I looked at her while she did what I knew she would do.

"The last time I saw my mother she was crying," said the funny little man in my brain. "A good title for a chapter in the diary." Then I seized up. It was almost like that unreal moment during the Kristallnacht, standing in the window, waiting for the man to smash down the glass on me; a suspension of reality. A timelessness. There seemed to be no other people or objects at the station. The only thing I saw was my mother, first with both hands to her mouth, as if stifling a scream, then with her hands reaching out to me, running after the train, tears stream-

217

ing down her face, running faster and faster until she no longer could keep up with it and dwindled rapidly into a tiny speck in the distance. After the first slam of pain I only saw, I didn't feel, I heard nothing. I turned to ice. Coldly angry with her . . . for having had her heart torn out.

We sat and watched the grimy railway view of Berlin passing outside. Our compartment with its two long benches, face to face, its sliding door to the corridor on one side, window on the other, was overheated, dry, smelled of fresh lacquer and sooty smoke. We said very little until we were well out of the city and I raised the question of the other kids. We decided to avoid them at all costs. Then I changed my mind. It was dumb not to talk to them. We didn't have to travel together, but perhaps we could help each other. Did they know about that Jewish hotel in Kleve? Did they know something or have ideas that could help us? Susi agreed and I set off along the swaying corridor. They too had a compartment to themselves and looked up anxiously as I knocked at the window of their sliding door, before pulling it open.

"*Schalom uv'rachot*" I greeted them in Hebrew. "Peace and Blessings."

They looked at me suspiciously. Anybody can learn that.

"You saw us before, on the station, my cousins and me, with our family, didn't you?"

They half-nodded and I continued, "I think we're all doing the same thing, aren't we, visiting our aunt in Holland?"

There was a weak grin, and we started talking. Yes, they knew about that unfortunate transport and had come to the same conclusion: now or never. Like us, they had been shocked to see competitors boarding the train and had decided to ignore us.

I sat with them and outlined our plan. Well yes, staying

218

at the hotel in Kleve, that was a good idea, but they barely had enough money to take the permitted ten marks across the border. And (hesitation) they had a plan.

There was a pause after that statement, and we looked at each other. I tried to appear nonchalant, just politely interested, with a sort of "Oh really?" look in my eyes.

Achim, obviously the leader or spokesman for the group, looked at the others briefly, looked at me, then decided to confide in me. Help me, in fact:

"Somebody we know got across easy. He jumped the fence at the railway station at Nijmegen, that's the first stop in Holland. It's only about five feet high, the fence, and there's a real dark street on the other side. You've got to be at the front of the train, the first wagon after the locomotive. That goes way past the station building at the middle of the platform. Our friend just hopped over the fence and walked into town. But he had somebody's address there."

"And you don't?"

Achim shook his head, and for a moment it flashed through my mind that I had something to barter for a share in their fence jumping. Instead, I just told them that I had some Nijmegen addresses they could have. Here.

They looked surprised, pleased, and when I got up to leave they invited our little group to come and join them. Well, why not, we're still hundreds of miles from the border.

Soon we were asking each other the obvious question.

"Where were *you* during the Kristallnacht?"

For Achim it was the Crystal Day, not night. He started talking, and I admired the broad Berlin dialect my mother never let me speak.

"Nothing happened during the night in our street, and I went to school as usual. We live near the S-Bahn station, and it wasn't until I got off and started walking to school that I saw somebody clearing up a lot of glass. But I barely took any notice, I was late. When I got to school there was hardly anybody there. *Then* I found out about the synagogues burning and all that other stuff. I went right back home and told my parents. And we thought, thank God, they missed us and the two other Jews in our street. Well, we were eating—we live in the store, my dad's a tailor—and we were sitting having lunch, and there was a terrible crash, and another crash, and we heard glass breaking. Suddenly three storm troopers came running into the room, kicked over the table with all our food on it and grabbed my father. They hit him and hit him, they dragged him out and my mother was screaming and crying and trying to hold on to him . . ." Achim looked at the floor in tears, sobbing, unable to continue. We all sat and said nothing.

I was afraid to ask, but when he finally looked up and saw my question he said quietly:

"Yes, he came back a week later. They had shaved his head, he was black and blue all over, he didn't have any front teeth. He looked like an old man, my dad."

Helmuth put his arm around Achim's shoulder for a moment, and we changed the subject. We talked about how funny it was not to have to go to school, and argued whether England or Italy had a better football team. Susi, bored, got out some food which we all shared. All those kids had on their bread was mustard. Nothing else, not even butter. Now mustard was the only thing we didn't have and we said we wanted some. So we swapped around until we all had cheese, salami, butter *and* mustard.

I had been brooding and finally spoke up. No harm in asking:

"Look you guys, I don't want to impose on you, and you can say 'no' and there's no sweat. I like your plan better than ours. We could do the same thing tomorrow . . . but we would have to wait until night to

220

jump the fence, and that'll delay us for a whole day. I'm wondering. If we join forces tonight there are some good things and some not so good. Perhaps seven people would call a little more attention to themselves than four, but each of us would have a better chance to get away if there was a cop around. Even two cops. Who can grab seven kids, going off like firecrackers in different directions, all at once? And if we organise this right, we can avoid calling attention to ourselves."

We discussed this for a bit and finally decided on joint action and a precise plan, a one-two-three crossing of the platform by small groups. First, the two toughies of the other group would cross the platform and stop on our side of the fence. Norbert and another boy would follow immediately and would be helped over the fence by the first two. Once across they would stay by the fence, and Susi would rush to the fence and be hoisted over by the boys on both sides. Then the toughies over the fence, followed by Achim and me, who fancied ourselves as leaders, fast runners and heroes. Once on the other side, the two groups would split up quickly and go separate ways. Depending on the terrain, we would keep as far to the left as possible without crossing the station entrance, and they would strike out to the right. No running. Walk as if you belong. If challenged, everybody for himself, scatter in all directions and run like hell. We did a few mock rehearsals of the fence thing in the narrow confines of our railway compartment. The door was the fence. "No, no running unless you're chased . . . now you two to the fence . . . watch, make a stirrup like this, with your hands . . . Norbert, put your foot here . . . heave . . . and you two on the other side . . ." Soon we all knew exactly what to do and when. We hoped.

Then it struck me that my group had far too much money to take across the border. I collected all the surplus so that each one of us had ten marks and the price of the ticket for the train over the border. Then I distributed the coins I had prepared for hiding in Kleve, enough for another ticket across. There were also a few extra coins for refreshments on the way.

We told the others about our second-chance money, but they were broke. So we gave them a ten-mark note and told them to get it changed. That left one hundred and ten marks in notes. Boy, were we rich. Our parents would be glad to have all that back. I wrapped it in note paper and addressed the envelope with the fountain pen so thoughtfully provided by my mother for just such an occasion. As I wrote the words Havelstrasse 20, sitting in the rattling train six hours out of Berlin, it came to me that it was no longer my address. I posted the letter at the next stop.

The train had made several earlier stops, and for a while we had other passengers in our compartment, most of whom gave us curious looks. They were surprised to see seven kids sitting together without a teacher or leader, and even more surprised how well-behaved and quiet we were. We hardly said a word while they travelled with us. Our answers to one, whose curiosity got the better of her, were decidedly odd, too.

"You're visiting your aunt in Kleve? What, the same aunt *all* of you? . . . cousins *all* of you? . . . She's very sick? . . . Your parents are coming later? . . . they're at work? But how about you, don't you have school?"

The more questions she asked, the sillier our story became. Once started we just didn't know how to extricate ourselves. Finally, the poor woman just sat there, silent, sorely puzzled, shaking her head. But we weren't laughing, we were scared and must have looked it, and that probably saved us from unpleasantness. She must have realised that we were not trying to ridicule her. To our relief, she left at the next station, still shaking her head sadly.

222

We quickly cooked up some separate aunts, uncles and cousins in case there was another curious questioner.

Seven hours out of Berlin, we started pacing up and down the compartment and corridor. Sitting on the blond, shiny wood benches for seven hours had been hard on our behinds, and every minute brought us closer to the moment of truth. We avoided each other's eyes so as not to show or see strain or fear. It was getting dark, and it was snowing heavily as we pulled into Krefeld. We were a little late and only just made the train to Kleve. Again, there was a compartment where, though there were other passengers, we could all sit together. We seemed to need each other more every minute.

As we had planned earlier, we all kept a sharp lookout for other Jewish-looking kids boarding the train. There were some older kids, locals, with untroubled faces. Good. Let's hope there aren't any with troubled faces like ours waiting at Kleve for our next train.

There were none; just a few Dutch teenagers and some grown-ups, looking us over curiously as we entered the warm little station house. After buying our tickets, we asked for the toilets and were directed to a small separate building quite a way further along the platform. Good, again. Inside, there were tiles and smells, but no safe places in which six boys could hide a little hoard of coins. However, surrounding the building, under a few inches of snow, there were tile-bordered groups of flowerbeds with many little bends and curves. I tested the soil beneath the snow. It was soft enough. So everyone picked a little corner, pressed his coins beneath the soil and pushed snow back over the site. Then we pretended to have a snowball fight to mess up the whole area, masking our hiding places, and to justify all our previous bending down.

Back in the station house a final check revealed that we were still two and a half marks over the limit. Might as well waste it nicely. The boys got chocolate, Susi a tiny bottle of eau de cologne. A lot of people were arriving in a bus, mostly Dutch workmen going home, and soon the train steamed into the station. The moment we heard it we moved quickly past the waiting groups all the way to the very front.

Again we were lucky and found a compartment to ourselves. We had learned that the train would make two stops in Germany and then stop in Nijmegen. Now, moving towards the border, I was trying to find out from two Dutch kids standing around in the corridor, where the train would go after Nijmegen. It wouldn't hurt to have all the answers; one never knew when they might come in handy. They couldn't understand what I wanted, and I couldn't understand what they were saying in return. They didn't even pronounce Nijmegen the way we did.

We all sat and pretended to be cool, calm and whatever else one was supposed to be in adversity. We had run out of conversation.

Before too long the train slowed down and stopped. Wiping the steam off the window, we saw nothing much on either side. Just snow, a long, empty platform and a few dim lanterns. Way back some people were moving along the platform swinging hand lanterns. They were coming our way.

"Come on, sit down, let's look normal . . . read the newspaper . . . you too!" Achim distributed pages from the two newspapers we bought on the way. I got the sports page and tried to read something about a football team. We waited, for hours it seemed, then, suddenly, the train started to move again.

They missed us. They didn't check on us. We smiled with relief. Suddenly a black shape appeared, and an SS man slid open the door, saluted and yelled, "*Heil* Hitler," as he entered.

He took one look, smiled a thin smile and said almost

to himself, *"Na ja, schon wieder."* "Well, well, there we are again."

Then he barked, "Where are you going?"

An instant jumble of seven voices, "Family, aunt, cousin, Holland," and almost as quickly, silence.

"Your family . . . in Holland . . . of course. Hand me your passports."

Just two of us answered this time, quietly, "Sorry, we're all under sixteen, we don't have passports."

"Then let's have your Hitler Youth leave passes."

We looked at each other. What was that?

"We don't have any of those. We're Jewish, we're not allowed in the Hitler Youth."

"Damn it, *Saujuden*," he screamed, "you have to have a Hitler Youth leave pass or else an official document that you're not eligible for service. *Eine Schweinerei*, you know very well that's the law! You have to have proof or you can't leave Germany. I'll have you arrested! Stay here and don't you dare move out of this compartment, I'll be right back! *Heil* Hitler!" And he stormed out of the door and slammed it shut.

We sat there looking at each other and not even attempting to hide our fear. We kept on waiting for him to return with reinforcements. But the train just went on ratatatting into the night.

We started whispering, "What could he possibly want, how were we to know about those leave passes, surely he knows we wouldn't have them."

"I bet he's just trying to scare us," said Achim. "What a mean bastard."

Then the brakes squealed and the train came to a halt. Holland? No, Kroningen, the last stop in Germany. Maybe that's where he was getting the reinforcements to arrest us.

We sat there scared, clutching our bits of newspapers, pretending to read. An endless wait. Suddenly a face, a

225

uniform and peaked cap appeared at the little window next to the sliding door. He turned away, called someone, and another, and then still another face appeared, and they whispered to each other at the door. They've come for us. The door slid open but only one officer entered. He wore a green uniform, not black! And he smiled and said:

"Good evening, children. Customs Service."

He had said, "good evening," not "*Heil* Hitler." And he had smiled!

"Good evening!" we echoed, tremendously relieved.

"Anything to declare?"

We jumped up, grabbing and holding out our little pieces of luggage, but he waved them aside.

"No, that's all right. How about money?"

"Just ten marks each." We were all eager to empty our pockets to show him, but he waved that aside too.

"*Schon gut.*" But he kept staring at me and then, pointing, said, "You've tried to cross before, haven't you? What happened?"

Absolutely horrified I protested, "No, not me. I've never tried before. Honestly. My word of honour."

But he was shaking his head disbelievingly.

"Don't worry. It's all right even if you tried before. I wish you luck, all of you." And he gave me another searching look.

"My word of honour . . ."

He waved that aside once more, moved to the door, and smiled sadly:

"Have a good trip, children, I hope you succeed!" And then, after a hesitation, "*Es tut mir so leid.*" "I'm so sorry."

Another ten minutes passed before the train moved.

Now Holland. After a while we looked out of the window but saw absolutely no sign that we were in another country. The snow was still falling. A last, quick review of the fence sequence and we tensed up for the real thing as the train drew into the Nijmegen station. First we let everybody else off. Then we drew together in a tight bunch at the carriage exit, like a compressed spring ready to uncoil. There was the fence, one lantern immediately on the left, one further back right . . . and almost simultaneously the two boys moving out at the front turned back exclaiming:

"Halt. Look. Look Achim!"

Achim and I leaned out and saw two men in uniform marching up and down outside, on the other side of the fence. And another further down. They wore unfamiliar uniforms. Soldiers? Police? And they were armed.

We didn't know which way to go and stood squashed together, heads waving, whispering anxiously, a frightened Hydra, talking to itself.

"*Raus!*" I heard myself say loudly. "Achim, our tickets only take us here. If we go any farther we'll be even more illegal!"

"Right, let's get on the platform."

We found ourselves standing in the snow in the middle of nowhere on the dark, practically deserted platform. The station building was a hundred feet ahead of us. The soldiers on the other side of the fence had stopped and were looking at us. In the light of the lantern, we saw their breath in the cold air. One of them shouted in German, pointing towards the building:

"*Pass Kontrolle* and customs, over there, if you please."

"What do we do now?"

"Give ourselves up Achim," I said, "like the others before. What else can we do?"

Achim nodded and whispered to the others, "Don't tell anyone we were going to jump that fence! Understand?"

"Did you hear that?" I whispered, looking hard at Norbert. "Right, let's go."

Slowly, hesitatingly, treading on each other's heels, we moved towards the brightly lit building.

The large, high-ceilinged space was almost empty. Just in front of us stood a large square table with an open centre, manned by a Dutch customs officer. We moved in slow motion to the table, spread out and presented our baggage. The whole lot would have fitted into a normal-sized suitcase. One look and the officer waved us wordlessly on, towards the exit behind him.

We looked where he pointed and saw a very tall expanding metal gate pulled almost closed, leaving just enough room for one person to exit by walking past the ticket collector guarding the narrow opening. Two people filed past him, and we saw them hand over their ticket and show identification papers.

Huddled together again, we slowly, slowly moved towards the man at the gate. I caught sight of a dapper little person on the other side. He looked excited, moving in a jumpy manner that reminded me of someone. Charlie Chaplin, that's it, a well-heeled Charlie Chaplin. He noticed me looking at him, returned the look with great intensity and raised his hand slightly as if in greeting. I raised my hand slightly too, looking at him wondering whether . . . then he called:

"*Joodsche Vluchtelingen?*"

That was close enough to the German *Juedische Fluechtlinge* for me to understand that he was asking whether we were Jewish refugees. I nodded vehemently, and he jumped up and down with excitement, calling:

"*Gut, gut, alles gut*, I'm here for you. Do not be afraid!"

He moved rapidly to the man who was collecting the ticket, spoke to him, pointed towards us. The man in uniform who had already eyed us with professional interest permitted our dapper "Charlie" to enter. He came rushing up to us with a big smile:

"*Willkommen in Holland*! I'm from the Nijmegen

228

Jewish refugee committee. *Alles gut.*" Pointing to the dark part of the station on our right, he beckoned us to follow him to the end and up a short wooden staircase that led to a softly lit office ten feet above the ground. As we started up the stairs, Norbert, on the other side of Susi, leaned towards me, eyes wide, and asked in a stage whisper that could be heard for two kilometres:

"But I thought we were going to smuggle ourselves in?"

I thought I'd die. After quickly looking to see whether we had been overheard I leaned towards him in turn and hissed:

"Shut up, you twit. Another word and I'll kill you!"

The small, overheated office smelled of railways and coffee and was lit by a few dim bulbs under conical green glass shades. A heavy moustachioed officer enthroned behind a large register asked all of us in turn our whats and wherefores, faithfully entering every little fact into the open book. He looked exactly like my image of Yehova, entering our good and bad deeds of the day into his big, blue-lined register. In this case the archangel standing at his side, interceding or interpreting for us, wore a dark overcoat and a natty little moustache. After the officer made a few telephone calls it was our protector's turn to speak:

"The immigration officer has told me that he has permission to release you into my custody, waiting for a decision regarding your stay in Holland. This will come from the government in den Haag. I'll sign and take responsibility for you if you promise to be led by me and not to run away."

We swore by all that was holy to us that we would follow his every wish and command. Since my most absolute swearing was always done "on my mother's head", it brought my parents to mind. I asked whether it was possible for the nice officer to telephone our parents that we were safe.

"You're a good boy," said our protector. "I'll make a list as soon as we get to the office of the refugee committee at the synagogue. We're going there now, and from there we'll send telegrams immediately. We can't use the phone here. Ah, that reminds me. I've got to call someone else to come; I can't get all of you into my car. There's a phone in the station hall. Let's go, please."

When the second car arrived, we drove through the snowy streets of Nijmegen, all lit up and glittering festively for Christmas. My car was a splendid black Renault. "*Wunderschoen*," says my diary. I could once more afford to be aware of the better things in life.

We arrived at the synagogue chambers that housed the refugee committee rooms. Dull, dignified, conservative, they looked so standardly institutional, they could have been in Spandau.

But these chambers also sported a big tiled bathroom complete with a buxom, shirt-sleeved Dutch matron who grabbed every one of us, stripped, dunked and scrubbed, regardless of indignant protests, until we glowed like polished, blushing apples. From her steamy inferno we were ferried to the doctor who thumped, prodded and "Ah'd" us most thoroughly.

After these ordeals, we were led into a spacious room with a large table laden with food. Someone brought in hot chocolate. In addition to my travel companions, I found three other occupants in the room when I entered: two plumpish young girls from Duisburg and a little boy, a very little boy, under the dining table looking up at me when I drew nearer. About two years old, or so, I thought. He looked at me with such undisguised intensity; he seemed to enter my head, and I saw and felt nothing but those eyes. I held out my hand, and he quickly

230

crawled out from under the table and held on to it, tightly, never taking his eyes off me.

Tearing myself away from that look I turned to the girls:

"Your brother?"

They shook their heads. The older one, Irma, about fourteen, answered, "His name is Ralph. They found him on the train we came on with a little bag hanging from his neck." She hesitated, looked at Ralph, came close and whispered in my ear, "There was a note in it. From his mother. She wrote her husband was in a KZ and that she was on the run herself . . . will the kind Dutch people please take care of Ralph. She had nowhere to turn, and this was the only way she could get him to safety. She would send his documents to the refugee committee soon."

We looked at Ralph, who looked back at us and seemed to know that he was the subject of our conversation. I didn't want to get all drippy, or stomp my foot and say shit, shit, shit—so I picked him up briskly and sat him on my knee telling him, with all the unconcern I could muster, that I hadn't eaten a thing and would he eat something with me. He smiled, and I became Papa of the day. Perhaps I looked a little like his father, perhaps he sensed in me a giver of security and love. If the latter, he was pretty smart. I loved and wanted to protect him forever from the moment I saw him and still feel sad that I could not do so.

They called us together for a little meeting and announced the next steps. We would stay with private families, mostly Jewish, who had volunteered to look after us until a decision was made regarding our stay. This could take a day, or even longer. We would have to be patient.

"But there are so few of us, surely they won't send us back, will they?" I asked.

231

"I don't think they will," he replied, but there was a tiny hesitation, a small frown, and he did not look at me directly until he remembered something, and said, "Oh yes, sorry I couldn't put you up with your cousins. Nobody had room for three. But you'll be with a very nice family. They've children your age. I'm sure you'll like them. And they speak German."

I thanked him, hesitated, not wanting to plague him, but finally reminded him of his promise to let our parents know that we were safe. He patted my head and assured me that someone was sending our parents telegrams that very moment.

After ten, I thought, it won't get there until early in the morning.

It got there at five in the morning, my sister told me later. They had stayed up very late, even Lilian. Just after they finally got to sleep, a banging at the door woke them up. Gestapo? God . . . Father was at home! It didn't sound hard enough. Perhaps Fred coming back? Lilian was sent to the door to find out who was knocking, and the answer was "Fred".

She yelled, "It's Fred. It's Fred!" and they opened the door. It was Fred, the other Fred, Cousin Alfred Axel, who had just arrived from Belgium to pick up some of his mother's belongings. There were tears of relief, and continued anxiety because my escape was still in progress. The telegram from Nijmegen, two hours later, brought elation.

"I knew my son would do it!" announced my father.

ROTTERDAM

They were waiting for me at 27 Pontanusstraat, the whole de Wyze family, all beaming with pleasure, glad of my escape. Their house was tidy, spotless and small; too small, in fact, for house guests. Louis, their sixteen-year-old son, had to sleep on a rickety cot among the bric-a-brac in the attic so I could have his room and bed.

They tried to make me feel at home, plying me with hot chocolate, cake and smiles. But I felt strangely uncomfortable and shy, keenly aware that I was an object of pity and charity. That's a new experience, I thought with gallows bravado, and one that I'd better get used to. So I sat there and tried to keep on smiling back, in a room full of well-meaning, gentle people looking at me with concern and sympathy, asking innumerable questions about how it had all been in Germany. Luckily, we soon retired for the night. Mr de Wyze, a cattle dealer, had to go off to an auction early the next morning, and the kids, Kitty, Elli and Louis had to go to school. Of course . . . school . . . tomorrow was Thursday. It had been a month of Sundays for me, but here Jewish kids could still go to school. What do you mean, "still", corrected the other voice in my head, this is Holland. For years everything had been getting steadily worse and I got used to thinking in terms of "still". Last year I could still go swimming. Until May I could still go to the cinema.

I'm in Holland, I told myself, as I lay in bed thinking,

exhausted, but too excited to sleep right away. I was inordinately proud of myself. I tried to conjure up my parents' and Aunt Leona's faces upon receiving the news that we had made the crossing safely. Just before I fell asleep, my father's image took on tangible shape in my mind and I could almost hear him say, "I knew my son would do it!"

I awoke early, knew immediately where I was, and went quickly to look out of the window to see Holland in daylight. Our neat, pretty little street was lined with glazed-tile two-storey buildings glistening with cleanliness. The snow had been swept off pavements that gleamed as if they had been polished. An older woman appeared, slowly pushing a large, three-wheeled cart. Raised on two supports, a curved, painted sign advertised her movable fish store. Different fish arranged in neat rows were marked by little hand-written price tags, and a scale dangled and jangled from the overhead sign. She was followed by a throng of miaouing cats.

I wondered whether my parents had received the telegram yet. There was a knock at the door, and Mrs de Wyze announced breakfast. The kids had already left and she sat with me because "she liked to have company". I rather suspected that it was because she thought I was a motherless son. We sat around waiting for THE phone call, the one that would announce whether or not I could stay in Holland. I jumped two feet into the air each time the phone rang. Every time Mrs de Wyze answered, she would look at me and shake her head as she talked in Dutch. No, not yet. Then she asked whether I wanted to go shopping with her. Of course I did, but what about the call? She assured me they would call again and that she would really like my company.

Nijmegen was a small, charming little market town with street after street of colourful, tile-fronted little houses. The modern stores at the centre of town were decorated

234

for Christmas, now only nine days away. As I walked next to Mrs de Wyze, I became aware that somehow people recognised what I was. At best, they would look politely out of the corner of an eye, not greeting me, but somehow conveying the impression that they knew me, or about me. Others looked openly, and some even turned back to stare some more after I passed. Mrs de Wyze noticed my discomfort and said:

"It's the way you're dressed, Fred. It's very German. Nobody wears knickerbockers in Holland, so they know where you're from and why you're here. Don't mind them, they're curious. They're shocked by what has happened on the other side, and they're your friends." She said this with a lovely, slow smile. A generous smile.

"Thank you," I said, and she took and held my hand for a while as we walked. I felt like a little boy again.

Back at the house, the waiting for the telephone call continued. When they were back from school, Kitty and Elli took turns at racing to the phone every time it rang and shook their heads quickly if it was not THE call.

To divert me, Louis took me off for a chilly afternoon walk. He explained that they could not let me go out on my own; they had promised not to let me out of sight. Besides, if I were walking alone, I would be picked up very soon. The police, in or out of uniform, were constantly on the lookout for refugees. I told him how we had originally planned to jump a fence, and he was quite sure we would not have got very far. I saw his sidelong glance at my knickerbockers. If they send me back to Germany and I tried again, what was I going to do about these telltale trousers? When we got back to the house, I showed Louis the address I had been given in Berlin, and he made some phone calls.

"No good, not any of them!" he pronounced, "At least the ones in Nijmegen."

Then I asked him whether he would lend me an old pair

of long trousers and give me a couple of good addresses if the answer from den Haag was "No". He looked at me curiously, and I told him about the money hidden next to the toilet at Kleve.

"Of course I will," he laughed and ran to tell the whole family about it.

We talked, ate, played cards and "Snip"—a game, played on the table, in which a plastic disc, the size of a thumbnail, pressed against a smaller chip, made it jump into a container. Louis, Kitty and Elli all played just to keep my mind off the telephone bell. It was after office hours, and it didn't look as if I would hear any news today.

It rang just after seven, and Kitty ran to answer. We all sat and watched her listen intently, one hand holding the receiver, the other raised. We saw her face light up with joy. Turning to us she nodded emphatically but continued to listen, saying, "yes", a few times before putting down the receiver.

"You can stay!" she beamed. "You can stay in Holland—and the other kids too!"

I must have looked quite dumbfounded. It had taken so long to get here, and my ears just weren't connecting to my mind.

"He can't believe it." They were laughing and then they crowded around me, crying, hugging and smiling through tears—and I realised how tense they, too, had been, on my behalf.

Kitty explained that my companions and I would all be sent to a children's summer-place, staffed by nuns, opened this winter by the Dutch Catholic Church to help Jewish refugee children. It was to be a kind of halfway house, to quarantine us briefly in case we were importing some dreadful disease, and to sort us out for more permanent accommodation.

Lying in bed that night, I felt another surge of inordi-

236

nate boyish pride. I sat up and actually patted myself on the back. "There, you've done it, you old chump."

I was sad that I could not stay with the de Wyzes. You'll never have it better, I thought. True.

I said good-bye to everybody after breakfast except Mrs de Wyze, who had told me that she would first take me to the Committee house, and then also see me off at the bus station.

When we got to the synagogue chambers the others were already standing around in their overcoats, all scarfed, hatted, and ready to go. Suddenly a bundled up little figure shot out of the group and flew up into my arms. Before I could say "Ralph", I was a father again.

Three of the four boys with whom we had crossed the border were being sent to a refugee camp in Rotterdam. The youngest of the four, the two girls, my cousins and two boys we had not met before were going to de Steeg with me.

Ralph sat on my lap incredibly well behaved—too well behaved perhaps—and we watched the snowy landscape. We were on a regular bus to Arnhem, mixed in among the Dutch passengers. Shortly after we started, someone from behind tapped me on the shoulder and told me in halting German that I was looking after my little brother very nicely.

I turned around and saw a heavy-set older man in rough clothing, with the leathery face of a peasant, crinkled up, smiling. I told him Ralph's story, with some uneasiness. I didn't know just how much Ralph understood.

After a silence the old man said, "Well, that's all over now. You're safe. The Germans will never get here. We'll open the dikes and drown them if they ever try!"

The bus stopped at a roadside coffee stall with a wide counter. There was steam rising from everything; from silver urns, copper tanks, and glass display cases. It was even curling up in the early morning sunlight from the

237

slushy snow. When I looked at the warmly dressed people standing there, drinking and munching, there was still more steam, from their cups and their breath. Then, I saw some of our fellow passengers, who had left to get refreshments, move cautiously through the crowd and climb back on the bus, laden with paper bags, packages and cups, similarly steaming. How can they drink on the moving bus, I thought, and how will they get the china cups back to the stall?

Suddenly someone was standing at my side handing me a cup of hot chocolate, cakes, biscuits and chocolate. This, it turned out, was not a regular stop. The passengers had asked the driver to halt so they could buy us presents, and the driver had contributed as well.

"Welcome to Holland," they said. The bus stood until we had downed our hot chocolate and had shaken a lot of hands. Ralph developed an instant passion for hand-shaking and for the next hour or so got off my knees several times to make his earnest hand-shaking rounds of the bus. I welcomed these much needed breaks from fatherhood. My legs had become quite numb from the unaccustomed load.

Well, at least he's toilet-trained, I thought. Well, almost, I decided a little later.

Ralph's passion was horses, and he got excited whenever we passed one, which was frequently. My thrill was skaters on the steel-grey frozen ponds in the hilly, wooded Arnhem landscape. We passed close enough for me to see the skates quite clearly. They were beautiful, so unlike the clumsy steel "clamp-ons" I used to attach to my boots. The Dutch skates, fastened to the boots with leather straps, had lovely, slim, wooden bodies from which a thin, bright steel blade protruded, curled up at the front like a Turkish slipper. I made a drawing of them while Ralph watched in fascination.

The nuns stood in the snow in a little welcoming circle.

Behind them spread the solemn Revierhuis of de Steeg, a children's resort, not far from Arnhem. First we were led into a room full of tiny tables laden with toys for very young children. Ralph immediately appropriated some of them with a whoop of delight. Our names were called one by one, and after handing over our luggage, we hung up our coats in a peculiar cupboard. It had rails at various heights, very low to still lower. That was our first intimation of the shape and height of things to come. Throughout the house, everything—toilets, washbasins, beds, towels, blankets, was scaled down to fit tiny tot sizes up to towering five-year-olds.

We felt like senior citizens. Very few of the thirty kids already there when our group arrived were over ten years old. The eight "Frauleins", as we called the nuns who looked after us, all spoke excellent German, were trained in children's care and "couldn't have been nicer", my diary notes. The Directriese, the director of the home, an older, greyer, stiffer Sister who walked around leaning on a heavy black cane, rated one star; "mostly pretty nice".

When a Fraulein tried to relieve me of Ralph, he raised such a hue and cry that the windows rattled, and he clutched on to my knee so ferociously that I was forced to continue my papadom. He wouldn't leave my side for even a second. I had to take him to the bathroom both when he had to go and when I had to go. That's the way he learned to pee into the pot standing up. None of the Frauleins could have shown him that. He didn't cry "Eureka" when he saw how I was doing it, but he got very excited, pulled out his little number, and standing right behind me peed all over the back of my pants.

"No Ralph, in here," I grabbed him and redirected his efforts in midstream. His enthusiasm knew no bounds, and for the next twenty-four hours I had to take him to the place every half hour and wait for him to squeeze out a few drops.

The tables and chairs were midget size, but happily the meals weren't. But the price of parenthood—feeding Ralph on my lap—put me at a decided disadvantage. By the time I was ready for seconds everything was gone. Nor could I play with the others after the meal. No, I had to drag Ralph up to his room to take a nap. I had to sit there under his beady, watchful eyes until he finally fell asleep. Strangely enough, I didn't mind. It felt good being his protector, looking after him, being needed, loving him. It also gave me something else, a greater sense of security: if I could look after him, then I must be all right too, mustn't I? I loved the way he fell asleep with his head on my shoulder and stayed asleep as I carried him up to his cot. And when he learned my name and kept saying "Fred, Fred," looking at me tenderly, that was the most thrilling thing I had ever known.

Irma, the older girl from Nijmegen, was the only other person who could do anything with Ralph. I was relieved to have her around, since I had already started to wonder what would happen if I had to leave him. That was inevitable, I was sure, and it would be terrible for the poor kid. I mustn't let him get too used to me.

Ralph permitting, I played chess, cards, or draughts with some of the older kids. There was very little else to do in the evening. That first night we all retired to bed and suffering in a newly "opened" room. My bed was made to fit a seven-year-old dwarf. Every time I stretched my legs I dented my skull. All the bedrooms were unheated. They didn't seem to know about featherbeds in Holland either, and the two thin midget blankets we were given failed to prevent us from freezing to the mattress. There was a lot of healthy fresh air in the room, admitted by rattling windows with unsealed gaps. The icy wind entered in gusts that constantly threatened to extinguish the flame of the candle that burned under the plaster statue of the Madonna and child in the room where Norbert, I and three others lay shivering.

The cold and candle kept me awake. I was also worried that Ralph might wake up and cry. It had been tough, getting him to sleep. He kept on holding my hand and staring at me. Maybe I should learn some lullabies.

"Damn it, I'm Jewish and I'm freezing," said one of the boys, who jumped out of bed and stomped out of the room, barefoot, wrapped in his blanket. I did not quite know how to reconcile those two statements. Did he mean Jews shouldn't be made to shiver?

A little later he was back with a heap of thin blankets, one more for each of us. That was for the freezing. Then he marched over to the Madonna and blew out her candle. That was for the Jews.

"I had to go to the Directriese," came his voice out of the dark. "You should have seen the look she gave me when I told her that the candle on the Madonna was against my religion."

The next morning the kids next door showed us a former glass of water on their window sill. During the night it had been transformed into a clump of ice and a dozen glass splinters. I too nearly turned into a clump of ice, on my knees in the unheated bathroom, washing myself with cold water. They had no warm water, and there was a line for the higher sinks.

It was Saturday and we met for prayers led by one of the older boys. The nuns looked on benignly, the head sister sternly. She always looked stern, even during breakfast in the dining room with the big windows that looked out on a lovely hilly landscape with a winding river, groups of pine trees and a red rising sun reflected in the snow. Every face glowed as we wolfed down the delicious buttered white bread strewn with chocolate flakes or flowing with honey. I thought the Dutch were absolutely

241

the most civilised people in the world . . . chocolate flakes on bread and hot chocolate. Even on *ordinary* days.

I discovered a small pile of German books in the Revierhuis, but they were mostly for kids. I missed my own books. Their presence in my room had been important to me. Playing dumb kids' games all day got boring. I missed my parents too, but not desperately so, yet. The relief of being out of Germany overshadowed everything. Besides, I had been away from home before and expected to see my parents again—sometime soon. It didn't occur to me that "sometime soon" could become "never again".

One aspect of being away from home did make itself felt that evening. It was Chanuka, but this year there were no presents. There was, however, a menorah, and when we lit the first light we were celebrating our own liberation.

There was a wind-up gramophone and some battered old records, and we were soon dancing to "Yes, we have no bananas, we have no bananas today". Not that any of us could really dance; kids didn't get to dances much in those days. But we needed the exercise and hopped around. Suddenly the festivities stopped, and we were standing in little groups exchanging contradictory rumours. We're all going to be sent to Rotterdam, to the big refugee camp. No, not all of us, only the older ones, over fifteen. No, only the younger ones.

The news was of great concern to Norbert and me because it sounded as if they meant to separate us from Susi, who was over fifteen. Sure enough, that's exactly what they were going to do. The Directriese appeared, raised her right hand majestically, and we fell silent. Yes, in a day or two, all the children over fifteen would be sent to Rotterdam; the others were to stay here. She read out the Rotterdam list and Susi's name was included.

Norbert and I formed a two-man protest and resistance movement and laid siege to the office. Three times they kicked us out firmly, and three times we went back, firmly.

They told us how unhappy we would be in that camp for older people. But we will be together, we argued. They told us we would be housed in old barracks, it would be cold, the food would be much worse.

"Then why are you sending Susi there?"

"That was not our decision. She's going there because she's over fifteen."

"But that's only one year older than us."

Finally I played my old trump card, the one I used at the railway station in Berlin. I looked the Directriese straight in the eyes and said:

"We escaped from Germany. How are you going to prevent us from running away to Rotterdam?"

She looked at me, and then at Norbert, and then again at me. "She's his sister," I said pointing at Norbert, adding as a clincher, "and she's my double cousin, that's just like a sister. Her father and my father are brothers, my mother and her mother are sisters."

Everybody in the office had stopped talking, and there was a long silence. Then she kicked us out of the office for the fourth time.

Norbert and I were standing around fighting down tears, having our heads patted by some compassionate kids when Susi came running in with the news that the Refugee Committee had decided to allow us to go to Rotterdam with her after all. We were delirious. And only then, with a pang, did I remember Ralph. I kept thinking about him and feeling sad. Irma too was being sent away. My God, that's terrible. That's awful. But what can I do?—I kept reminding myself.

Then I thought about Rotterdam and got excited about going to a big harbour with all those ships. We would be reunited with the three boys who had crossed the border with us who had been sent to Rotterdam directly from

243

Nijmegen. That night, still shivering with cold, my last thought before dozing off was that I hoped the rooms would be heated in Rotterdam.

Next morning I asked the Directriese whether I could take Ralph with me to Rotterdam. I would look after him.

At first she was going to give me a quick, snappy "certainly not" reply. I could see it in her face. But she relented and I saw the first sign of warmth I had yet seen in her eyes:

"You've been very good with him," she said, "but he needs grown-up parents, a father *and* a mother. It would be an impossible burden for you . . ." She held up her hand, stopping my protest. "Besides, we have had news about him from den Haag. His mother wrote to the government the day she put him on the train. His name is Fraenkel and the mother asked whether he could be found a foster home until she could get him back again."

"He's going to cry a lot."

"You're not leaving until the day after tomorrow. I'm going to get sister Antje to take care of him most of the time today and tomorrow, and you can help by including her as much as possible from now on, gradually leaving them alone together for longer and longer periods. Will you do that?"

I did, reluctantly, for his sake, but it didn't work all that well. He still called for me all the time, and I had to put him to bed, feed him, and put him on the potty. But he did accept sister Antje as a friend and she was permitted to help me feed, dress, undress and bathe him.

Luckily, the bus came for us after lunch on Tuesday, after I had put him to bed for his nap. I hugged and kissed him—and tried to tell him that I had to leave him. I wanted him to forgive me. But he didn't understand and just pulled my ear as I bent over him. He was sweetly asleep when I sneaked away and boarded the bus to Rotterdam.

I had a good window seat directly behind the driver. It was a new bus, gleamingly modern, with a radio and, what joy, heaters. I was warm for the first time in days. The driver, who spoke pretty good German, started to point things out to us as we travelled.

"These are the Dutch Alps," he said with a chuckle, pointing at the little snow-covered hills we were passing. "The rest of Holland is flat . . . ," and he talked about the Zuider Zee, the dikes, the windmills, tulips and wooden clogs.

We were an appreciative audience. He knew it and talked with gusto. It was dark by the time we got into Rotterdam, and the driver kept having to stop to ask the way before he finally set us down. I was disappointed. We were way out of the city, in the middle of nowhere, far from the harbour and ships. We stood in front of a tall fence with barbed wire, gate and guard-house. The guard, accompanied by a German shepherd on a leash, looked at the documents offered by our driver, opened the gate and admitted us, counting heads as we entered. We stood in the strong, icy, cutting wind until someone arrived and marched us through the dark towards the lights of the camp commander's office. After a lot of questioning and entries in a big book, we were assigned to our barracks; Norbert and I being quartered together in a boys' enclave. Susi was sent off in a different direction.

Our barracks had two huge bedrooms, one at either end, each with its own washrooms, small kitchen and day-room/dining-room. They could be operated as two independent units, or as ours was now, as one giant unit. Our "bedroom" alone contained over eighty bunks, and I immediately commandeered an upper one. There were girls quartered at the other end of the barracks, in the

245

women's section. We all met and mingled in the central common rooms.

"Fred Zeller. What on earth are you doing here?"

Just about the very first person I ran into on arrival was Ruth Haarpuder, a cousin of my friend Fred Weil, the other inner-tube sailor on the Havel. She could not tell me where Weil was. I told her my story, and then she asked me:

"So, where are you going now?"

"Where am I going?"

"From here, I mean. Where will you go from here?"

And then it occurred to me, indeed, where was I going? All that mattered had been to get out of Germany. And now that I was out . . . what?

"I've no idea," I said. "How about you?"

"We're waiting for a visa to the United States. It's been months already. I'm with my parents, in one of the family barracks."

An off-stage clamour announced the evening meal, a noisy affair at the long tables and benches in the big common room. Most of the boys at the table came from Vienna, and I could hardly believe their dialect. They had the strangest words for ordinary things . . . why, they called *Kartoffel* (potatoes) *Erdaepfel*, apples of the earth . . . and tomatoes were *Paradeisos*. They called us Germans *Piefkes*, not a pleasant name judging by the contemptuous look that went with it. We didn't know what to call them, not that I wanted to call them anything at first. It struck me as decidedly odd that common fate had not bound us together more firmly. Soon I was arguing as idiotically as the rest about who had had a tougher time under Hitler.

"You've had them longer, true" admitted the Viennese, "but we, we had it worse than you ever did, and right from the start, too; the full measure right off."

"Ridiculous," we replied. "Full measure! You mean it

hurt less in 1934 when they beat the shit out of you than in 1938?"

It reminded me of the German-first versus Zionist fights in Berlin. I found myself sucked into it. Stupid, stupid, stupid. At first I shrugged it off with a humorous, "Well I was born in Berlin, but I'm really Austro-Hungarian-Czech-Polish by parentage." It didn't work. Minor differences in dialect and attitude became quite grating, and there was at best a humorous, patronising tolerance, at worst outright hostility between the factions. Perhaps underneath it all was that tinge of arrogance displayed by quite a number of Germans who considered themselves superior to the "indolent" races of the South. Not surprisingly, some German Jews had inherited a tinge of that tinge too, considering themselves superior to those Eastern Jews, including Austrians who, as everybody knew, were just slightly cleaned up Eastern Jews.

The Directriese of de Steeg was right about one thing, the camp food was awful. But the beds were long enough, the camel-hair blankets grown-up size, the toilet seats regular height, and the place was heated better than my parents' house.

In bed that night, I again started thinking about the question Ruth Haarpuder had raised. OK, I'm out, terrific. But now what? I wished my parents would send Lilian and then come out themselves. Not that I was all that crazy to have Lilian with me—she was a royal pain—but I had started to miss my parents and I wanted them out NOW. But in the meantime? Must talk to the camp commander soon and ask him what they have in mind for us.

When I woke the next morning, I did some calculating. Let's see, we left last Wednesday . . . Nijmegen one night, de Steeg six, that takes me up to Tuesday . . . right. Today is Wednesday, a week since I left Berlin and still not one word from home. Home, I thought, hell,

Berlin wasn't home any longer, was it? Suddenly, for no
reason at all a melody came into my mind, a stupid song
that I used to sing *con brio* long time ago, when I was a
kid.

"Berlin, du bist die schoenste Stadt der Welt.
Berlin, du bist die Stadt die mir gefaellt."
(Berlin, you're the loveliest city in the world.
Berlin, you are the town I like.)

"Berlin sssshit," I spat like an angry cat.

Calculating . . . even if they had answered the postcards I sent immediately, the post would still be in
Nijmegen or de Steeg.

"How do you get post here?" I asked my neighbour as
I climbed out of bed.

"At breakfast. They call your name."

They called my name. There was a postcard for me that
morning and one for my cousins, too. In this first card,
which had followed me from Nijmegen, my mother
rejoiced that I was "in good hands", asked whether we
were all still together, and exhorted me to be "good and
nice to other people". My father too, was happy for me,
and asked whether those other four boys had arrived
safely also. I was touched by his concern. What a nice
man, my father. He must have heard about the others at
the station from Mother. All seven of us signed greetings
to him on my next postcard.

After breakfast we had our first reunion, the three of
our train companions who had come here from Nijmegen
directly showed us around the camp. Pretty dreary. A
snowy, treeless landscape, flat as far as the eye could see,
blending into the river, with that endless, tall, chain-link,
barbed-wire topped fence stretching around us on all
sides. Inside, a dozen large, brick barracks spread out
over the banks of the Maas which was so wide, that
one could hardly see the other side. We were west of

Rotterdam, well on the way down river towards the Hook of Holland and the open sea. Every large ship coming in or going out of the harbour had to pass us; the camp had been built but a few years earlier to serve as a quarantine station for incoming ships. There was a sizeable pier, now blocked off by three layers of barbed wire in case we felt tempted to jump into the icy Maas and swim to the other side. In addition to the barracks, there were a few official or service buildings, like the boiler plant building, all dreary and lonely-looking because everything was spaced so far apart.

A couple of days later I received a second postcard from home, via de Steeg. My mother was happy that I had obtained permission to stay in Holland and exhorted me to be "worthy of this privilege by becoming a good person, making myself, as well as my parents, happy. Always be nice and polite to peers and grown-ups alike . . . it can only bring you joy." Parents are *always* exhorting kids to be good. Sickening.

But there was good news, too. Mother offered to send me ten marks every month. She warned me to be frugal with it, but in the same breath told me not to deprive myself. And, I must write every day. She would send me international postage coupons which I could exchange for stamps. Should she send me some clothing, or wait until I had a more permanent address? "Do write to Uncle Max in Palestine. But he mustn't know I told you to write! Tell him how things are with us. And please do convey my best wishes to the Directriese."

My sister scrawled in wavy lines that she would really like to come and join me. Pity we could not spend Chanuka together, but maybe we would Purim, 5 March, though that was a long time away still. Would I like her to make a hat for me? (Good heavens, no!) She would send me my best fountain pen with their first package, and did I also want my "Stempel"? My stempel . . .

rubber stamp? What on earth was she talking about? Did she mean my little printing set with the ink pad and movable rubber type? And then it came to me. Very smart, my little sister . . . rubber stamp, stamp, postage stamp, my postage stamps, my stamp collection sitting in envelopes, ready to go. Even kids knew how to read and write "between the lines". Caution had become such a habit that we even wrote "between the lines" when there was no need for it.

"No thanks," I told Lilian, "I'll want my stempel soon, but not yet. I still have no idea where I will be next."

My visit to the camp commander's office a few days later, after Christmas, brought no revelations on this subject. I marched into his office with a breezy:

"*Goede morgen! Als tu blieft.* If you please, may I speak with Mijnheer Commandant?"

That did it. Had I just said "good morning" in German he might have let his secretary deal with me. But apparently not many of his wards tried a little Dutch. He looked up curiously, came over, and after listening to my "Where do I go from here?" threw out some vague hints that England or America might take some of us. No, there was nothing definite, and no again, they were not thinking of placing us with Dutch families. That was only for the very young without parents.

I asked him about Ralph, but neither he nor his staff knew anything about him. I also wrote to Sister Antje in de Steeg without success.

"Might we be able to stay in Holland for good, Mijnheer Commandant?"

"Some of you, perhaps."

"*Dank u.* Well, then I had better learn some *Hollandsch*," I said, knowing just where I could do that.

"It won't break your leg. You're doing well already," smiled the commander.

I knew where, because I had already started my Dutch

lessons. I had met big Piet and little Piet. Within a day of arriving at the camp my stick-your-nose-into-everything personality had reasserted itself. Formerly the explorer of darkest Berlin, now discoverer of the exotic, mysterious Rotterdam Hyplaat Camp. I followed trails in the snow leading to the kitchen, laundry, mortuary, watch-room, electrical distribution centre . . . and the boiler plant. Right from the start I became most curious about the boiler plant, that stubby, steamy, tall-chimneyed building in the middle of the camp. It rumbled the way I thought a whale should rumble. It sang the siren song of an over-sized mermaid. I was forever hanging around the door trying to take a peek inside. It was best at night when the interior was lit. Then you saw two monstrously big, round, silver shapes, whales definitely, spouting streams of gleaming copper tubing.

I could usually make out two or three people inside, but they never seemed to notice me, not until Christmas Day, that is. I was doing my usual sideways ogling when suddenly a tall, older man in overalls arose out of the ground in front of me: Big Piet, the stoker, ugly as hell, sporting a wall-to-wall grin that revealed the most tobacco stained teeth I had ever seen, with more gaps visible than teeth. Some rasping, guttural sounds issued from that grin:

"*Goeie morgen, vrolijk Kerstfeest* . . . something, something, something . . ." which turned out to be "Happy Christmas from all of us here." An unmistakable big-handed gesture invited me to enter the sanctum.

Wasting no time on decorum, I grinned my best grin, said the four Dutch words I had learned from the de Wyzes, "*Goede dag, dank u*", and entered the promised land. In the centre of the huge hall, side by side were my silver whales, two giant boilers padded with silver-covered insulation. Out of them issued enough gleaming copper tubing, valves, gauges with dancing needles, ther-

mometers and heaven knows what to delight any technic-
ally-minded kid. The whole place was humming, hot, and
smelled of steam and engine oil.

I was led to a little table on which two candles were
burning. They had noticed me hanging out daily, decided
to take pity on me and got together a little Christmas
treat of hot chocolate, biscuits, sweets and a couple of
second-hand books in German. One was a mystery, the
other about travels in Bohemia at the turn of the century.
The books came from little Piet, another stoker. Being
somewhat of a student, attending evening classes "to get
out of the coal shovelling business", he thought I might
need something to read. About twenty-five, slim, short
little Piet was as handsome as big Piet was ugly, as quiet
as big Piet was noisy. And he had the most perfect teeth
I had ever seen, as strong as steel—he cracked hazel
nuts with them. There were other stokers, but I don't
remember them at all, neither what they looked like, nor
what they said. But the two Piets are with me still.

My parents wrote that they were trying to get to Bolivia
". . . There's little hope, but we must try anything and
everything." I remembered that Bolivia was high on my
favoured nations list. It had real live Indians. But hadn't
I already submitted an application years ago? I had, but
things had changed. Bolivian visas were being sold on the
black market, and their price depended on how much
despair there was at any given location . . . Germany,
Austria, or where Uncle Mulu was, at the Zbaszyn Polish
border camp.

I thought of my father making the rounds of consulates
as I had done. The rounds of "so sorry" shoulder-shrug-
gers. I missed my parents, but was I homesick? Not yet.
The new faces and places, my adventurousness and insati-
able curiosity all helped to keep such feelings at bay. But
I was beginning to realise that this wasn't just another
holiday, that I wouldn't be back home tomorrow. I had

known this in my mind, but it was only just starting to put cold steel into my soul.

The conditions at the camp did not exactly help to dispel anxiety. There were practically no medical services, dentists, chemists, nurses or barbers. We had to rely on amateur self-help and aspirin. Food was not the main attraction either, and it seemed to get worse every day. We lived on potatoes and fish. Clean, healthy, monotonous food but barely enough to keep hunger away. There were very few other vegetables, little bread, no butter, hardly any milk, no fruit. Just fish, fish and fish. As a Berliner of modest means, familiar with just a few types of fish, I marvelled at the many species the Dutch had discovered and at the many ways they had found to disguise them. We had fish steamed, sautéd, grilled, chopped, breaded, pickled, salted, smoked, fried, dried, swimming in oil, in tomato, and innumerable other sauces, served hot, cold, made into paste, "fish-balls", sandwich spreads, stews. We started growing fins and gills.

Our guards with their police dogs and barbed wire, the regimentation of all our activities, eating, sleeping, cleaning, none of it was inspiring. We weren't even allowed to approach the fence closely. Since we had only "temporary status", the authorities feared that some of us might try to escape, mingle and disappear in the population. Not a bad idea, actually.

But the Dutch were doing all they could, and much more than any other nation in Europe or for that matter, in the world. They had taken us, penniless, when no one else would. They looked after us as best they could, even though they had grave unemployment problems and there were many needy Dutchmen. Most of us realised this, were grateful, and felt we could put up with a little temporary starvation and lack of freedom.

I felt the lack of food, clothing or barbers less trying

253

than the lack of books, or having something interesting to do with my head or hands. But now, just about all we had was conversation, soccer in the snowy fields and occasional table-tennis games when some kind outside donor supplied the too, too fragile balls.

Later, in the spring, when people found themselves still behind barbed wire, some self-help was organised by the grown-ups. In response to our appeals, the camp commander put an unoccupied barracks at our disposal. It became The Cultural Centre, with a makeshift theatre/ concert hall, table-tennis room, photographer's corner and barber shop. A man from Vienna had joined us recently, bringing with him a pair of barber's scissors and thus civilisation.

In the mortuary, the only vacant small room in the camp, there were classes for the very young. Older children, like me, were considered smart enough already.

Local talent was recruited: anyone who played fiddle, piano or could sing, anyone who could juggle, dance, or do magic tricks. Local talent fixed and tuned the battered piano, made stage lights out of tin foil, and once a week there was Gala Night for all who wished to attend. Life was definitely looking up.

A kind Rotterdam cinema owner invited the entire camp, guards and all, to his theatre. We travelled in a fleet of buses to a special showing of Disney's *Snow White*. Ralph would have loved it. I missed him.

Then we had visitors. A marvellous troupe of volunteers, regular employees, organised, financed and delivered to our doors by "De Bijenkorf". The Beehive— Rotterdam's big department store. They descended from their bus one by one, hunched up, grey, weary after a day's work. Bundled up in winter woollens, they trundled through the dark and snowy lanes to our "theatre". Thirty minutes later they emerged from behind the scenes, scintillating, radiant, their faces flashing crimson smiles. They performed wild vaudeville acts with magnificent jugglers and magicians and comedians. They played, sang, joked and Fred Astaired their hearts out. They sang risqué songs (*kom naar boven, ik bin alleen* . . . come upstairs, I'm alone, I have a jojo . . .) There was culture too, serious stuff at the piano, chunks of Beethoven and Chopin and people like that.

Everything was done with love, enthusiasm and devotion. We adored them and gave them endless standing ovations. After their positively final and last encore, sweaty and glowing, they joined their audience, handing out sweets and fruit to the children, cigarettes and cigars to the grown-ups. They shared with us photos of their children, families and homes. There was banter, joking and smiling. A green oasis in our horizonless wintry desert of boredom.

At least I had my "honorary stoker" appointment. Nobody's idle mascot, I was up there, fifteen feet off the ground, like a sailor, straddling the asbestos-padded silver-cloth jacket of the big boilers, polishing brass and copper with the best of them. I learned to tighten valve packings, read gauges and shovel coal straight and deep into the small heat chamber opening. I often did the rounds with little Piet. In addition to the central boilers, each distant barracks had a steam re-heating plant that needed checking and feeding. As we walked through the slushy snow, Piet sang. That was his great passion and I was his best audience. His current favourites were songs from *Snow White* and Friml's "Donkey Serenade" which he delivered with flowing hand movements, in English. When he wasn't singing he taught me Dutch. The clean kind, not the "*God ver* . . ." stuff I had learnt from brown-toothed big Piet.

The Piets must have known about the camp's food shortages. They frequently offered me a share of their lunch or came with little gifts, but most of the time I refused their offers. I didn't want them to think I hung out with them because I wanted to be fed. One day big Piet got that out of me, told the others, and they all threatened to damage me seriously if I didn't accept their little offers. Of course they knew I was their pal, a stoker just like them. And didn't I help plenty? They were a warm, kind, generous lot.

I wish I could say the same for myself and my cousins.

It's obvious to me now, as I look through the letters and postcards my parents sent to Rotterdam, that we constantly made life harder for them and plagued them with unreasonable demands.

We complained about the food, not to the Dutch, but to them. I kept worrying about my bicycle and asked them not to sell it. Ridiculous. They offered to send it by rail. Equally ridiculous. Where would I keep it and ride it?

My cousins and I fought as never before and constantly complained about each other to our parents.

There was cousin Rudi's package from Belgium, for instance. At my mother's request he had sent us some dried fruit, nuts, and sweets. It was addressed to Susi who, being the eldest and female, represented, to Rudi at least, "motherhood". I knew nothing about that package until my mother wrote asking how I had liked it. I asked Norbert first. He hadn't received it, but Susi had, sure. He had caught her chewing the sweets.

"Share? She never shares," he explained cheerfully. "She didn't in Berlin either. Whenever she got some chocolate she'd eat it by herself and hide what was left in stupid places where I'd always find it. And then I ate it."

She told him the package was sent to HER! Then he had bluffed his way into the girls' dormitory, filled his pockets and mouth twice. It had not occurred to him to share with me either. I was utterly disgusted with both of

256

them. Of course, my poor parents had to share the burden of my anger.

Susi, at the time, was quite spoiled and selfish. She pestered her mother with incessant requests for clothing and other personal items, even after being told that it was now most difficult to send packages abroad. There were endless forms to complete, inspections, approvals needed. It took weeks. Even my discreet mother, who had never interfered before, blasted Susi in a letter, telling her not to make her mother's life miserable over a few rags, reminding her of the pain and loneliness Leona had to bear.

"Dear Susi," she concluded, "you do not seem to comprehend, my child, that times have changed most drastically for us. No matter how painful it is for your mother, she can no longer fulfill all your wishes at once."

Was it uncertainty? Loss of love? The loneliness of our situation? Was it the numbing boredom? Or just that kids are thoughtless, selfish little monsters?

And then there was Tilly Schanzer from New York, who brought sudden light, hope and a terrible family scandal. She had been Uncle Mulu's long-time mistress, secretly visiting him in Berlin once every year or so. It turned out that my dashing, handsome, vital uncle was quite a ladies' man. We knew nothing of all this or of her existence until we saw her at the camp commander's office. She had come to sign us out and take us for tea in Rotterdam. All three of us. When I walked into the office there was Susi, sitting with this very colourful lady who wore strange clothes and more lipstick and other goo on her face than I had ever seen on anybody else. "*Frisch gestrichen*", freshly painted, my mother would have said. Wearing makeup and pretty clothes was almost sinful in dowdy pre-war Germany. Tilly looked very much like the very embodiment of a scarlet woman, a marriage breaker. But all we knew then was just what she said—that she

257

was a friend of the family and, on her way to New York, had come to Rotterdam especially to take us out of the camp for an afternoon.

We had a wonderful time with her at an expensive hotel in town having tea and eating things we didn't know still existed. But when she offered us a special treat, smoked salmon, she was a little taken aback with our chorus of "Oh no!" and look of horror. Fish again? Grrr!

Before departing she promised that she would do all she could to help us and our parents, and since she had taken us around town in a huge, chauffeured limousine we believed every word she said. If she couldn't do it who could? For days we were euphoric. We'll all be together in America, perhaps Aunt Cilly too, maybe everybody, a real, complete family again.

Eventually the whole scandal became common family property. It had started to surface a month or so earlier, when Uncle Mulu, rotting away in his Polish detention camp, had appealed everywhere for help. Tilly Schanzer responded promptly and actually dropped in on him in Poland. Appalled by what she saw of the conditions in the camp, she offered to help Mulu and his children. She did not mention Leona apparently . . . or did she? Here family chroniclers part company. Some say Mulu did a dastardly, unforgivable thing by deserting, for Tilly, his wife who had crossed the border illegally to join him. They called him a murderer. Others point out that Mulu never even went to New York to see Tilly, but went via London straight to South America, fully intending to send for his wife and children the moment he was established there.

The correspondence I still have shows that my mother and Leona were fully informed about Tilly's visits to Poland and Rotterdam, that Mulu's entire family was originally going to New York, and that my mother thought Tilly might help to get our family to America, too. Reading between the lines, I sensed that neither sister cherished Tilly's presence on the scene, but both were so desperate that they were willing to appeal for help even to a potential marriage breaker. Tilly had the means to write us all affidavits. In several letters my mother urged me to write her nice letters, with thanks for her kindness, asking her to remember my family, too. She was our one hope to be together again.

As so often, there are many truths. Tilly could have provided the affidavits, but she didn't. Perhaps she played a role in getting Susi and Norbert to England. Perhaps she even exerted some influence to get my sister and myself there. Perhaps. I did have a letter at the end of February, in which Aunt Leona consoled me for Norbert and Susi's imminent departure for England, saying that she would "cause us to follow very quickly. I promise you this absolutely". Poor Aunt Leona. She certainly had not been able to "cause" anything much thus far. The only new ingredient was Tilly.

But then things changed. My theory is that Tilly wanted Mulu and offered to rescue his family if he left his wife for her when they got to New York. At first Mulu might have tentatively agreed, and they were all scheduled to go to New York. Then he must have balked at actually promising to walk out on his family there, at which point Tilly disowned him. End of theory. The hard facts remain that Mulu wound up having to rescue his family himself. Before joining him in Poland Aunt Leona raised money by selling their furniture and remaining store merchandise at give-away prices. She found a German railway engineer who regularly took his train from Berlin past Posen, Poland, a town very close to Mulu's camp. For every hundred marks he received from Leona he gave Mulu fifty. Not that the mark was worth a lot, but it was better in Poland than elsewhere because Polish currency was weaker still. An out-and-out wheeler-dealer and a born survivor, Uncle Mulu started selling the only thing he had—money. He became a dealer in foreign currency, and he made out quite well.

According to Mulu, Leona, losing her nerve about Tilly, suddenly and unexpectedly arrived at his doorstep, having crossed the border illegally. Mulu had just bought one of those famous Bolivian visas for one hundred and fifty pounds sterling which left him with a little passage money, a Leica, and a Contax camera. He told Leona, who had risked jail bringing what little cash they had left in Germany, to stay with distant relatives in Poland until he had sufficient income to feed and shelter his family. Then he would try to get his brother and family to South America, too.

It never happened. Three months after Mulu left, Poland was overrun and Leona disappeared. Had he "loyally" stayed with her, they would both have perished. Before boarding his ship to Bolivia in Liverpool, he stayed over with my cousins in a cheap boarding house in London, sharing a room with Norbert.

Weeks later, arriving penniless at the railway station in La Paz, Bolivia, right there, on the arrival platform, he sold his somewhat shabby Stetson hat to a couple of Indians. He sold his Leica and Contax cameras to a photo dealer in town. This money permitted him to wait for a visa to Chile, promised him by a chance acquaintance, a kindred soul, another wheeler-dealer he had met on the boat. This man, who happened to be the Belgian Ambassador to Chile, pulled a few strings. Mulu got to Chile, and with the very small capital left from his cameras started a tiny business. When he was finally well established, towards the end of the war, he got his children to join him in Santiago. He helped his estranged brother Monio to go there too, shortly after the war. Monio and his Christian wife, Mina, had spent the entire war years hidden by Christian friends in a basement right in the centre of Berlin.

But Tilly Schanzer was only one of the events of February which had profound consequences. My stateless parents were *"ausgewiesen"*, expelled, by order of the Nazi government. They were told to leave Germany within eight weeks.

Father went to the Berlin Hilfsverein, a Jewish self-help agency, that told him to apply for an extension of the deadline like the tens of thousands of other Jews who were expelled at the same time and had nowhere to go.

"How about Shanghai?" he was asked. "The Japanese are admitting some Jews there."

"Shanghai?" said my parents. "Without money? We'll never see our children again."

Until now I had asked my parents to send out my sister in just about every postcard or letter home. I repeated emphatically that she should be sent to her "aunt" in Holland who would come to the station at Nijmegen to meet her, provided she had some advance notice. Her "aunt" wanted her to come right now, before all the rest of the family came visiting and she would have no time for Lilian. But my parents did not respond. The idea of having no child left, or letting such a young girl go alone, must have seemed unbearable. Immediately after hearing from my father that they had been expelled and did not know where to turn, I wrote to Lilian directly, saying, "Come now. Once more, here's all you need to know . . ."

Late one February Friday, someone called my name in the common room. I was told to report immediately to the camp commander. I ran through the windy, icy dark all the way to his office. A week ago, after hearing that my parents had been expelled, I had gone to see him.

"Help me, please!"

Was there anything he could do? Did he know anyone

261

who could help them find shelter in Holland, at least for a little while? They were desperate. He looked at me sadly and promised, without sounding hopeful, to try. Could I get him a photocopy of the expulsion order? I wrote immediately for one. Did he have news for me now?

He had news for me. A telegram had just arrived from Germany. Fearful, I tore it open and read, "Going Halle tonight, your beloved sister Lilian."

Before I understood what those words really implied I shook my head sadly. How often did I have to tell that girl to sign your loving sister, and not your beloved sister?

Then the meanings got through—all of them. That grammatical error made it obvious that Lilian herself, not my parents, had sent the telegram. She had run away. And Halle, a town known to Lilian, was not meant to be "Halle" but her secret code for "Holla" . . . Holland. She must be on the Krefeld train right now, I concluded, and told the commander my news.

"How old? Twelve? Yes. I'll call Nijmegen so someone will be on the lookout for her at the station. But as for getting her to Rotterdam . . ." He just shrugged his shoulders and shook his head.

"She's too young; she doesn't have parents to look after her, like the other kids here."

"I'm parents. She's my little sister, and I can look after her."

He smiled, doubted, but at my insistence promised to try anyway. There was no news of her the whole next day, Saturday. Nor on Sunday. But, of course, she would be waiting for permission to stay, and it was a weekend.

Monday morning there was a letter from Berlin, Father asking why I had requested a photocopy of the expulsion order. Was someone offering help? Next, he said he would leave it to Mother to deal with my request to send Lilian out at once. And then, written in haste: "Since I left this letter unfinished yesterday, Lilian has run away to join you. She left with a hundred marks, and I hope something remains of this money. Please do immediately get in touch with your aunt to look after her."

And then Mother: "Unintentionally you have caused me great grief. Lilian has had no peace since you called her. She left with nothing, without clothing, without food; she didn't even take her night-things. I sent her shopping at three, and she never came back. In the evening we had a telegram saying she was on her way to Halle to join you. Since we knew she would never get to you via Halle we were terribly worried. We looked for her at Charlottenburg station until after midnight. May God forgive her for the pain she caused us. This morning we had a telegram that she is safe in Holland. I don't know how I'm going to send her clothing and other things. The formalities are more difficult every day. My dear son, look after your sister. Protect her, because you must now be everything to her and are responsible for her. How I wish I could go to Holland and we could all be together, but that's out of the question. A dream too good to be true. We have no idea where fate will take us, but we must leave here soon. The only way we can get out is to find someone abroad willing to help us. But there is no one."

My camp commander succeeded in getting Lilian to Rotterdam. I was overjoyed to see her, asked a lot of questions and made notes of her answers. "Why are you writing it all down?" she wanted to know.

"I'm putting you in my diary."

Not to be outdone, she immediately asked me to lend her my pen and paper and sat down to write her own diary. Here it is in its glorious entirety.

"HOW I RUN AWAY FROM HOME

It was a big excitement at home. My brother is going to Holland.

I cried when I saw the train leave. From now on I cried every day and every night. I had begged my parents on my knees to let me go along, but they were always afraid.

I said to my mother six days after my brother's departure: 'Mutti, I'm going to scram from home.' My mother laughed. I could just remember that my mother had said there is money at this place, take it if something happens to us. I thought my parents were stateless and expelled and had to be out by 2 April.

One day I took the money and took another fifty pfenning for the trip to the station. I bought a ticket to Kleve and left at 11:45 p.m. and travelled until the morning. In the morning I changed trains at Kleve but had no ticket to travel to Nijmegen. Later the committee came for me and paid the ticket and I was sent to rich foster parents for two days. From there (who could be happier than I) I was sent to my brother in Rotterdam at the quarantine in Beneden. We went with a committee car to the quarantine station in Rotterdam. I had to go to the camp commander's office. When I was inside, a boy stormed into the room, I saw only tousled hair and freckles, and he embraced me quickly and kissed me. I had a big shock, could this be my brother? It was him. 'How on earth did you do it?' he kept on asking.

I begged him to be silent. The whole place knew it already. I had to tell them all until my mouth hurt in the evening. Every day I had to tell it again." (Signed) L. Zeller.

Lilian had waited to make her break until after her birthday, on 6 February. Nothing was going to make her miss the birthday presents. Three days later, having finished the consumable gifts, she quietly removed the money my mother kept under the lining of a chest of drawers, emergency money if something terrible were to happen to both parents. Getting out of Germany was an emergency, Lilian felt. She admitted, later, that there had also been a few other little "emergencies" previously, and that she had "borrowed" from this fund. Taking what was left and going off to Holland neatly covered her tracks and resolved her constant fear of being found out.

The rich young lady went into town and hung around the big stores for a while. After sending my parents and me telegrams, she bought a carrying net, food for the journey, a few magazines and miniature German-English and German-Dutch dictionaries. She went to a public bath to "clean up for the journey", had herself a nice haircut and saw a film.

My mother, quite desperate waiting for her at home, finally got in touch with Father. Just moments after he arrived at the Havelstrasse, so did Lilian's telegram. My parents did not recognise Halle being Lilian's code for Holland. Was she going to Margot, my girlfriend, who had occasionally sent a note to Lilian? Eisleben near Halle, that's where I had gone in August when I ran away. Lilian is only a little girl, she may have been confused, thought Mother, rushing to the Papiermeisters to phone Margot's parents while Father waited at home in case Lilian returned. She called the railway to check on Halle and Holland and found out that there had been no train either to Halle or Krefeld since Lilian left, but that there would be trains later that evening. Mother ran back home, and both parents set out to try and intercept Lilian at Charlottenburg, the station from which I had set out.

But her "only a little girl" Lilian, after enjoying the film, quite deliberately went to the other station from which the same Krefeld train left, Bahnhof Zoologischer Garten. There she ran into an unexpected problem getting her ticket. She was tiny and looked much younger than her twelve years. The man at the counter wanted to know why she was travelling all alone, without any guardian, in the middle of the night. Lilian explained sadly that her parents were dead, that she was being sent to an aunt in Krefeld who would come to the train in the morning before work. Her aunt here in Berlin, who had just brought her to the station, worked nights and started at midnight so she couldn't wait here with her. After a long look and a little hesitation, the man handed her the ticket and change.

A couple of minutes before departure, after checking out the train most carefully, Lilian boarded the train and locked herself into the toilet. The train started, and after what seemed to her like ages, stopped at Charlottenburg. She stayed locked in the toilet with a wildly beating heart until the train was way out of Berlin. Squinting out of the window she actually caught a glimpse of our parents looking for her, pacing up and down the platform with worried faces.

A few days after Lilian's arrival in Rotterdam, I had a most puzzling letter from my mother. Looking at it now, I understand it better. For a moment she must have lost touch with reality and escaped into a dream world.

First she talked about Tilly, a wonderful person. Both she and Leona would help us all get to America. Then she wondered whether I could not ask the Refugee Committee to send me to America to study engineering—or perhaps I should ask the Dutch whether I could do so in Holland. (She probably thought America and Holland felt the way she did about education and that these countries would be only too happy to support a child who wanted to study.) She mentioned again how terribly difficult it was for them to get out of Germany. And then, as if any of us had the slightest control over our fate, she proposed that if Aunt Leona's Polish passport could not get her into Holland to say goodbye to her children before they left for America, we should all meet at the Dutch border; she would go there with Leona. Lilian had better stay near the border too.

Here we were, penniless, behind barbed wire not even permitted to go near the fence, never mind the Dutch border. How she envisaged such a meeting, I couldn't imagine. Waving to each other at a distance across no-man's land? She couldn't cross over, and I certainly would not set foot in Germany again.

I was most disturbed reading her lines and had a nightmarish flight of fancy in which I saw the two bent, forlorn shapes of Leona and my mother standing in the snow, holding on to each other, while far, far away, across the fields, on the other side of the border, under the pine trees, we four children silently waved to them.

But then, happily, Mother's letter ended in a more realistic vein with the usual reminders to always be nice, good, helpful to others and industrious.

Father, too, had his flight of fancy at about this time. He asked whether we had a large garden at the internment camp: working the soil in spring would be such fun, he suggested. I always suspected that my father was a farmer at heart. He grew up on his father's dairy farm in the Carpathian mountains. No, I wrote back, no planting, no reaping, this is a transit camp; there's no tomorrow here.

That February things were moving at an incredible pace, as my family disintegrated. Every one seemed to be on the move, except my parents. Some were even on their second move.

The Bobaths were running from Czechoslovakia on the eve of the German invasion. On his way to New York, Arthur Bobath "the immigrant", *en route* to his ship in Rotterdam, briefly met his brother Karl Bobath "the tourist from Czechoslovakia", headed for London. They were carrying all their worldly goods. Arthur came to the camp and took his four little cousins into Rotterdam for a moment of liberty and a meal. He was flat broke but, to buy food, he handed us a five dollar bill, a very considerable part of his total remaining fortune. Then he kissed us goodbye and sailed off in his big ship.

I remember very little of teatime with Arthur, but his passage through Holland had an important consequence. It brought us Freek Adriaans. Arthur can't remember how or through whom he briefly met this tall Dutchman. But, asked to look up Arthur's little cousins, this total stranger who lived and worked in Rotterdam came to the camp almost immediately. In his thirties, spindly, slightly stooped, wearing metal-rimmed glasses, vaguely apologetic in posture, he became the pivot about which my life and that of my immediate family was to turn for quite a while.

By chance I was near the camp gate when this elongated apparition rolled up on bicycle wheels, stopped at the gate and bent low to talk to the short guard. He walked right past me to the office, clutching a couple of bulging paper bags. These turned out to contain little luxuries: cake, biscuits, raisins, chocolate. Freek worked as an engineer and regretted that he could only visit us at weekends. But he came just about every weekend. When he saw how bored and how eager I was to learn something, he brought books and spent a great deal of time teaching me maths and some engineering. I told him how desperate my parents were, and he said he would write to them. They not only corresponded frequently, but he tried to get them an impossible visa for Holland. He even went to Berlin and risked serious consequences smuggling some of their few remaining valuables out of the country.

My parents had given up their apartment in Spandau and moved in with Aunt Leona, "to share their unhappiness". Leona was at a breaking point; her children were in Holland, her husband in Poland, apparently in the process of being enticed away from her by a woman who could help us all.

Thank heaven for Freek, he became my big brother. A few weeks after Tilly's visit, Norbert and Susi were informed that they were leaving Holland. First it was to go to America, then that was changed to England. With all our quarrelling, I missed them terribly when they had gone and felt more alone than ever before. Lilian was too young to be able to make up for their loss.

Suddenly, in the middle of April, I was called to see the camp commander.

"*Jongen*," (young man), he said, "we're going to lose you. They're sending you to England shortly."

"But what about my sister? I'm not leaving without my sister!" I protested.

He gave me his word that she was already scheduled to follow me shortly. We talked for a short while and shook hands solemnly. He was a fine man.

The night before my departure, lying in the dark, staring at an invisible ceiling, I took a tally of my family. Good God! What next?

"I'm being shipped off to some camp in England, that's what's next," I thought with a pang of sudden fear, but how can we ever get together again, in one place?

My last and most lasting impression of Holland was not the lamp-lit harbour at the Hook, with its light-flashing, bobbing, black water and squealing cranes. Nor was it the engine-throbbing, salt-smelly iron tub as it sailed out of the harbour for Harwich.

Lit in my mind like a stage is the classroom for younger children at the Rotterdam camp, the morgue, the only small teaching space available at the time. I went there to get Lilian, so that after her class we could be together on my last afternoon in Holland. I entered to the sound of chirpy, shrill voices singing in rhythm, and then I saw them. Five little creatures, snapping their fingers and swaying around the raised, white, mortuary slab with its run-off channels for embalming fluid. On this marble stage clickety-clicked my black-eyed, tiny sister, concentrating intently, her thin arms spread out as if to fly, doing

an imitation tap dance to the beat of the latest *"schlager"*,
the latest Yiddish hit from New York:

"Bei mir bist die schein,
Please let me explain,
Bei mir bist die schein,
Means wunderbar."

EPILOGUE

THE CHILDREN:

Lilian Zeller, sister, got to England just before the war broke out. Now the mother of four grown children, she is living with her second husband in Los Angeles.

Norbert Zeller, cousin, joined his father in Chile, then lived in Mexico with his wife and two children. Moved to Los Angeles where he died of cancer in 1988.

Susi Zeller, cousin, after living with her father in Chile married an Englishman and now lives in London and Wales.

Frederic Zeller, the author, sculptor/writer, lived in England until 1957, now divides his time between his house in Noyac near Sag Harbor and loft in New York City.

The Others. I lost all contact with little Ralph and our other travelling companions on the children's railway.

MY PARENTS:

Fanny Zeller, née Gottesmann, was to join my father in Antwerp, but the German invasion prevented it. She remained alone in Berlin until arrested in 1941. Sent to the Maidanek extermination camp, she did not survive.

271

Heinrich Zeller fled to Belgium in 1940, just before the invasion. Walked to the South of France where he was arrested and interned by the Vichy government who delivered him back into German hands in 1943. Transported to Auschwitz. Did not survive.

FATHER'S FAMILY:

Emmanuel (Mulu) Zeller, brother died in Chile where he established a successful business similar to the one he had in Berlin.

Dasha Dresner, née Zeller, sister, escaped in 1940 to Belgium with her husband and then disappeared.

Edek Zeller, consumptive brother, last known in Berlin. Disappeared.

Monio Zeller, oldest brother, and his Christian wife Mina survived the Nazis, war, and bombs in a Berlin basement, hidden by Christian friends. Joined Mulu in Chile later.

MOTHER'S FAMILY:

Leona Zeller, née Gottesmann, sister, joined her husband Mulu, interned in Poland 1938. He escaped to Chile 1939. Before she could join him, Poland was overrun. Disappeared.

Bertha Axel, née Gottesmann, sister, fled in 1938 to Belgium, then in 1940 to the South of France. Interned by the Vichy government and delivered back to the Germans in 1943. Disappeared.

Max Gottesman, brother, went to Haifa, Palestine, with his wife and two sons early enough to save most of his wealth. He is survived by his children and their families.

Cilly Bobath, née Gottesmann, sister, fled to Prague with her husband Ignatz and daughter Lotte, then to Denmark. All three smuggled into Sweden by the Danish Underground. Survived husband and daughter, and died in Copenhagen at age 103.

Lotte Mork, née Bobath, niece, married Louis in 1939 to save her own and her parents' lives. (See Cilly Bobath.) The marriage lasted until her death. Her husband still lives in Copenhagen.

Carl and Berti and Arthur and Erika Bobath, Cilly's sons Carl and Arthur and their wives, survived in London and upstate New York respectively. Now retired from practising medicine.

Nina Sanderling, née Bobath, niece, fled to Moscow with her first husband. He disappeared in one of Stalin's purges, and she married Kurt Sanderling. After living in East Berlin she defected to the West with her son Thomas.

Maecky and Gerda Gottesman survived in Haifa, Israel, where Maecky died a few years ago.

FRIENDS:

The Papiermeisters escaped to the United States in 1939 and settled in Baltimore. Joseph, Benno and Ruth are still alive, I believe, but I have lost contact with them.

The Kachels survived the war and I was in touch with them for a while, unable to send them much help from rationed England.

The de Wyze family disappeared in the holocaust, except for one of the daughters with whom I corresponded briefly after the war.

Freek Adriaans survived forced labour, married a widow with two lovely young daughters. Saw them in 1947, lost contact and have since tried to find them unsuccessfully.

Gotthart Blenn and his father, the former minister of the Nikolai Church in Spandau, were not known to the present minister of the church when I tried to find traces of them in 1982, during my first look at Spandau since 1938.

APPENDIX

A Resume of Laws, Ordinances and Actions of the Nazi State from 1933 to 1938.

Jews had equal rights with other German citizens through laws established in Prussia in 1869. Immediately on taking power the National Socialists denied civil liberty to all and systematically continued to introduce legislation denying Jews the most basic human rights and protection under the law.

1933

4 January	Hitler appointed Chancellor.
2 February	Public demonstrations outlawed.
4 February	Over 40,000 SS and SA men given police power.
27 February	The Reichstag fire followed by mass arrests of political opponents.
28 February	Presidential decree (Hindenburg) gives Hitler emergency powers he never relinquishes. Prohibited: Free Speech. The right to privacy including mail and telephone. The State given rights of house search and confiscation of property beyond existing laws.
21 March	Special courts for prosecuting dissidents.
24 March	The "Enabling Act" voted by the Reichstag gives Hitler power to institute legislation without recourse to the Reichstag.

	First Concentration Camp established, Oranienburg, near Berlin.
1 April	State-organised boycott of Jewish business.
7 April	Ordinances dismiss Jews from Civil Service in wide variety of professional employment (example: Medical and legal services).
2 May	Dissolution of all labour unions.
10 May	The burning of 'Un-German' books.
14 July	All political parties banned.
22 September	The nationalisation of Press, Literature, Film, Music. Obligatory membership excludes Jews. Mass dismissals of Jews follow.

1934

Ordinances denying Jews the right to qualify as dentists, doctors, apothecaries, university lecturers etc.

| 30 June | Blood purge. SA chief Ernest Roehm killed. |
| 19 August | On President Hindenburg's death Hitler takes over armed forces. |

1935

16 March	Military conscription started.
6 September	Jewish newspapers banned from street sale.
15 September	The Nuremberg Laws. Legalisation of anti-Semitic measures. Apart from banning inter-marriage, they set Jews apart from the Aryan Germans legally, put them outside the protection of the state and deny them access to law and law courts.
14 November	Expansion of the Nuremberg laws banning Jews (now including front-line vet-

erans) from all official functions or employment. Gradually this exclusion is extended to the medical, legal, financial and other professions.

1937   Jews no longer permitted to graduate.

1938

26 April   Exclusion of Jews from the German economy. Jews and Aryans married to Jews must declare all property or capital they own in or out of Germany.

15 June   All previously convicted Jews re-arrested.

17 August   Jews must add a second name to their documents. 'Israel' for males. 'Sarah' for females.

5 October   Jewish travel documents marked with a "J".

9 November   Kristallnacht pogrom.

12 November   Jews may no longer operate any business, trade or independent profession. Jews fined 1,000,000,000 marks.

28 November   Local authority given the power to restrict when or where Jews may be seen in public.

3 December   Jews must surrender their driving licences.

6 December   Jews banned from all public places such as theatres, museums, concert halls . . . as well as certain streets or sections of town. Jews must surrender, within one week, to a special bank, all their invested financial assets, including stock shares, bank accounts. Jews may not acquire, pledge or sell gold, platinum, silver,

pearls or precious stones.
Compulsory Aryanisation of all Jewish
enterprises and shops.

*(Main source for the above: Official catalogue of the exhibition
"Jews in Prussia" [Berlin 1981], published by Bildarchiv Preus-
sischer Kulturbesitz.)*